In Translation

In Translation

Positions and Paradigms

Anisur Rahman

Orient BlackSwan

IN TRANSLATION: POSITIONS AND PARADIGMS

ORIENT BLACKSWAN PRIVATE LIMITED

Registered Office
3-6-752 Himayatnagar, Hyderabad 500 029, Telangana, India
Email: centraloffice@orientblackswan.com

Other Offices
Bengaluru, Bhopal, Chennai, Guwahati,
Hyderabad, Jaipur, Kolkata, Lucknow, Mumbai,
New Delhi, Noida, Patna, Vijayawada

First published 2019

028661

ISBN 978 93 5287 462 0

Typeset in Book Antiqua 12/14 *by*
PrePSol Enterprises Pvt. Ltd., Faridabad, Haryana 121002

Printed in India at
Glorious Printers, Delhi

Published by
Orient Blackswan Private Limited
3-6-752 Himayatnagar, Hyderabad 500 029
Email: info@orientblackswan.com

Contents

Preface

A gradual distancing from generality has come to mark the state of knowledge today. We no longer inhabit a world of ubiquitous constructs. With change in the world order, knowledge is more particular now than before; it draws upon its own contexts, identifies its own resources, and creates its own paradigms of signification. The trajectory of what we know as Translation Studies now is redefining itself; it is developing alongside identified locations and configuring its contours with particularity but also with larger relevance to other sites of life and living. This implies in a major way that it is the distinctiveness of the context, location and their multiple markers that determine the condition of secular knowledge in today's world of multiple affiliations.

Translation Studies now must also follow the newly carved path that insists on particularity but with a critical concern for larger relevance beyond the particular. While the individual fields may grow their crops, the larger fields may see sharecropping. This means that in the domains of translation theory and practice both the particular and the universal may bear upon one another with equal indulgence to each other. The four-dimensional issues of language, culture, location and identity that have ever defined and redefined the poetics and practice of translation reflect upon our translational and theoretical engagements both in local and global terms. These have also led to a critical consideration of another set of references that relate with pre-colonial, colonial, postcolonial histories, and the versions of modernism and postmodernism.

These may lead us to address the overwhelming questions posed by globalisation which also relate with translation in general and postcolonial translation in particular. Being identified with modern capitalism, technological developments, and new world order, is globalisation a gift or a bane, one may ask, since it camouflages diversities presented by sub-cultures and less powerful languages in order to hegemonise and homogenise. One may argue that even while the cultural and linguistic diversities of India do not necessarily present a case against globalisation, they make a case regarding the role of translation in contemporary times, and raise intimate questions whether English is an empowering language in itself, or whether it gets empowered when a text is translated into it. By implication, it also raises another important question whether an Indian text really gets empowered only when translated into English and not other Indian languages. It may be argued further in this context that translation empowers two languages simultaneously, and it does not prosper at the cost of any of them.

The ten chapters included in this volume hark back to the issues mentioned above and present a case for India as a major site of translational activities unlike any other site for reasons of its remarkable diversities, each one of which calls for wider negotiations. Divided into two sections – Positions and Paradigms – the chapters raise theoretical issues in one part and engage with the paradigms of representations in the other. The first section of the book engages with multiple issues concerning the theory and practice of translation. The chapter on "Author, Text, Translator, Reader: The New Indian Context" examines the symbiotic relationship amongst the four and their contribution towards creating a new literary culture in India. This makes a case for five models of empowerment and the need for contextualisation, theorisation and canonisation of the acts of writing, reading, and translating. "Changing the Order: The Problem of Translatability" examines the problematic of language, writing, and translation in relation to text and translation types. It argues that the text enters into a dialogic relationship with the author and the translator who develop collaborative linkages with multiple agencies during which the elements of fluidity and fantasy mark the two acts of writing and translation. "Translation as Dialogue: Aesthetics of Collaboration" projects the problematic of collaboration in the acts of writing and translation. It traces the genealogy of the Indian text and the lineage of the Indian author, and posits that the collaborative act is also an interrogative act with social history and textual formation on the part of the author and the translator. "Translation as Discourse: Notes on Intent Formation" is an inquiry into language as repository of discourse and translation as a mode of discourse formation and dissemination. This has been demonstrated with reference to *sutras* and *malfoozat* which, disseminated through translation, led to a critical engagement with the semantics and morphology of the text on the part of the translator. "Broadening the Frontier: Towards a Poetics of Painting and Architecture" posits a case concerning the practice and evaluation of translation with reference to other arts. In drawing upon parallels from translation, painting and architecture, it has been argued that all these three aspire to develop a pattern language by developing a delicate balance amongst language, grammar, density and design in order to achieve a level of excellence and acceptability.

The second section of the book develops a set of translational paradigms with reference to different kinds of writing and translation. "Translation as Empowerment: The College of Fort William" draws upon the idea of multiple empowerments and examines them in the context of a variety of writings and translations undertaken during a particular period of colonial history in India. Drawing upon texts, translators, policies and politics, it has been said that translation as a politico-scholastic engagement led to defining the Indian literary tradition by proxy. "Translating Representation: The Problematic of Indian Literature" examines the concept of literary representation and tries to develop the idea of literature as representation and translation as re-representation. With reference to text, tradition and history in comparative and contrastive terms, it has been argued that the representations of India by Western and Indian scholars underline their politics of writing and translation which defined the idea of India and Indian literature. "Translating the Urdu Ghazal: The Classical contexts of Meer and Ghalib" makes a case for primary and secondary translation as the two acts of speech and examines the principles and practices of translation at a broader level. It also defines the ghazal for its nature and form and attempts a verbal evaluation of the translations of Meer Taqi Meer and Asadullah Khan Ghalib into English to underscore the possible value of translating a poet from the classical past representing a tradition that is peculiarly alien to the English sensibility. "Translating Modern Urdu Poetry: Creating Canons in Translation" proposes the idea of translation as a way of dissemination and canon formation. It traces the trajectory of modernism in Urdu poetry to make a case for its dissemination in the English language since recent translations have already made way for its acceptance in the larger and secular literary habitats of our times. "Translating a Form: The Possible/ Impossible Ghazal in English" is an inquiry into the possibility of translating a form which turns out to be the most difficult when it comes to translating the form of the ghazal and writing a ghazal in the English language. This has been done with reference to the multiple contexts of the ghazal and its divergent configurations which also show the complex and enriching process of literary impact and response. The ten chapters of this book, taken together, create a paradigm of translation poetics and practice which has now become a major academic concern in India today.

Anisur Rahman

Acknowledgements

"Author, Text, Translator, Reader: The New Indian Context" was presented at an International Conference on *Diverse Harmonies: Literary and Cultural Confluences* in University of Hyderabad, 28–31 January 2009. It was later published in *Translation and Culture: Indian Perspectives* (ed.) G. J. V. Prasad, New Delhi: Pencraft International, 2010. I would like to thank G. J. V. Prasad and Pencraft International for permission to use this essay.

"Changing the Order: The Problem of Translatability" was delivered as keynote address at a national seminar on *The Literary and Linguistic Terrain of Translation* in Salesian College, Sonada, July 31 2010.

"Translation as Dialogue: Aesthetics of Collaboration" was presented as a plenary address at a national seminar on *Translation and Indian Culture* in Banaras Hindu University, Varanasi, 15–16 November, 2010.

"Translation as Discourse: Notes on Intent Formation" was presented at a national seminar on *Translating Cultures* in Indira Gandhi National Open University, New Delhi, 17–18 February 2011.

"Broadening the Frontier: Towards a Poetics of Painting and Architecture" was delivered as keynote address at a national seminar on *Issues and Challenges in Translation* in Aligarh Muslim University, 29–30 March 2012. It was later published as "Revisiting Translation: Towards Fine Arts and Architecture", in the collection *Literary Culture and Translation: New Aspects of Comparative Literature* edited by Dorothy M. Figueira and Chandra Mohan (Primus Books 2017). I thank Primus Books for permission to include this essay.

"Translation as Empowerment: The College of Fort William" was presented at a seminar on *Translation and Empowerment* in Osmania University, Hyderabad, 20–22

March 2003. It was later published in *CIEFL Bulletin*, Vol. 12, Numbers 1 and 2, 2002.

"Translating Representation: The Problematic of Indian Literature" was first presented at an international seminar on *Literature as Resistance: Challenging Religious, Linguistic, Casteist, and Sexist Essentialism* in University of Mumbai, 2–4 February 2006. It was subsequently presented as a public lecture in Purdue University (USA) on 16 April 2007 and University of Wisconsin (USA) on 3 May 2007. It was later published as "Indian Literatures in English Translation: The Discourse of Resistance and Representation" in *Journal of Postcolonial Writing*, Vol. 43, No. 2, August 2007.

"Translating the Urdu Ghazal: The Classical Contexts of Meer and Ghalib" was published in *Literature in Translation* (ed.) Pramod Talgeri and S. B. Verma, Bombay: Popular Prakashan, 1988.

"Translating Modern Urdu Poetry: Creating Canons in Translation" was published in *Indian Literature*, 185, Vol. XLII, No. 3, May–June 1998.

"Translating a Form: The Possible/Impossible Ghazal in English" was published in *Translation: Poetics and Practice* (ed.) Anisur Rahman, New Delhi: Creative Books, 2001.

All the essays have since been thoroughly revised for this book. Some of the titles have been changed in accordance with the revisions made in the chapters.

I gratefully acknowledge the invitation of the academics who reposed their faith in me for making these presentations in their seminars or conferences, and the publishers and editors of the volumes where some of these essays appeared. In collecting all these ten essays together, I relate my interest to the current appeal and relevance of Translation Studies in the Indian academia that took me along and helped me locate some of the positions and paradigms that this volume tries to project. I would also like to thank Padmaja Anant and Sreenath S of Orient BlackSwan for their efforts in putting this volume together.

Positions

ONE

Author, Text, Translator, Reader: The New Indian Context

The new Indian literary context has redefined the modern Indian author, the text, the translator and the reader. It is a complex and symbiotic relationship that these four have entered into in the recent past. This chapter seeks to address the parameters of this relationship and to examine how the four have contributed towards the emergence of a new literary culture in India.

In order to understand the predominant features of the four-dimensional relationship between the author, the text, the translator and the reader, an attempt has been made in this chapter to understand each one of them individually in precise terms and then to relate them with the broader Indian context. It is suggested that while the broad parameters of the four remain the same in theoretical terms, they differ with respect to locational variation, as may be seen in the context of the modern Indian literary tradition. This has led to the development of five models that empower the author, the text, the translator and the reader, distinctly and separately, in various combinations. The argument, so formulated, makes way for a proposition that there is a need to contextualise, theorise and canonise our activities of writing, reading and translating in India today.

Literary criticism and theory have engaged variously, and in varying degrees, with the idea of the author, the text, the translator and the reader over a large period of time, representing the classical, the romantic, the modernist and the postmodernist phases of literary history. It may be noticed, however, that greater attention has been paid to the author and the text, both being perennially significant points of reference for multiple discourses on the acts of writing/authoring. While developing a view on the multiple approaches to the four points of our reference, it may be possible to create a perspective on the modern Indian authorial and translational negotiations which, it must be posited, is essentially an act of multiple empowerments in the Indian context. In order to establish how the author, the text, the translator and the reader[1] stand individually and interact symbiotically, the following sections engage with these to arrive at a point of convergence which makes way for the empowerment of the four, both separately and together.

AUTHOR

Questions like who/what is an author and what does authorship/authority over text imply have been addressed variously in literary/intellectual history for a very long time, although the answers have differed substantially over the ages. We may appreciate that the relationship between the author and the text can hardly ever be severed but it has been argued lately that it is the text that ultimately proclaims its independence even though the trace of the author remains within the text in many ambiguous ways. We are also aware that there is a real or historical author, as against a masked, imagined or implied author, which Gérard Genette has defined as the "image of the author in the text" (41). He/she is now a scripter, now a narrator, now an interpreter, but it is the sensibility of the age that finally defines and redefines an author according to the predominant poetics of the times. Both Roland Barthes and Michel Foucault seem to agree that the idea of the author and authorship started getting concretised only since the late eighteenth and early nineteenth centuries. This implies that the debate on the subject can be traced with certain clarity only since then.

Alexander Pope in his "Essay on Criticism" (1711) projected the author as seeking his "light" from the heavens and marked his significance for the quality of his wit. The Neoclassical emphasis on wit along with restraint, refinement and art that defined the author's obligation came to be replaced with emphasis on the role of imagination during the Romantic revival.[2] Wordsworth's definition of poetry in his "Preface to Lyrical Ballads" (1800), drawing upon spontaneity, powerful feelings, and their recollection in a moment of tranquillity, largely represented the stock response of the period with regard to the author (poet). An entirely different response in the early twentieth century came from Sigmund Freud, who said that both the creative writer and the child indulge in day-dreaming. The writer, he posited, "creates a world of fantasy which he takes very seriously—that is, which he invests with large amounts of emotion—while separating it sharply from reality" (36). Yet another view on the author was developed by T. S. Eliot in relation to the presence of the poet (author) at multiple levels:

> The first voice is the voice of the poet talking to himself—or to nobody. The second is the voice of the poet addressing an audience, whether large or small. The third is the voice of the poet when he attempts to create a dramatic character speaking in verse; when he is saying, not what he would say in his own person, but only what he can say within the limits of one imaginary character addressing another imaginary character. (1957, 89)

Eliot's engagement with the role of the author seems to have made way for further serious deliberations in a theoretical framework subsequently. Interestingly enough, the revision/editing of his own poem *The Waste Land* by Ezra Pound[3] raises an important question regarding the problem of authorship, as Pound may be considered to be sharing the authorship of this modern classic with his radical editing that may be seen in the facsimile and transcript of the original draft developed by Eliot. These advancements towards defining the author and authorship made way for deliberations like those by Barthes and Foucault at a later stage.

Barthes opened a new argument in "The Death of the Author" by separating the author, his world, and his worldview from the text. By declaring the death of the author, he privileged language and the structure of writing over the author as the one who only scripted a moment, or a context, in time and history. In underlining the movement from the author to the text, he relegated the author to the background and initiated a fresh discourse:

> The image of literature to be found in ordinary culture is tyrannically centred on the author.... The explanation of a work is always sought in the man or woman who produced it, as if it were always in the end, through the more or less transparent allegory of the fiction, the voice of a single person, the author 'confiding' in us. (126)

Showing a certain proximity, as well as distance from Barthes, Foucault engaged with undoing the author–reader hierarchy, negated the identity of the author as a historical personage, and subscribed to the configurations of history beyond the structures of language. More importantly, he deliberated upon the function of the author towards developing a discourse which accounts for yet another discourse. He summarised his argument on author function in "What is an Author" in these terms:

> (1) The author function is linked to the juridical and institutional system that encompasses, determines, and articulates the universe of discourses; (2) it does not affect all discourses in the same way at all times and in all types of civilisations; (3) it is not defined by the spontaneous attribution of a discourse to its producer, but rather by a series of specific and complex operations; (4) it does not refer purely and simply to a real individual, since it can give rise simultaneously to several

> selves, to several subjects—positions that can be occupied by different classes of individuals. (113)

Author, author function and the production of discourse have since acquired larger dimensions. Now, the author operates beyond language; he writes the world at large; he is, for example, an architect, a painter, a sculptor, and develops discourse in his own medium while privileging the medium rather than the message.

Let us now think of the modern Indian author in the context created above. This author is a potential literary entity today, and of much greater consequence than ever before. He/she is a cultural icon, an informed individual, a political being, an economic creature.[4] He/she draws upon the multiple contexts of his/her being and belonging, as also the complicated contexts of time – both past and present, myriad traditions of the land – both ancient and modern, and the regions of this land representing diverse languages and cultures. He/she incorporates within himself/herself a continuous tradition of social and intellectual evolution handed down through a long line, beginning with the saint–scholars of the past, symbolising *gyan* or *'ilm*, to the modern author constructing and disseminating an amazing variety of knowledge through electronic means. Descending through a line of *gyan-gurus* to *e-gurus*, he/she strikes a balance and acquires an individual identity. He/she traverses through a maze of time and place; he/she represents a part that aspires to reflect the broad Indian sociocultural reality as a whole that is both diverse and united; the economic condition that is now stressed, now relaxed; and the political situation that now causes conflict, now achieves a compromise to suit narrow ends. While incorporating many voices, he/she works as a mediator in disguise to evolve his/her own narrative. He/she historicises the land and its people; he/she projects a broader perception of truth and a broader kind of knowledge with reference to the Indian nation – its racial predicaments, cultural configurations and linguistic interfaces.

As a phenomenon on the literary map, this modern Indian author is on a continuous quest for particularising and indigenising his/her literary representation. He/she seeks an idiom and a text that may be unambiguously called Indian in its form and value. He/she resists, reclaims, reconfigures; he/she evolves new structures of art and meaning. He/she enters into broad collaborations with other Indian literary and linguistic traditions – canonical formulations as well as other texts, genres, ages, and milieu. At the turn of the century, this author emerged as the one who constructed co-texts and sub-texts in the process of creating his/her text. This author is now intertextual, heterogeneous and multilayered. He/she may be read best along a complex web of references, and also as the one who can assimilate multiple traditions while creating one of his/her own kind and make.

Today, this modern Indian author reflects a rich tradition of the sacred, the secular, and the profane writings of a nation that expresses itself in two thousand dialects and eight hundred languages, out of which twenty-two are its official languages. He/she acquires his/her special strength from heterogeneous perceptions, narrative forms, cross-cultural identities and interconnections, given to him/her by both the past and the present.[5] This author is clearly distinguishable from any other author of any postcolonial site in how he/she figures his/her modernism and postmodernism,[6] how he/she approaches his/her language, defines his/her location, and expresses his/her ideology, in how he/she uses his/her history and memory and in how he/she constructs his/her own myths of belonging.

TEXT

The discourse on the status of the author in the modern times appeared after New Criticism prioritised the text over the author and made way for a fuller theoretical engagement with the subject. A stock response came from T. S. Eliot in his 1919 essay "Tradition and the Individual Talent" where he proclaimed: "Honest criticism and sensitive appreciation is directed not upon the poet but upon the poetry" (1953, 25). Later, W. K. Wimsatt and M. C. Beardsley in "The Intentional Fallacy" (1946) also argued that the "design or intention of the author is neither available nor desirable as a standard for judging the success of a work of literary art" (16). This amounted to clearly proclaiming that the text could not be justifiably subjected to authorial intention as it stood on its own, and retained its status despite the author being its creator.[7]

Following Eliot, Wimsatt and Beardsley, it would be appropriate now to engage with the idea of the text as problematised by at least two of the theorists referred to frequently in this regard. In works like "The Death of the Author" (1967), "From Work to Text" (1971), *The Pleasure of the Text* (1973) and "Theory of the Text" (1973), Barthes problematised the idea of the author and the text in order to develop a fuller discourse on their nature, role and status. He emphasised the plurality of the text and the extension of one into many other texts, giving it an intertextual character. A text, to Barthes, was a "multidimensional space in which a variety of writings, none of them original, blend and clash. The text is a tissue of quotations drawn from the innumerable centres of cultures" (128). This was an exercise in rewriting that went on endlessly. He also gave precedence to text over the author as it is the language that is the repository of a supposed message rather than the author, who is only a medium. Barthes also considered text either as "readerly" or "writerly", by which he meant that the readerly text was one in which the reader remained a passive recipient while in the writerly text the reader is an active participant; a decoder of the text. Furthermore, being different from "work" which has a physical form, a text is a linguistic manifestation with a structure that strikes a balance between the text (language) and the reader (receiver). The text is thus a manifestation of multiple signifiers.

This aligns further with Derrida's idea that a text spills over the margin and the binding of the book; it embodies the trace of the other text(s) with certain difference, and bears the burden of arbitrariness, absences and deferments as language remains ever unstable. To Derrida, a text is thus not "a finished corpus of writing…but a differential network, a fabric of traces referring endlessly to something other than itself, to other differential traces." (84). Both Barthes and Derrida marked a keen relationship between language and text and underlined the instability of both language and meaning. Octavio Paz developed a thesis closer to this with regard to translation which opens to the reader a world composed of texts over texts:

> Each text is unique, yet at the same time it is the translation of another text. No text can be completely original because language itself, in its very essence, is already a translation—first from the non-verbal world, and then, because each sign and each phrase is a translation of another sign, another phrase. (154)

As the romantic notion of text as a body of literal meaning matured into a discourse, it became a complex figural representation, and finally reached a stage where it was completely liberated and became an open site of possible meaning. The idea of text turned into a subject of philosophical inquiry with Barthes and Derrida who transformed it ultimately into a critical discourse. Literary theory liberated text from the traditionally defined literary expression of the verbal kind. As such, the world itself, with all its signs and symbols, came to be problematised as text.

Considering the above in the context of the multiplicity of his/her belonging, one could pertinently ask what kind of a text the modern Indian author creates. Does he/she create *many texts in many languages* or just *one text but in many languages*? Understandably, he/she constructs one that represents many as he/she exists both unilaterally and multilaterally. I have mentioned sacred, secular and profane categories above.[8] They broadly represent the large variety of texts the modern Indian author produces today, as well as texts the authors in the past produced. It must, however, be posited that the modern Indian author sets the parameters of his/her writing with greater clarity now than his/her predecessors did.

Having passed through diverse periods of our history (ancient, medieval, modern and contemporary), phases of linguistic predominance (Sanskrit, Pali, Prakrit, Tamil, Persian and English), cultural identities (North, East, Northeast, West and South), communal configurations (Hindu, Muslim, Sikh, Christian, etc.), and thematic diversities (gender, subaltern, regional and national), Indian literatures are now clubbed into different linguistic clusters for the sake of convenience (Hindi-Urdu-Punjabi, Bangla-Odiya-Ahomiya, Tamil-Telugu-Kannada-Malayalam, and so on). Even while being a part of the larger whole, Indian texts differ from one another as they represent ideological/thematic/experiential varieties and stylistic modes/movements/milieus. Such a thesis may be testified best in the context of many Indias representing multiple literary traditions. Historical, linguistic, cultural, communal and thematic clustering, however, have their limitations as they create barriers and boundaries which translation alone is capable of breaking. It is, to some extent, already doing this. It is in this process of breaking barriers, developing resistance and reconfiguring the very act of writing that a sense of the "Indian" has been created and a new literary culture has come into being.

Thinking of the modern Indian text, one may thus assert that it incorporates co-text(s) and sub-text(s), as has been suggested earlier, precisely because it draws upon hybrid linguistic patterns, cultural configurations and historical predicaments. Most appropriately, it is at this stage that the author finds the translator as a co-author of his text. This co-author/translator takes the author's text beyond the confines of a given language for broader negotiation with other readers. This renders the whole process of authoring, co-authoring and reading quite complicated in the new literary context and redefines the role and nature of the author, the text, the translator and the reader.[9] In other words, the four enter into a complex relationship of shared empowerment in which one draws upon the other only to create multiple levels of writing and reading.

TRANSLATOR

A translator is a curious being between the author and the reader of a translated text. He/she has been in existence perennially, as the history of translation in world languages shows, which establishes that he/she forges and determines multiple relationships among communities of readers, a melange of messages, and clusters of languages. These easy-to-arrive-at conclusions, however, lead to some serious questions. One: is the translator an author too, and if so, must he/she also be declared dead like the author; two: how much of theory does he/she know, if that be a requirement, and how does he/she benefit from it to execute his/her job; three: what is his/her motivation to do what he/she does, and what method does he/she apply; four: does he/she have a reader in mind, and a set of ethics to follow; five: does he/she also vie with the author to project his/her own discourse; and six, does he/she really create a community of compatible readers, a habitat of the likes, a small democracy of commons, of his/her own hegemonic order with his/her own ideology and idealism?

In more ways than one, these questions underscore the method and methodology of translation and translation studies. To answer the first question, it may be proposed that one may not logically deny that a translator is an author but he/she has limitations in the sense he/she is an author's author, a demi/semi-god, the author's other.[10] As such, his/her death may be more immanent than the author's, and his/her life less eminent than that of the one whose shadow he/she bears. To address the second question, it may said that the translator may be inwardly aware of the critical demands of his/her job but may not necessarily be a translation theorist to be able to translate, just as the author was not inevitably required to undergo lessons in creative writing to write his/her text. It is only proper to assert that practice leads to theory and not the other way round, as can be testified by referring to creative writing as writing independent of all constraints.[11] The answer to the third question regarding motives and methods is closely related with the answer to the second question. Both the author and the translator configure a language to their purposes and unless otherwise motivated to write/translate a text, are not dictated by any reason except their own to appropriate a language for themselves, as it is finally the language that speaks rather than the author/translator. The problem of readership and ethics which constitutes the fourth question can be addressed with reference to the predominant sensibility to which a language/text, and by implication the author/translator, caters. The text, in the act of being, brings its own ethical parameters of authoring which relates with the issues of thematic preferences and linguistic nuances to create a certain desired condition. Answers to the fifth and the sixth questions are interrelated and complex. Translators are known to have moved away from their authors, manipulated the text, and misrepresented them. Such an act on the translator's part may be directed towards projecting his/her own discourse at the author's cost, which is essentially a matter of ethics in translation. While he/she indulges in violating the text/author, he/she does create a community of his/her own readers who may be misled while trusting the translator. This may lead to the creation of an exclusive habitat of individuals of a certain orientation and create a hegemonic structure of a given ideology.

Let us now examine how this complex relationship has come into being in the context of the Indian translator. We should do well to remind ourselves that in the eighteenth and nineteenth centuries both religious and secular texts, being considered as literary texts of remarkable merit, were translated by the Orientalists and other Western translators for English language readers.[12] Not concerned or aware of the theoretical issues involved, they were trying, at best, to present the great literary curiosity of India to the West with respect to themes, characterisation, taste and style. They were interested in bringing out the Hindu notion of the sacred, the profane and the secular, and in reflecting the great variety of Indian life, beliefs and manners that were of interest to their new-found readership. Their efforts, however, essentialised India as a land of spiritualism, exotica, grandeur and romance, a notion which postcolonial theory resisted, although much later.

The early twentieth century saw the emergence of Indian translators on the scene[13] but they too were acutely aware of the fact that the West mattered and translators needed to seek acceptance from those quarters. This is quite understandable in view of the colonial discourse that held sway during those days. Postcolonial India, however, saw a remarkable change with the context of translation growing more complex.[14] In the wake of postcolonial studies emerging as a new theoretical domain, it became a political agenda to foreground resistance against essentialist positions and to create new paradigms of writing and reading. There was now a need to evolve a definition of the Indian Postcolonial in particular, and Indian Literature in general, in order to establish its individual nature and relevance and to create its post-independence, pan-Indian identity. Translation, as such, became a serious engagement with young academics, established writers, translation experts and critics.[15] They engaged themselves with retrieving and reviving the past, reinventing the form of the ancient and the classical Indian texts, turning the exotic into what is strikingly real for contemporary relevance, and finally, developing new resistances and new representations for the contemporary reader.

READER

At the end of his essay "Why Write", Jean-Paul Sartre posed a rather philosophical question: "For whom does one write?" (384). He finds an answer in the relationship between the author and the reader who keep the writing alive. Following a detailed discussion, he makes a precise point:

> Thus, reading is a pact of generosity between author and reader. Each one trusts the other; each one counts on the other, demands of the other as much as he demands of himself. For this confidence is itself generosity. Nothing can force the author to believe that his reader will use freedom; nothing can force the reader to believe that the author has used his. Both of them make a free decision. There is then established a dialectical going-and-coming; when I read, I make demands; if my demands are met, what I am then reading provokes me to demand more of the author, which

> means to demand of the author that he demand more of me. And vice versa, the author's demand is that I carry my demands to the highest pitch. Thus, my freedom, by revealing itself, reveals the freedom of the other. (379)

The idea of the author–reader nexus may be problematised further by proposing that both the author and the translator have an imagined reader to themselves, although this reader would differ from the author depending on the constituency of the language into which the text is translated and the community of readers which, as the Reader Response theory suggests, generates meaning. The Structuralists, on the other hand, would argue that it is the narrative that creates the reader and that the reader is thus a construction, an implied entity who is created by the author and is not a real reader. This corresponds with the construction of the implied author by the real author within the body of the text who carries forward the narrative to the reader. Extending this logic further, it may be posited that it is not the author alone who constructs a reader; the translator does the same. This brings us to Barthes who invested the reader with a unique strength in proclaiming that "the birth of the reader must be at the cost of the death of the Author". (130)

In relation to the theoretical argument, one could posit that the new Indian reader is one who generally reads in more than one language. There is, however, a class in metropolitan India that can read only in the English language.[16] There are many, however, who willingly read across languages, negotiate between literary cultures and evolve their own responses. The act of reading is a conscious and political act, just as the acts of writing and translating are conscious and political acts. There are vital questions involved in this process, like who is the reader of a given text, how that reader approaches that text and at what point of time. This process also redefines the role of the reader, the intellectual climate around, and the nature of the text he/she chooses to approach. The text is configured many a time: first by the author, then by the translator, and at both times by the respective readers in the source language as well as in the target language. The multiplicity of responses can be figured out in the following five models.

FIVE MODELS OF WRITING AND EMPOWERMENT

The very act of writing is an act of empowerment in itself and it empowers all four: the author, the text, the translator, and the reader, quite distinctly. They develop a complex relationship in various combinations and permutations as may be seen in the following proposed models of writing and empowerment:

Model 1: Empowerment of the Author

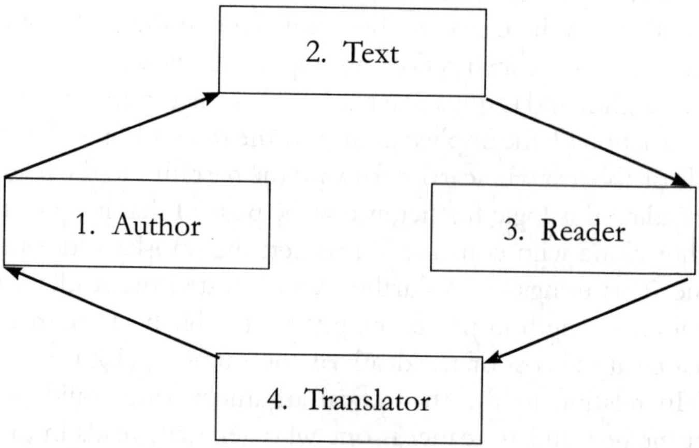

(i) The figure shows that the author has a text, a reader, and a translator.

(ii) It also shows that the author has a text, the text a reader, and the reader a translator for himself/herself who would deliver him/her to the author.

(iii) In both the options, the author stands empowered. He/she is the prime mover as he/she first creates a text, then calls for a reader, and then earns a translator. In this process, he/she calls upon his/her readers at two different levels: first, to negotiate with the text in the source language, and then in the target language.

Model 2: Empowerment of the Text

(i) The figure shows that the text has an author, a translator, and a reader.

(ii) It also shows that the text has an author, the author a translator, and the translator a reader for himself/ herself who he/she delivers to the target language text.

(iii) In both cases, the text stands empowered. The text is the prime mover as it controls its author, then calls for a translator, and then earns a reader. In this process, the text also calls upon its readers at two different levels: first, to negotiate with it in the source language, and then in the target language

Model 3: Empowerment of the Translator

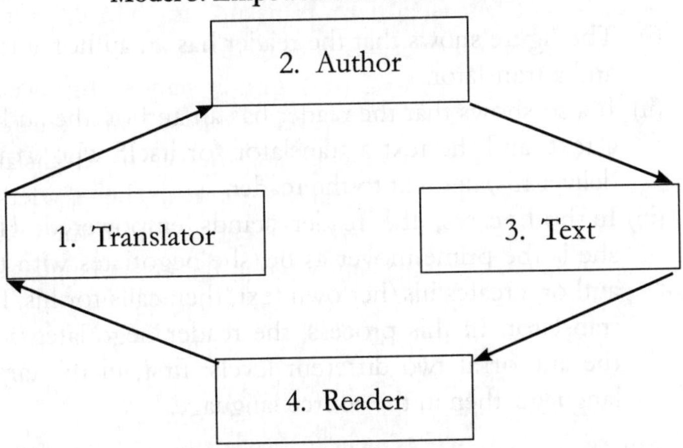

(i) The figure shows that the translator has an author, a text, and a reader.
(ii) It also shows that the translator has an author, the author a text, and the text a reader for himself/herself who would deliver him/her to the translator.
(iii) In both cases, the translator stands empowered. He/she is the prime mover as he/she negotiates with the author, creates his/her own text, and then calls for his/her reader. In this process, the translator, like the author, calls upon his/her readers at two levels: first, to negotiate with it in the target language, then in the source language.

Model 4: Empowerment of the Reader

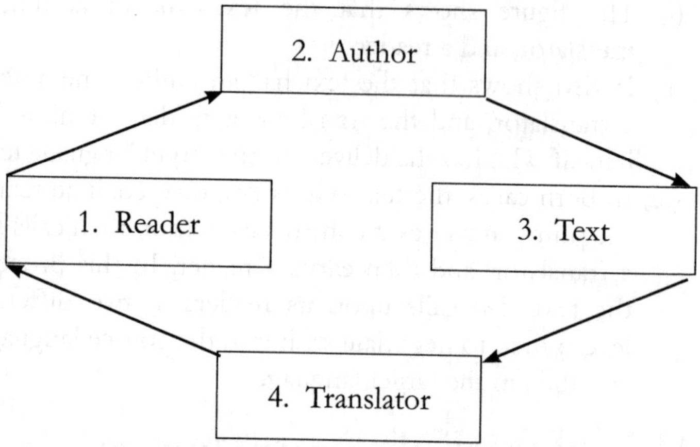

(i) The figure shows that the reader has an author, a text, and a translator.
(ii) It also shows that the reader has an author, the author a text, and the text a translator for itself who would deliver his/her text to the reader.
(iii) In both cases, the reader stands empowered. He/she is the prime mover as he/she negotiates with the author, creates his/her own text, then calls for his/her translator. In this process, the reader negotiates with the author at two different levels: first, in the target language, then in the source language.

Model 5: Multiple Empowerments

The author has	→	Text of one kind
The translator has	→	Text of another kind
The reader has	→	Text of yet another kind

The text is again empowered here because of the multiple natures it acquires in multiple hands. While the text remains the prime mover, the three addressees or recipients of the text approach it in three different ways.

This raises the theoretical question of the multiplicities of text, authorship, and readership.[17] As there are two texts, one in the source language and another in the target language, there are two authors, one being the source language author and the other being the target language author. Ultimately, when the text moves to the readers, it gathers infinite responses both in the source language text, as well as in the target language. At this stage, both the author and the translator lose control over their work and remain subjected to unpredictable responses from a variety of readers.

CONTEXTUALISATION, THEORISATION, CANONISATION

Drawing upon the issues raised above, I would like to posit that the whole process of writing, reading and translating today has to be approached with reference to three vital factors – *context, theory* and *canon.* An understanding of the context – both past and present – is important to redefine one's location in it. Similarly, there has to be a theoretical basis for choosing a text to read for valid reasons and to translate that text for the contemporary reader with a valid methodology in hand. An understanding of the context and the evolution of theory, as proposed, would lead naturally to the formation of a canon that would sustain both Indian literatures and Indian literatures in English translation.

All three – context, theory and canon – I would suggest, are in the process of acquiring their certain concrescence.[18] The three vital figures of the author, the reader, and the translator are constantly engaged in locating, identifying, and shaping their texts. The text is their forte, the sign and the signal of their identity that sustains them as it grows over them. It is in a continuous process of configurations and re-configurations. This text evolves on its own as it draws its spirit from the people it represents, the language it chooses, the location it concerns, the history it constructs, and the ideology it nurtures. The author, the reader and the translator partake in its organic growth. The new Indian postcolonial condition is yet another reality that it incorporates in its web of myriad references which it draws from history.

Even a general appraisal of the present literary scenario would suggest that the conditions for writing and reading have changed remarkably, the space for translation has increased manifold, and the parameters of acceptance have broken new ground. As a result, a new literary culture has come to stay. In this new scenario, literary and popular texts are no longer alien neighbours; they find a liberal space on private and public shelves together. Genres and forms, narratives and structures are not sacrosanct any further, and do not have to be kept from mixing with one another. The new canon departs from traditional norms in critical ways in order to create new ones. The new literary culture admits new discourses, new bodies of knowledge and new modes of dissemination. The new Indian text that is historically, politically and socially conscious is intertextual, interdisciplinary and comparative; it affords individual space to the author, the reader and the translator who construct a text together. This text remains in flux as it reconstructs the past for the present, the present for the future – a future which is likely to repeat the process incessantly.

NOTES

1. Much theoretical discussion has gone into the nature, concept and role of the author, the text, the translator and the reader during the past decades in Western academia and intellectual circles. Some of the seminal contributions on these may be found in the works of Andrew Sarris ("Notes on the Auteur Theory", 1962), Jacques Derrida ("Structure, Sign, and Play in the Discourse of the Human Sciences", 1966), Roland Barthes ("The Death of the Author", 1968, "From Work to Text", 1971), Michel Foucault ("What is an Author?", 1969), Alexander Nehamas ("What an Author Is", 1986), Sara Mills ed. (*Gendering the Reader*, 1994), Andrew Bennett ed. *(Readers and Reading*, 1995) and Harold Bloom *(How to Read and Why*, 2000). Issues concerning these four have not been, however, debated in the Indian context, although there is a need to do so with reference to the singular nature of India's linguistic and cultural multiplicity, as also the fast changing literary scenario in India. This chapter makes an attempt to lay down certain parameters concerning the complex relationship that the author the text, the reader and the translator foreground.
2. For a comprehensive treatment of the ways of imagination, especially in relation to Coleridge, see John Livingston Lowes, *The Road to Xanadu* (Constable and Company: Great Britain, 1927).
3. See the newer facsimile edition of *The Waste Land: A Facsimile and transcript of the original drafts including the annotations of Ezra Pound*, ed. Valerie Eliot (London: Faber and Faber, 2011).
4. This is clearly borne out by the changing socio-economic scenario. References may be made to the increasing per capita income of Indians, their migration from rural to urban areas, the phenomenon of urbanisation, increasing expenditure on infrastructure by the state and broader accessibility to the larger world by electronic media, popular culture, internet, etc.
5. A reference may be made to the literary history of India which showcases a rich and diverse fare of writings in many languages and in many styles, representing many voices.
6. The labels of "modernism", "postmodernism" and "postcolonialism" have been used rather loosely with reference to the Indian context. Indian versions of these are different as they came to be used in India much later, acquired their roots differently and developed under different circumstances.
7. An interesting parallel may be found in W. H. Auden's poem "In Memory of W. B. Yeats" where the idea of life's transience and art's (text's) permanence is projected: "The death of the poet was kept from his poems". This is further reiterated metaphorically: "The words of a dead man/Are modified in the guts of the living" (107).

8. Traditionally, these broad categories have been used to mark the variety of Indian literary writings. It is, however, important to note that these categories stand open to revision in view of the new writings that India has produced during the past few decades.
9. These issues that primarily concern the theory of translation may be examined with great relevance and profit with reference to the Indian context. This is so precisely because of the difference that India as a literary site represents in terms of linguistic multiplicity, cultural variety and the narrative strategies employed.
10. The appearance of the translator's name in print is a rather recent phenomenon. It has been a prolonged and delayed process. Once the translator asserted his/her "right", his/her name was mentioned in small print at the end of the text; then it started appearing on the inner pages, and now it appears on the title page, though less prominently, although some publishers are yet to allow this space to him/her. The translator today is vying for a much larger space; he/she seeks prominence, no less than the author, to the extent that, metaphorically speaking, he/she tills someone else's soil and claims the harvest as his/her own. Translation awards being offered now give a fillip to his/her desire to acquire an identity of his/her own, parallel to the author.
11. One might suggest that one learns driving while sitting in the driver's seat and not by taking theoretical lessons in driving. This is not to undermine the role of theory but only to suggest that theory is an academic engagement of a very respectable kind but its knowledge is not a necessary condition for competent writing and/or translating.
12. Charles Wilkins: *Bhagavad Gita*, Sir William Jones: *Abhignansakuntalam*, W. Franklin: *The Love of Kamarupa and Kamalata*, Nathaniel Halhed: *Upanishads*, Horace Hayman Wilson: *The Megha Duta*, C. A. Elliott: *Chronicles of Oonao*, T. H. Griffith: *Ramayana*, M. Kempson: *Taubat-un-Nasuh*, H. A. D. Phillips: *Kopal-Kundala*, W. Dumorgue: *Indulekha.*
13. Romesh Chundur Dutt translated his own Bangla novel into English as *The Lake of Palms,* as did Tagore his poems. Another interesting example is that of Purohit Swami who translated *Ten Principal Upanishads* with the assistance of W. B. Yeats.
14. Only a brief account of translation activities in India in various phases has been given here but it would be highly instructive to study the history of translation in India. This would also highlight the changing notions of the text as developed by the translator, his/her choice for a particular text against the other, and his/her methodology of translation.
15. A. K. Ramanujan chose to translate ancient classics from Tamil and Telugu, Gayatri Chakravorty Spivak decided to do so for Mahasweta Devi, William Radice for Tagore, Ralph Russell for Ghalib, Qurratulain Hyder for her own work, Dilip Chitre for Tukaram, Linda Hess for Kabir, Agha Shahid Ali for Faiz, and so on.

16. This underlines the problematic of class difference in India, the rural–urban divide, as also the acquired and the imposed norms of behaviour and language use.
17. This is also related primarily with the theory of translation but it acquires greater relevance when considered in relation to the Indian author, text, reader, and translator.
18. Although translation has emerged as a major literary activity in India and critical writings related to the theory and practice of translation have multiplied during the past decade, they are yet to achieve a mark of authenticity and broader acceptability as compared to similar activities in the Western world. It is thus imperative that the whole enterprise of translating and understanding translation is critically formulated and assessed in the Indian context.

WORKS CITED

Auden, W. H. 1940. *In memory of W. B. Yeats. In another time.* London: Faber and Faber.

Barthes, Roland. 1995. The death of the author. In *Authorship: From Plato to the postmodern: A reader,* ed. Seán Burke. Edinburgh: Edinburgh University Press.

Derrida, Jacques. 1979. Living on/Border lines. In *Deconstruction and criticism*, ed. Harold Bloom, Paul de Man, Jacques Derrida, Geoffrey H. Hartman and J. Hillis Miller. London: Routledge.

Eliot, T. S. 1953. Tradition and the individual talent. In *Selected prose*, ed. John Hayward. London: Penguin.

———. 1957. Three voices of poetry. In *On poetry and poets.* London: Faber and Faber.

Foucault, Michel. 1984. What is an author? In *The Foucault reader*, ed. Paul Rabinow. New York: Pantheon Books.

Freud, Sigmund. [1908] 1972. Creative writers and day-dreaming. In *20th century literary criticism: A reader*, ed. David Lodge. London: Longman.

Genette, Gérard. 1988. *Narrative discourse revisited.* Trans. Jane E. Lewin. Ithaca, NY: Cornell University Press.

Paz, Octavio. 1992. Translation: Literature and letters. In *Theories of translation from Dryden to Derrida*, ed. R. Schule and J. Bigunete. Chicago: University of Chicago Press.

Sartre, Jean-Paul. 1972. Why write. In *20th century literary criticism: A reader*, ed. David Lodge. London: Longman.

Wimsatt, W. K. and M. C. Beardsley. 1954. The intentional fallacy. In *The verbal icon: Studies in the meaning of poetry*. Lexington: University of Kentucky Press.

TWO

Changing the Order: The Problem of Translatability

The recent proliferation of translation activities in India calls for a serious academic examination. It is a phenomenon of great literary merit and a marketable proposition of considerable worth. I have posited in this chapter that all discussions concerning literary translation, in one way or another, revolve around the larger questions of language, writing and translatability which, in turn, relate to various text and translation types.

A literary piece of writing is a phenomenon of veritable significance. It is a complex construct of cultural significations, political connotations and historical implications. This writing acquires greater magnitude if it hails from a multilingual and multicultural site like India. It tests and tries a translator – it is elusive at times, familiar and easily penetrable, at others. Its translatability remains, at best, a possible/impossible proposition.

Further, a piece of writing enters into a dialogue with the reader and the translator at diverse levels. It collaborates with other languages, authors, ages, canons and genres. Just as the concept of original writing is illusory, so is the concept of originality in translation. Since no writing is a complete entity unto itself, no translation can ever be an absolute unit. This chapter posits that there is as much of an element of fluidity and fantasy in writing as in the act of translation, since both are mutable insofar as one puts language in order, and the other changes that order.

Although generalised statements may sound banal at times, they also help to initiate an argument and to make a point. As I wish to do both here, I would like to begin by positing certain primary issues concerning writing as language in order, translation as changing the order, and translatability as a larger problem of negotiation between (a) language and intent, (b) sound and meaning, (c) form and structure, and finally (d) culture, history and politics. In this regard, I would like to posit that the history of putting language in order to construct a piece of writing, and translation as a piece of rewriting by changing that order, is as old as human consciousness. This argument may be carried further by saying that all human expressions are essentially an effort at putting a language in order, and finding ways to translate it by changing that order. These propositions make way for an extended argument that sheer human necessity, irrespective of its magnitude, led to the need for creating a certain order of words to convey a message. Thereafter, this order was changed through translation to reach newer areas of readership/reception. With these points of reference in mind, I would like to proceed further and examine the ways language is conducted through the process of writing, and how in the subsequent stages of rewriting – of translating one writing into another – the issues of translation and translatability emerge from multiple domains of human communication and trajectories of civilisation.

WRITING AS LANGUAGE IN ORDER

Let it be said at the beginning that all our acts with letters and words put in different combinations that result in the acts of noting, drafting, messaging, scripting and so on are, broadly speaking, various acts of writing. Although each one is a different act from the other, done in a different manner and with a different purpose, each one uses language in some order which may or may not follow a given or standard practice of writing. This order is determined by the varying linguistic principles followed consciously or unconsciously by a people, the rules of their grammar, and their larger sociocultural and psychological conditions that cause the construction of a supposed meaning. In the literary domain, the act of writing is a much more complicated act than others as it involves the use of imagination, employment of rhetorical devices and an understanding of linguistic manoeuvres. An individual who produces a literary piece of writing graduates from being a writer to being an author[1] which subsumes the act of languaging an idea and developing a discourse. For the purpose of this chapter, I would like to neutrally designate all literary production as writing which puts language in a well-wrought order, as defined by the processes of historical, political and sociocultural evolution of a people.

Going back to the broader idea of writing as language in order, I would argue that seeking expression has been a basic need and desire of human beings ever since they came into existence. Born in a physical image, they have expressed themselves through two modes – gesture and language – and these two modes of expression, both separately and together, have evolved larger modes of human expression. Further, words or counters of expression that formulate a language, when put in various orders, have emerged from the dual needs of mankind: the need to broaden the frontiers of knowledge, and the need to establish communication with others. Human beings naturally desire knowledge, said Aristotle, and this desire to acquire knowledge got manifested in their psychological need to explore new areas of awareness, to extend the limits of human relationships, and to communicate beyond the confines of the self, for which purpose language, both communicative and dialogic in nature, was devised.

This need to communicate beyond the confines of the self led men and women to discover their own imaginative counters of linguistic expression in the later stages of the development of a civilisation. This resulted, ultimately, in the emergence of organised writing, over a long-drawn process of historical evolution. It was in this process of growth and development of a people that a working lexicon acquired concrescence, which later gave birth to a language, then the language to a grammar, and the grammar to a pattern of expression, and finally that pattern of expression to a style. Writing, therefore, is a complex phenomenon – it has grown and concretised over a prolonged span of time, and it has emerged as the sign of a people and their essential character. Thus, the huge legacy of writing created by the geniuses of various languages was bound to be as varied as human needs. Writing came to be created as per the needs of a given place, and its various purposes included imparting knowledge, creating a political order, running a social structure, establishing a legal system, colonising a people, running a market, propagating a religious faith, evolving a healthy message, spreading a vicious propaganda, integrating or disintegrating a people, and so on. In a different parlance, writings of innumerable types came to be created which included secular and religious, social and political, cultural and philosophical, legal and administrative, scientific and technical kinds of writing, as also those kinds generated and conditioned by the market and propagandist forces.

This brings us to the idea of various kinds of writing designated as "types" of writing. These types, generated by various societies, mark their social and intellectual conditions in general. They fall into two broad categories of imaginative and non-imaginative kinds of writing, and are caused and conditioned by the common sensibility of the age. Trying to put them in a larger context, Hatim and Mason mention the types of writing and their supposed function:

> Classifying texts according to criteria such as 'field of discourse' alone amounts to little more than a statement of subject matter, with examples such as 'journalistic', 'religious', 'scientific' text types. Defined in this way, text type, like register, is so broad as to have no predictive value. Yet when attempts are made to narrow the focus of

> description, we run the risk of ending up with virtually as many text types as there are texts.
>
> Another approach based on an over-general notion of text 'function' leads to text types such as 'literary', 'poetic', 'didactic'. Again the categories are too broad and do not admit the possibility of a literary text being didactic and vice versa. (138)

Hatim and Mason engage with the typology of writing and their functionality in a larger perspective by examining the issues of textuality, contextuality, intertextuality, textual interaction, textual hybridity, ideology and thematic variety. Albrecht Neubert and Gregory M. Shreve problematise it further by positing that the types of writing are "labels for complexes of receptive expectations and productive procedures. Writing types act to define sets of socially situated textual instances which share certain features" (127). They elaborate on the idea that the text types "operate as procedural knowledge because configurations of textual markers (patterns of linguistic material) are associated with abstract frames" (128). They develop these propositions still further with reference to prototypes of writing, their meaning, macrostructures and macrorules, communicative value, writing and communicative equivalence, and finally, with writing in relation to translation theory.

All these formulations have been carried forward in yet another direction by Susan Bassnett in her essay "Culture and Translation" with reference to writing grids, where she draws upon her earlier work, *Constructing Cultures: Essays on Literary Translation*, to make a different point. She writes:

> In formulating our notion of textual grids, we pointed out (Bassnett & Lefevere, 1998:5) that some cultures (such as French, German and English) share a common textual grid that derives from the Christian and Greco-Roman traditions. Other cultures (such as Chinese and Japanese) share less with others. But the textual grids seem to exist in all cultures in ways that pre-exist language. The grids are

> constructs; they reflect patterns of expectations that have been interiorised by members of a given culture. (19)

One may, therefore, argue that writing grids define a culture as much as a culture determines the nature and character of its writing grids. These grids also determine the contours of individual and collective writings produced in a culture and they ultimately characterise a literary history. Writing types and writing grids, taken together, seem to make way for a kind of thesis that Terry Eagleton has projected while answering what is both an ever-old and ever-current question as to what it is that we call literature, or literary writing. He has developed a liberal approach towards various kinds of writing based both on fact and fiction and interrogated the very role of language, the place of ideology, the problem of value judgement, and the use of literary devices in a very broad framework of literary and extra-literary references. Keeping his ideological position in abeyance until the essay's conclusion, he finally draws upon it at the end of the essay and seemingly suggests that all types of writings, if they need to be classified at all, may be classified as literary writing. He writes,

> It is true that that many of the works studied as literature in academic institutions were 'constructed' to be read as literature, but it is also true many of them were not. A piece of writing may start off as history or philosophy and then come to be ranked as literature; or it may start off as literature and then come to be valued for its archaeological significance. Some texts are born literary, some achieve literariness, and some have literariness thrust upon them. (7)

While Eagleton harked back to Shakespeare rather lightly to make his point, it may be appreciated that he underscored the significance of the varieties of writing produced over a period of time and how they have been perceived differently at different time periods. Drawing upon the types and grids of writing, as also the open definition of writing proposed by Eagleton, it should be possible to assert that written works have been produced variously in various ages and cultures in the past, and would continue to be produced in the future as well. They would, in the process, contribute towards the making of literary cultures generation after generation. These literary cultures would, consequently, define and redefine the acts of putting a language in order, and changing that order to produce a work in translation.

All these varied kinds of writing ultimately helped identify a people and their major characteristics. Difficulties in the process of producing a piece of writing arose when human concerns multiplied and grew intricate with the passage of time. Writing, therefore, was no longer the result of an individual's experience or indulgence; it became a serious critical and theoretical concern as it turned into a complex construction of disparate constituents. It reflected the growth of a language, as much as it represented the complicated thematic or ideological concerns of a people. It also became intertwined with the progress of a culture, the preservation of knowledge and cross-cultural communications. Thus, writing became an iconic activity, a certain measure of the growth and development of a social conglomeration or habitat. In this process of growth and development, a literary piece of writing turned, ultimately, to be a phenomenon of veritable significance, a complex construction of cultural significations, political connotations and historical implications. This writing acquired varying degrees of significance depending on the site from where it emerged. Cultures with a more unified pattern of history produced writings which were relatively simple and less layered, while cultures with more complex patterns of history produced more complex and nuanced kinds of writings to negotiate with. In the case of the latter, highly diverse and variegated types of writing came to be handed down. These writings were bound to evade a concrete and broader definition of their essential nature, as would be borne out by the case of the multilayered writings from a multilingual and multicultural site like India. Indian exercises in literary writing, I would submit, have tested and tried a translator more than any other kind of writing, especially when an effort was made to translate it into a non-Indian language.

It must be further added that a piece of writing could not have been constituted unless it entered into a dialogue with its co-relates at diverse levels. This dialogue had to be established with the reader, as also with other languages and ages, authors and writings, canons and customs, forms and genres. It implies that no writing has a unitary life of its own, nor does it stand alone in isolation. As such, literary texts can never be said to be entirely independent and original in their make-up, character and cumulative impact. Let me assert that writings sustain a culture, and as cultures do not survive in isolation, the writings too do not live a unitary life. This amounts to an assertion that the writings that grow in shared, dialogic and communicative relationships in and beyond time, grow organically as writings of power representing an advanced cultural condition with greater authenticity. This writing of power is characterised by its ability to wield influence in and outside the peripheries of its origin; it creates new canons, and seeks new identities.

These arguments lead us to think of what has been posited by theorists as the instability of language, causing indeterminacy and unreliability of meaning in a piece of writing. As all writings remain open, they generate questions about language itself as the carrier of a supposed discourse. For Barthes in "The Death of the Author", writing is "neutral, composite, oblique space where our subject slips away…where all identity is lost" (125). This has been interrogated further by Michel Foucault in "What is an Author" to develop a revisionist stance and to posit that

> writing has freed itself from the dimensions of expression. Referring only to itself, but without being restricted to the confines of its interiority, writing is identified with its own unfolded exteriority. This means that it is an interplay of signs arranged less according to its signified content than according to the very nature of the signifier. Writing unfolds like a game (*jeu*) that invariably goes beyond its own rules and transgresses its limits. In writing, the point is not to manifest or exalt the act of writing, nor is it to pin a subject within language; it is rather, a question of creating a space into which the writing subject constantly disappears. (102)

Foucault's reference to the liberation of text, its engagement with signs, and its transgressing its own rules underline the nature of modern literary writing. Modern literary writing, however, may not be seen in isolation as it constitutes a part of a larger tradition which began in an oral form and grew to concertise in written forms which developed diversely with time.

Let me now elaborate upon the relationship between the oral and the written forms of literary expression. I would like to do this with reference to two analogous Indian narratives – *Baitaal Pacheesi* and *Singhasan Batteesi.* These two narratives have passed from the oral to a variety of written forms over a period of time, defying the preordained stature of the sacrosanct narrative which is necessarily assigned to an author. These two narratives, like many others, are typical examples of cultural configuration that define a characteristically Indian textual grid like the one referred to by Bassnett with reference to French, German, English, Chinese and Japanese. To contextualise this argument, a brief discussion of the two narratives is necessary.

Let me first discuss *Singhasan Batteesi.* Before it came to be recorded variously in prose and poetry, especially in the Persian, Urdu and Hindi languages, it took its birth as an oral tale in the typical Oriental tradition. With the dates of its composition and authorship unconfirmed,[2] it acquired a definite form only when it was transferred from the oral to the written word in Sanskrit. At a later date, it was translated from Sanskrit into Braj Bhasha and from Braj Bhasha into Nagri. It was then translated into Hindustani, a hybrid of Urdu and Hindi, and written in the Persian script. When published by the College of Fort William in 1805,[3] it became the prototypical copy from which it was published several times, at least in the Urdu language. In the latest edition of *Singhasan Batteesi* in Urdu, Intizar Hussain has recorded that it is a co-text of *Baitaal Pacheesi* and the two stories should be read together as one relates Vikramaditya's story during his lifetime and another, the period after his death (5–18). While *Baitaal Pacheesi* is a collection of twenty-five stories told by a demon called Baital to King Vikramaditya,[4] *Singhasan Batteesi* is a collection of thirty-two stories told by thirty-two statues to the same king. Finally, Hussain argues that they take us back, rather metaphorically, to *Katha Sarit Sagar* which is the great storehouse of tales from where they emerge and take various shapes. It is not surprising to find that the stories vary across different narrations but what is remarkable is that they mark a cultural trajectory which traces the continuity of a great tradition of building, telling, listening, writing and publishing stories which found popular appeal with the masses. This is well substantiated by the fact that *Singhasan Batteesi* was narrated, heard and recorded in different forms (prose and poetry), different scripts (Nagri and Persian), and different languages (Urdu and Hindi) at different points of time (medieval and modern) with larger appeal to a substantial mass of readers.[5] Subsequently, this made way for the emergence of a narrative technique and prose style in the Urdu language which could not have been possible had the stories been recorded in a sacrosanct Sanskritised or Persianised language.

With the examples of *Baitaal Pacheesi* and *Singhasan Batteesi* in hand, I would like to argue further that as oral traditions make way for written narratives, they also discover language in a certain order meant especially for narratives which keep changing with changes in the manner and conditions of their reception. As these two narratives demonstrate this process, they also bring to the fore how narratives acquire a new form by shedding old methods of language and narration and acquiring new ones, a process which creates new forms and intents during the act of retelling/rewriting. This trajectory shows a change of order during the process of translation from one language into another, and this act of changing the order, with newer appropriations of language, underlines further that they also make way for the writing of a new sociocultural and literary history.

In the proposition that writing, particularly literary writing, is the act of putting a language in order, there may be a risk of assuming, incorrectly, that it can be read only in linguistic terms which, in fact, is neither the case nor the proposition being made. The idea is to posit, rather broadly, that language carries a huge baggage with itself; it grows gradually by shedding many of its habits while acquiring newer ones, and it reflects a literary sensibility, an intellectual tradition, and most cumulatively a range of cultural identifiers that distinguish a literature, as in the case of *Baitaal Pacheesi* and *Singhasan Batteesi*. As a language grows, it acquires and consolidates a culture of its own which remains subject to constant change. As it changes with time, it produces various versions that are different from those of the past. Thus, both language and literature being repositories of inclusive consciousness of a culture, remain in a constant state of flux at both the levels – when a piece of writing is produced, and when that writing is translated into another language. These two texts only substantiate what Steiner said – "translation exists because men speak different languages" (49). What I have posited extends this logic with reference to *Singhasan Batteesi* and *Baitaal Pacheesi*, that languages need to undergo a change of order in the act of translation. This is also borne out by what contemporary theory also emphasises, that language remains in a perpetual state of change, and that possible interpretations and supposed meanings vary. This leads us to deliberate upon the very business of translation itself which involves an examination of theories developed around it and which should also help us appreciate issues relating to the problem of translatability.

TRANSLATION AS CHANGING THE ORDER

Drawing upon the premise made earlier that translation is a process of changing the order, it is worth proposing in this section that changing the order may not necessarily involve only the changing of lexical or syntactical order, or grammatical or semantic structures. It is also not about producing all discursive writing literally, or rewriting of writing as an organic whole. Further, translation cannot be viewed as a purely literary exercise undertaken for imparting aesthetic pleasure. It involves, at a much larger level, several simultaneous acts of negotiation between a huge variety of issues related to language and intent, sound and meaning, form and structure, and culture, history and politics. A closer study of the issues would reveal that all these are ultimately related to translation theories which, directly or indirectly, address issues of translatability.

In order to appreciate this aspect, a brief reference to various translation theories would be in place here. In his introduction to *Contemporary Translation Theory*, Edwin Gentzler proposes that those who work "monolingually may purport no need for translation theory; yet translation inheres in every language by its relationship to other signifying systems both past and present" (1). He refers to Roman Jakobson's "intralingual", "interlingual", and "intersemiotic" classification of translation practice and their intersection with various cultures, disciplines, and discourses. Before drawing upon the development of modern translation theory, which, he said, began with structuralism, he sums up the earlier developments rather succinctly. To make his point he refers to George Steiner who "characterized the history of translation theory until Jakobson as a continual rehashing of the same formal (consistent with the form of the original) versus free (using innovative forms to simulate the original's intent) theoretical distinction" (1). He goes on to make his point by referring to some of the major theoretical engagements under five different headings: the North American translation workshop, the science of translation, early translation studies, polysystem theory, and deconstruction.[6] While discussing the North American translation workshop he refers to the approaches adopted by I. A. Richards, Ezra Pound, and Frederic Will with reference to language, and later to more focused translation theory developed fully by Lawrence Venuti with his problematisation of ideology, self effacement, domestication and foreignisation (5–43). Discussing the "science" of translation, he analyses the business of translation with reference to its linguistic turn, as reflected in Noam Chomsky's preference for "underlying" structures of language, and Eugene Nida's choice to apply the rules of generative grammar in the act of translation, as also Wolfram Wilss' theoretical practices in Germany and the functionalist theories in German language countries (44–76). In discussing early translation studies, he emphasises the efforts made by André Lefevere and Susan Bassnett towards maturing the existing models of evaluative practice as a critical activity (77–105). He then examines the polysystem theory evolved by Itamar Even-Zohar as the sum total of overarching and all-inclusive literary systems which was further developed by Gideon Toury (106–144), and finally, discusses deconstruction as a theory applicable to the business of translation (145–186). With reference to all these Western approaches to translation theories, it may be surmised that translation theory is now in a state of great flux, with multiple approaches being adopted at different Western and non-Western sites of translational engagement. He does not, however, take note of the non-Western postcolonial theory of translation which distinguishes translation theory and practice with respect to translatability in an altered historical-cum-cultural perspective.

Let us remind ourselves at this point of what Gentzler has said about the place of translation among monolingual people and how that point has been taken up in a reverse order by Steiner with reference to multilingual people. Steiner makes his point by posing a question:

> How does a multilingual sensibility internalize translation, the actual passage from one of its first languages to another? Certain experts in the field of simultaneous translation declare that a native bilingual speaker does not make for an outstanding interpreter. The best man will be one who has consciously gained fluency in his second language. (119)

This mention of multilingualism with reference to translation can best be appreciated in the Indian context which is characterised by multiplicities/diversities of language, culture, ethnicity, region and religion. Appropriately enough, all these points of postcolonial reference also define the concerns of postcolonial translation that engages with difference rather than universality. Apart from seeking authenticity, postcolonial translation raises newer issues of translatability in relation to a new set of readers other than those trained in English and other European languages.

In the context of the current trajectory that translation theory has created, certain questions like what does language carry – a truth or a supposition – and how does a writing make sense beyond its typologies and grids, its cultural markers and historical predicaments, its locational variations and multilingual postcolonial conditions, also call for attention. Today, translation is more of a philosophical engagement of the postcolonial and postmodern moment of history; it is closely related with the problem of identity and assertion, with the sociology and politics of writing as acts of coding and decoding, and with the act of making literary choices and creating canons. It is also an act of interrogating hegemonic translational strategies canonised by the centres of power and to write back, as also to discover the dialectics of literary writing in the modern age. With the contemporary advocacy for a cultural turn in humanities and social sciences, it is now a political act as both the acts of writing and translating are themselves rooted in cultural and political systems.

Supported by a variety of arguments, it may be asserted that all writings are eminently translatable, just in the same way as one may counter-assert that no writing is truly translatable. A general survey of the issue would reveal that the two opposite views regarding translatability come primarily from the linguistic and cultural approaches to the problem of translation. Linguists argue that no translation may be successfully undertaken because no two words, in two different languages, are ever the same in their meanings, in spite of all the approximation regarding their possible intent. It is so because the base units in two languages are incongruous and because there are no lexical or syntactical substitutes available to the translator which could help the reconfiguration of any writing in the target language. Those who would not agree with the linguists would posit that it is not the language that poses a barrier in translation but metalanguage, allusions and sociolinguistic dialectics that make a translational negotiation problematic. They would also assert that experiences of a private and personal nature do not lend themselves easily to the translator. Since discussions on translation theory have generally tended to be normative, translators look for optimal solutions to work out a strategy and enter this tough terrain of linguistic and literary translation. They depend largely on the functionality of language in its most liberal sense and exploit the same in the target language. They trust the referentiality of the source language writing and work to create conceptual wholes which the reader in the target language may possibly relate with.

To extend the argument concerning translatability still further, I may also posit that translation has long been held to be only a partial act of textual negotiation primarily because of the disparities in languages and cultures. This amounts to saying that the related codes cannot be switched with any degree of success. Given the complexity of translatability, one is naturally tempted to ask as to what constitutes translatability in actual terms and how the parameters of translatability can be authenticated in the act of translating. To find answers to these questions, we shall have to engage with the writing and the writer – the two prime sources – and examine the dynamics of writing which include the issues of historicity and metaphoricity, myth and mythopoeia, texture and structure, as also the very nature of the writing in hand, and the language employed to recreate or reconfigure that writing in translation.

At the very basic level, translatability depends, as we are quite aware, on how well a translator may negotiate with the devices employed in the original writing, and how best the figures of speech may be reconfigured in a translated piece of writing. These basics, however, lead to more complicated issues like how the cultural specificity of any piece of writing preserved, for example, in the figures of speech, may possibly be dealt with in yet another language. This brings one to the question as to how the ideological formations, enmeshed in the original writing, may best be incorporated to sound plausible after changing the order in a work of translation. As ideological bases also define the form, and as forms are quite often best suited to a language and achieve their perfection only in the source language, the problem of the form is yet another issue to be taken into consideration. The roots of the particularity of form in a given language attest to the richness of the language in which the writing is originally created. In translation, the form is recreated and in the process, it is quite likely that the form acquires a different *avatar*. A very appropriate example in this context may be of those forms which are rooted in a literary tradition and cultural history that created those forms. Here, one may think of the ghazal which had its origin in seventh-century Arabia and travelled through Persia before it came to India after following a circuitous route through several other sites. It found its zenith in Arabic, Persian and Urdu, emerging essentially as the poetry of love, and reflected the Islamic/Muslim sensibility of the time. Rubai is yet another example which is also rooted in the Persian and Urdu literary traditions. Other examples are those of the sonnet and haiku which originated in Italy and Japan respectively, but travelled to newer literary locations over a long period of time. All these forms share many traits: they follow a defined form; they have gone beyond their own literary and cultural habitats and all of them have found acceptance in the English language. A close study would show that when these forms take root in other climes, they differ from their original forms, like a fruit that grows well in a particular climate grows differently in taste, shape, and size in other climates. The ghazal, rubai, sonnet and haiku in English, therefore, differ from their forms in their original languages.

With the issues raised so far, it would appear that translatability has to be the most important concern for the translator, and not that a particular piece of writing is worthy of translation due to its content, or its status as a canonical text in its source language, and other factors of this nature. It is worth arguing that the choice of a piece of writing made by the translator must depend on the possibility and degree of translatability that the translator may possibly see in it. It depends on how the translator reads that piece of writing, and how the supposed reader may possibly approach the same writing in translation.

This issue is also related with a subsidiary issue that concerns the very purpose of translating a piece of writing. It has to be asserted here that no translation may be undertaken without an adequate examination of how far a piece of writing from one language would ultimately matter in another language. In other words, it needs to be assessed as to how a piece of writing from one language would confer with its counterpart in another language, which may have its own codes of identity and its own marks of individuality. A good example in this case would be that of Omar Khayyam's *Rubaiyat.* The questions to be asked in this regard could be: does the translation of this text succeed because it is a cultural curiosity, or because it represents a unique literary tradition, or because it negotiates well with the challenges of a constraining form, or because it is the simple lure of the Orient which takes the reader in its fold? A poetical work like this may pose several problems of this kind and they cannot be answered partially but only cumulatively. This would mean that the translator would only be obliged to negotiate with the demands of linguistic equivalence, cultural specificity, literary tradition, poetic devices, and a well-defined form before arriving at a point of larger negotiation.

This example of the *Rubaiyat* may be carried forward to test if this kind of poetical creation may develop a dialogue with the reader in the target language. As every piece of writing speaks differently to different readers, translatability also depends on the nature of the dialogic relationship the translator develops with the piece of writing in hand. The author of the original writing initiates a multilayered dialogue while producing a piece of writing, which takes into account the configurations of time, place, milieu, tradition, canon, and the very experiential capital that may inhabit a writing in the process of its making. In the process of translating a critically chosen piece of writing, a translator relives the source text and recreates the same in the target language for a different readership with the intention that the reader may possibly establish a level of congruence with the codes of experience and expression contained in the original piece of writing and finally enter into a dialogue with the text in translation and all its constituents.

In a broader perspective, the issue of translatability relates with a huge variety of elements that render the domain of translation problematic. Keeping in mind the example of the *Rubaiyat*, these would include the problems at the semantic, phonetic and morphological levels, that would further call for negotiations with (a) intent, idea, ideology, and interpretation; (b) literary tradition, forms, genres, and canon; (c) text typologies, grids, textuality and intertextuality; (d) figures of speech, metre, sound, and style; (e) contexts of history, location and culture; and (f) linguistic and paralinguistic systems. The translator strikes a balance to arrive at a possible version of the text chosen for translation. Discussing the translation of poetry, Susan Bassnett in *Translation Studies* (1980) has referred to André Lefevere's cataloguing of seven kinds of strategies employed by the English translators of a poem by Cattulus. He classifies the translations thus: "phonemic" for those which reproduce the sound, "literal" for those that choose a word for word, "metrical" for those that reproduce the source language metre, and then mentions "poetry into prose" which leads to distortions of sense, "rhymed" which goes for double adherence to metre and rhyme, "blank verse" which is determined by structural principle, and "interpretation" which turns a text into a version and an imitation (81–82). This process is replicated in these and several other ways with individual differences that the translator chooses as a strategy to re-produce a piece of writing, which I have called changing the order. A pertinent question that a translator needs to answer for himself/herself is whether there is a need to discover a separate language for translation. This is a vital question a translator of *Rubaiyat* would need to ask more pertinently than others. As every translation is ultimately an engagement with language, the answer to this question again relates with my proposition that every translation is an act of changing the order which subsumes most of the issues raised above.

These issues are buttressed further in the argument that J. C. Catford develops in relation to translatability and identifies the problems residing in the domains of language and culture. While the non-availability of a counterword poses a problem in linguistic translation, it gets much more complicated in the context of cultural translation. This argument may be understood with reference to the translation of a piece of writing into an alien language for an alien reader; for example, the translation of a certain work representing a certain grid, like the *Rubaiyat*, or an Indian text into a European language which exhibits its own marks of multiple differences. Another aspect of this problem, as argued by Anthony Pym, can also be traced in Derrida who acknowledged the "plurality" (38) of the source, and wondered if a writing could make any possible sense to readers "beyond its original historical and cultural location" (38). This is resolved by Pym in Derridean terms: "…literature is a system of operating with ideals other than the constant process of deconstruction" (38). Thus, writings with their linguistic and cultural baggage determine the ways of its rewriting, or changing the order in the act of translation.

Both the acts of putting a language in an order to produce a piece of writing and changing that order to produce a piece of translation are essentially acts of developing a dialogue with the reader. As the intent or meaning behind a dialogue cannot be guaranteed to have reached the reader with exactness even in the original text, there is a great possibility of its being lost, misunderstood or even misconstrued in the act of translation. There are multiple reasons for this miscommunication from linguistic and psychological points of view that reflect the larger makeup of the author and the translator. Any act of translation, as such, may best be interpreted as a partial act. One of the major reasons why it remains partial concerns the problem of translatability. This leads the translator to re-think his/her strategy and reinvent his/her methodology. The translator leaves the text unfinished in certain ways, just as the source-language author does at times. As such, both the author and translator testify to the fact that many writings, like many translations, remain unfinished and both make way for subsequent works to follow and for literary traditions to grow.

Just as the concept of original writing is contestable, so is the concept of originality in translation. Since no piece of writing is a complete entity unto itself, no translation can ever be an absolute unit. My argument is that all writings are essentially about the fluidity and fantasy of experience and expression, just as all translations are about the indeterminacy and mutability of life and language as lived and contained in the original piece of writing. The creation of a piece of writing and its translatability are possible–impossible projects worth attempting and worth failing at, and vice-versa.

NOTES

1. While a writer is a scripter or a recorder of acts and events in a language, the author performs many more roles of deeper significance. He/she codes and decodes; he/she works with metaphors, symbols, myths and archetypes. He/she creates concrete universals and distinguishes them distinctly one from the other. He/she turns into a philosopher of language as he/she finds an expression for the manifestations of the physical universe.
2. There is a lot of conjecture regarding the date of composition and the authorship of *Singhasan Batteesi.* Urdu critics like Gyan Chand Jain (*Urdu ki Nasri Dastanen*) Gopi Chand Narang (*Urdu Mathnawiyan*), and Jameel Jalibi (*Tareekh-e Adab Urdu*), in particular, have engaged with issues related to *dastan* and this text. With reference to Garcin de Tassy, Narang records that it owes its origin to a Sanskrit text called *Vikramacharitram.* It is also conjectured that this text was written in Braj Bhasha in the early seventeenth century. Later, it found its way into other Indian languages and also into French. Other works of interest include those by Gauhar Naushahi (*Baital Pacheesi*), Sohail Ahmed Khan (*Majmoo'aa* and *Dastan Dar Dastan*), Haider Bakhsh Haidari (*Aaraish-e Mehfil*), Faqeer Deccani (*Singhasan Batteesi*), and V. A. K. Aiyer (*Stories of Vikramaditya: Simhasana Dwatrimsaka*).
3. *Baitaal Pacheesi* was translated by Mazhar Ali Khan and Lallulal-ji and *Singhasan Batteesi* was done by Mirza Kazim Ali Jawan and Lallulal-ji. They were assisted by other *munshis* of the college and supervised by John Borthwick Gilchrist who was a Professor of Hindustani at the College of Fort William in Calcutta.
4. In Urdu works, Vikramaditya is written as Vikramajeet. Intizar Hussain says that Bikram is the abbreviated form of Bikramajeet which could then be called Bikramajeet.
5. He defined them as follows: "[...] *intralingual* translation, a rewording of signs in one language with signs from the same language; *interlingual* translation, or the interpretation of signs in one language with signs from another language (translation 'proper); and *intersemiotic* translation,

or the transfer ('transmutation') of the signs in one language to non-verbal sign systems (from language into art or music)."

6. See for example: F. R. Amos *Early Theories of Translation* (Columbia University Press, 1920), Hilaire Belloc *On Translation* (Oxford University Press, 1931), Herbert Grierson *Verse Translation* (Oxford University Press, 1948), T. H. Savory *The Art of Translation* (Jonathan Cape, 1957), A. H. Smith (ed.) *Aspects of Translation* (Secker and Warburg, 1958), Reuben A. Brower *On Translation* (Harvard University Press, 1959), C. Day Lewis *On Translating Poetry* (Abbey Press, 1970). A major shift may be seen since George Steiner's *After Babel* (Oxford University Press, 1975) where he examined language and culture specifically in relation to translation, making way for more specialised studies in relation to history, philosophy, culture, linguistics, gender, and postcolonialism.

WORKS CITED

Barthes, Roland. 1995. The death of the author. In *Authorship: From Plato to the postmodern: A reader,* ed. Seán Burke. Edinburgh: Edinburgh University Press.

Bassnett-McGuire, Susan. 1980. *Translation studies*. London: Methuen.

Bassnett, Susan. [2007] 2011. Culture and translation. In *A companion to translation studies*, ed. Piotr Kuhiwczak and Karin Littau. New Delhi: Orient BlackSwan.

Eagleton, Terry. [1983] 2012. *Literary theory: An introduction.* New Delhi: Wiley India.

Foucault, Michel. 1984. What is an author. In *The Foucault reader*, ed. Paul Rabinow. New York: Pantheon Books.

Gentzler, Edwin. [2001] 2010. *Contemporary translation theories.* Rev second edition. New Delhi: Viva Books.

Hatim, Basil and Ian Mason. 1990. *Discourse and the translator*. London: Longman.

Hussain, Intizar, trans. 2014. *Singhasan battisi.* Lahore: Sang-e-Meel Publications.

Neubert, Albrecht and Gregory M. Shreve. 1992. *Translation as text.* Kent: Kent State University Press.

Pym, Anthony. [2007] 2011. Philosophy and translation. In *A companion to translation studies*, ed. Piotr Kuhiwczak and Karin Littau. New Delhi: Orient BlackSwan.

Steiner, George. 1975. *After Babel: Aspects of language and translation.* London: Oxford University Press.

THREE

Translation as Dialogue: Aesthetics of Collaboration

This chapter engages with the idea of writing and translation taking shape in a dialogic and collaborative process. As this happens at two levels – creation and translation – the author and the translator act as prime collaborators at two different levels and in a variety of ways. This argument is taken further to trace the genealogy of the Indian text and the lineage of the Indian author.

The role of the translator as a collaborator in today's Indian context is more complex than ever before. As texts in the Indian contexts have developed, both thematically and stylistically, through a dialogic process spread over centuries, the translator too can work best using a collaborative approach. While collaboration on the part of the translator happens at myriad levels, he/she approaches a text to help create a new literary condition.

Dialogic and collaborative acts, being interrogative acts on the parts of the author and the translator, create ways of negotiating with the history of social and political formations, as also of formulating narratives of identity. Finally, as Indian culture is plural and diverse, collaborative engagements make them homogenous and accessible which is so central to the sustenance of a cultural and literary life.

Translation studies, heavily laden with theoretical baggage and contextual references, have developed a complex discourse around the issues involving text and translation. As I underscore their seminality, I wish to build an argument around two of the more significant issues, *dialogue* and *collaboration*, which, I posit, define the processes of creative writing and, subsequently, of its translation. I would do so in order to demonstrate that (a) a veritable text remains in a constant dialogue in several stages of its *pre-life*, *life*, and *afterlife*, that (b) translation is essentially an act of collaboration, and that (c) this argument is nowhere as appropriately applicable as it is in the case of India today, where translation constitutes a major point of reference in literary practice and studies. I would do so by proposing a paradigm that underscores the significance of dialogic and collaborative engagements in relation to the writing and translation of a text through historical periods and literary spaces.

TEXT IN DIALOGUE: PRE-LIFE, LIFE, AFTER-LIFE

In order to provide a framework for my argument, I would draw upon the metaphors of *insemination*, *conception* and *delivery* to suggest that a text also passes through three stages which I should like to designate, with a little difference,[1] as the *pre-natal, natal* and *post-natal* stages in the life of a text. I would suggest further that all texts pass through this cycle while some of them which qualify for larger readership beyond the source language also enter into another cycle of life along the same lines, as I have argued below. Let us consider the three stages in the first cycle of a text's life followed by the next three stages in the second cycle of its life.

Just as a life starts taking shape right from the embryonic stage, a text in its *pre-natal stage* is first conceived in the mind of the author.[2] I would argue that in order to configure a text, the author initiates a curious dialogic process at multiple levels at this stage of textual formation. It begins with the author entering into a dialogue with a body of language from which he/she chooses his/her counters of expression. In choosing those counters of expression, he/she also enters simultaneously into a series of dialogues with a rewarding idea, a suggestive image, a promising metaphor, a substantial symbol, and a potential myth that lie in a limbo of personal and collective consciousness, or cultural storehouse.[3] They remain in suspended animation till the author happens to employ them to express his/her experiential capital in the text.

Having passed through the *pre-natal stage* where the text has taken a certain physical form, it arrives at the *natal stage* where the author enters into the actual process of delivery by entering into another set of multiple dialogues first with himself/herself, then the possible form and the possible reader. It is at this critical and final moment of delivery, which is also the moment of deliverance for the author, that he/she tests his/her control over form and tries his/her capability to articulate himself/herself through words with critical caution. This is akin to the ultimate moment in the state of labour which brings forth a new life upon this earth. After the text reaches its point of delivery, and once it is finally delivered on paper, or put in print, the author loses control over his/her creation.[4]

Once the text is born, and once it disengages from authorial control, it reaches the *post-natal stage* where it enters the third stage of dialogic enterprise. Now, it opens itself up to a new sphere of interaction, not with the author this time but with the reader who receives, negotiates and evaluates it for all its worth. This reader initiates a new set of dialogues with the text which varies according to individual responses. As no text is unitary and complete unto itself, it seeks its individual or relative merit in association with other texts, written in the same language. Seeking its sustenance in a community of same-language texts, it compares its mythologies, motifs, signs and symbols to confirm where it is situated. This process may be appreciated with reference to the figure on the following page:

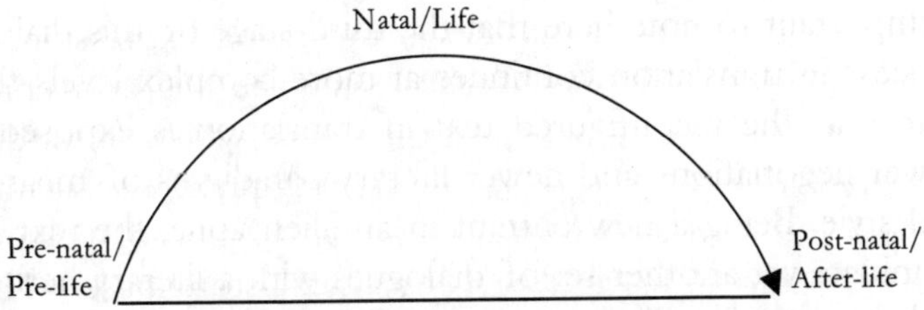

Figure 1: Text in dialogue in the process of writing and delivery (First cycle)

Let me carry this argument further by suggesting that it is with the third and the *post-natal phase* in the life of the text that it enters into the second cycle of its life in a set of new conditions. It happens only when the text outgrows its linguistic periphery through translation to enter into yet another dialogic continuum beyond the source language. This time, it develops a dialogue with texts in other language(s). In cohabiting with another set of texts marked by a plethora of differences in content and style, it gets contextualised in a broader perspective. It is now comparatively assessed for its literary and contextual merit and meaning. Depending on how veritable the text is, it acquires a span of life for itself and qualifies to remain in constant dialogue with readers and literary establishments beyond a given time and space. In the second cycle of its life, to put it differently, the three dialogic stages are once again replicated with three major differences – the author is replaced by a translator, the source language with a target language, and the source language reader with the target language reader. Now the translator reconceives and rewrites a text by collaborating with its constituents as the author did in the first cycle by collaborating with an idea, image, metaphor, symbol, myth and language. As it happened in the first cycle, the *pre-natal stage* in the second cycle of the text's life makes way for the *natal stage* in which the translator re-writes the text by engaging with himself/herself, the possible form, and the possible language for a possible readership in another language. As it happened in the first cycle, the text ultimately enters into a *post-natal stage* where the translator loses control over his/her work and leaves it to the reader for larger negotiations. It is important to note here that the third stage of this dialogic process in translation continues at more complex levels than before as the reconfigured text in translation is exposed to newer negotiations and newer literary paradigms of meaning and style. Being a new entrant in an alien zone, the text has to initiate yet another set of dialogues with a literary heritage and the prevalent literary taste, to discover its moorings, and to find a hospitable habitat for itself. In sum, the three stages in the life of the text in the first cycle are followed by yet another three stages in the life of the text in translation which largely accounts for the text's *pre-life*, *life*, and *after-life* in two cycles. This process may be represented with the help of the following figure:

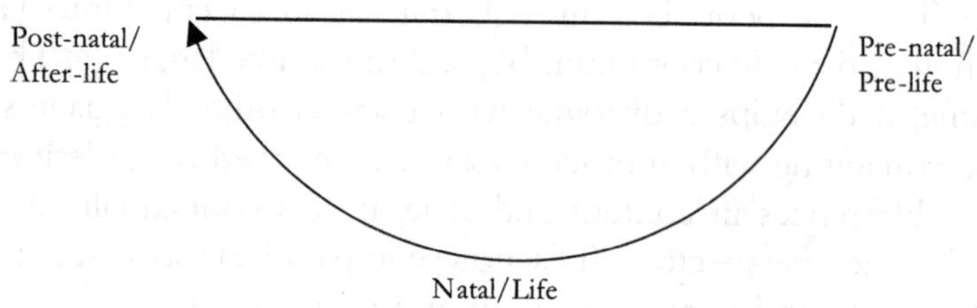

Figure 2: Text in dialogue in the process of translation (Second cycle)

Once we know that it is the author who creates a text by entering into a complex creative process, the pertinent question to understand this paradigm further is to ask how the author makes way for the translator to join him/her in the sharing of a text beyond the confines of a given language. We are aware of the primal position of the author as the sole creator of a text, who either denies or subsumes all other agencies that contribute towards the concrescence of a text. We also acknowledge that the author is the only one who negotiates with the possible constituents of his/her text from the very beginning (which I have called the pre-natal stage) in the conception and development of a text. We have also for long subscribed to the romantic theory of the creative process that places a premium on the overpowering nature of imagination and the controlling hand of the author. I must add now that the text is always born in a process that involves dialogic negotiation. This is carried forward by the translator into another domain of language and readership. This translational negotiation results in re-writing, re-viewing and re-visioning the text which qualifies it to stay plausible with the readers beyond the source language.

Thus, even while a text passes through three dialogic stages in its life in the source language, it actually passes through more than three once a text is chosen to be translated. As such, a text in translation bears the marks of six dialogic stages in which the first three stages relate with the author's involvement and the next three, with the translator's intervention.

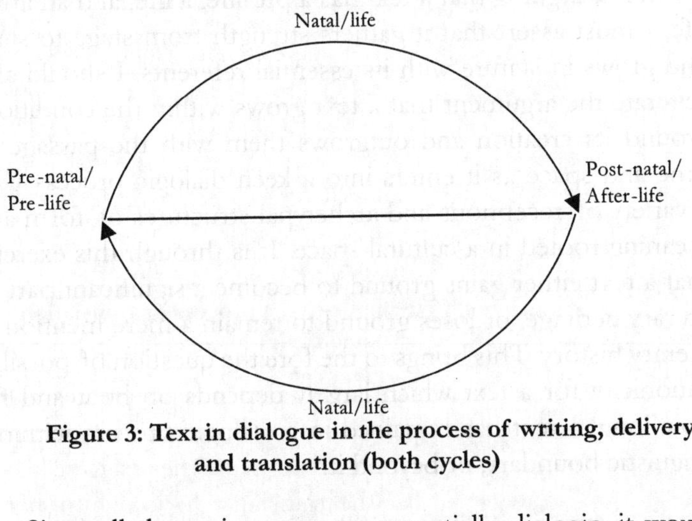

Figure 3: Text in dialogue in the process of writing, delivery and translation (both cycles)

Since all these six stages are essentially dialogic, it would be proper to reflect upon the phenomenon of dialogue itself in order to relate it with the acts of writing and translating. It may be easily surmised that dialogue presupposes a relationship between two or more participants and it develops between the intending parties involved in the act who may either agree on the basic premises, or assert their position in disagreement. A dialogue so initiated makes way for the development of a discourse which may, once again, acquire its field of acceptability or retain its individuality in difference. Mikhail Bakhtin, who introduced the concepts of dialogism, heteroglossia and chronotope in *Dialogic Imagination: Four*

Essays[5] has underscored the nature of dialogue and said that (a) dialogue presupposes a *relationship*, (b) its development is based on the cardinal principle of *difference*, (c) its difference may be marked in human *speech* which retains within itself an element of the "other", (d) it generates a *response* from the parties involved in order to create a discourse, and (e) it is conditioned by a *social context*. Extending his thesis further, he has evolved the idea of "heteroglossia", which implies the simultaneous existence of multiple layers of dialogues and linguistic expressions, and "chronotope" which suggests interconnectedness of multiple referents in a time–space narrative.

While arguing that a text has a pre-life, a life, and an after-life, I must assert that it gathers strength from stage to stage and grows in stature with its essential referents. I should also reiterate the argument that a text grows within the conditions around its creation and outgrows them with the passage of time and space as it enters into a keen dialogic process with a variety of receptions and archetypal structures of form and meaning rooted in a cultural space. It is through this exercise that a text either gains ground to become a significant part of literary heritage, or loses ground to remain a mere mention in literary history. This brings to the fore the question of possible canonicity for a text which largely depends on how, and for how long, a text has remained in a dialogic process within a linguistic boundary, or beyond it.

TRANSLATION AS COLLABORATION

Extending this argument, it may be posited that translation is essentially an act of collaboration which happens at a variety of levels with the translator playing the role of a prime collaborator. Earlier we asked who creates a text and how he/she does it, now we engage with another question: with whom does the translator collaborate, and how does he/she pursue that collaboration? There are several answers to this question which I would like to divide into three broad categories as they operate in unison at three interconnected levels. At the first level, the translator collaborates primarily with (a) himself/

herself, his/her chosen text, and the chosen author, before he/she collaborates at the secondary level with the (b) literary cultures in the source and target languages, and finally with (c) several subsidiary and even unacknowledged agencies that contribute towards larger literary production.

At the first level the translator begins this collaboration first and foremost with himself/herself[6] by assessing his/her own merits and skills before approaching the author.[7] He/she then collaborates with the nature of the text,[8] its language and form, rooted and constructed metaphors, and symbols and myths. He/she collaborates with both the author and the text to examine how far they lend themselves to translational negotiation in the target language. The translator thus emerges as the second author of the first text and develops his/her intimacy with that text to be able to collaborate well with multiple agencies involved in the process.

This opens up possibilities of further collaborations at the second level with the literary culture[9] that the text represents in the source language. Entering into this vast domain, he/she collaborates primarily with the co-texts and the counter-texts of the text chosen for translation. This implies that he/she collaborates with the literary canon of the source language, as well as with the age and milieu that produce the text. This implies further that he/she collaborates holistically with the atmosphere, the climate, and the temper of the source language's literary history. He/she begins this negotiation in the process to ensure, to the best of his/her ability, that a text from one literary culture appeals to the readers of another literary culture. This leads him/her to assess the acceptability of the source language's literary culture and all its constituents in the target language's literary culture. He/she thus collaborates simultaneously with two literary cultures to authenticate his/her effort.

At the third level, the translator collaborates with his/her fellow translators,[10] and possible and imagined readers.[11] Fellow translators provide models of success or failure depending on the age they lived in and the methodology they followed. They also help subsequent translators evolve new translation poetics and rewrite their texts with difference. The new translator strikes a balance between his/her translation and the one already available to readers from the earlier translator(s). As such, translating a text in a collaborative mode is also a way of marking the differences in reading strategies and reconciling them afresh in the translated text. This makes way for the acceptance of their work by the possible or imagined readers in whom the power of the translated text has to be finally invested. The translator, thus, develops an imagined dialogue with that reader and collaborates with him/her to produce a translation that would approximate with the literary choices the reader would make. Even while many collaborations remain unacknowledged, like those with the publisher and the market,[12] they register their presence in the production of the text that finally appears in translated form. Thus, the translator determines his/her own aims and methods through multiple collaborations and develops his/her own poetics for this purpose.

By entering into a new linguistic domain through collaborative negotiations initiated by the translator, the text is reborn and gains an *after-life*. In this phase of life, the text initiates a fresh course of dialogue with the new recipients, just as the text in the source language had done earlier with the readers of its own linguistic, literary and cultural stock. The collaborative method of translation, thus, results in reconfiguration of a language, idea and image. The process gets all the more complicated when the translator initiates his/her collaborative engagement with literary history and tradition of the text in question, as also its iconic and cultural significance. The translator thus, as the second author of the first text, turns into an iconographer of complex literary and philosophical configurations, as he/she aspires to create an intellectual condition by making a choice of the text for translation and developing a methodology to do the same.

In this process of multiple collaborations, the text is problematised by the translator, just as the original author and the reader are also problematised in the process. As an eminently possible way of refiguring a text, collaboration does not interfere with the myth woven around the author as akin to God. It does not interrogate the notion of "pure author" and "pure text"; rather it underlines the idea that every text is, in a major way, an "unfinished text", which is written and re-written again and again in the source language, as also the target language. From this perspective, collaboration is not a passive but an interrogative act aimed at defining the broader bases of a literary condition. Collaboration also contributes towards the text acquiring a double identity, and a double life, at least on two levels. Even if the source and the target language texts be twins, each one lives by its own identity, and each one is distinguishable from the other; each one creates its own autonomous space for itself and acquires its own life and afterlife.

Collaboration not only brings to terms different cultures and language systems, it also contributes to their individual and mutual development. It helps construct, disseminate and preserve knowledge in a variety of literary and extra-literary domains, as well as bridges gaps among people of various affiliations. Collaboration redefines geopolitical and socio-literary spaces, re-examines the modes of human apprehension, and reconsiders the paradigms of life and living, nation and narration.

Dialogue and Collaboration: The Indian Context

While the issue of translation as collaboration eminently qualifies for a detailed discourse, what calls for much greater attention is its added relevance in the Indian context. Decidedly, India is a different site – linguistically, culturally, ethnically, religiously, politically, philosophically – and it calls for a different paradigm of reading and critiquing. Passing through clearly demarcated phases of history, it has emerged as a major site of contestations and reconciliations. While all other cultures represent multiplicity within a unitary structure, India represents a unitary structure within its multiplicity which only goes to show that this has happened through a long-drawn collaborative engagement with homogeneous traditions and literary cultures. This tradition has produced texts that are unified at their core in their essential sensibility and are distinct from texts of all other sociocultural locations. Even its postcolonial literature, which is so divergent in its concerns, is clearly distinguishable from the literatures of other postcolonial sites principally because the Indian postcolonial texts show a certain contiguity marked by a persistent dialogic pattern. The very notion of Indian literature along with Indian literatures in English translation is, thus, required to be problematised.

There are two major issues that call for closer scrutiny: the genealogy of the Indian text and the lineage of the Indian author. A closer view of these two aspects would show that the interminability of the Indian text and the continuing legacy of the Indian author are traceable through a complex literary tradition which is based essentially in dialogic and collaborative enterprises. In order to contextualise this tradition, spread over several centuries, it would be important to develop a comparative perspective to see how the literature of India got configured through various ages of Indian history, how it retained its great continuity, and how it built a grand tradition through dialogic and collaborative efforts on the part of the authors and translators. Let me develop a broad view to illustrate this argument.

The Indian literary tradition[13] began with the construction and preservation of religio-philosophical knowledge since the later Vedic period (1000–600 BC) and continued till the middle of the eighth century in ancient India in a preeminently dialogic mode. During this period, Indian texts underscored the evolution and growth of a civilisation, the sanctity of the divine truth, the value of human wisdom, the yearning for spirituality, and a holistic understanding of life. These texts got their first configurations in the great *guru–shishya* interaction as they emerged out of the guru's *tapasya* and *sadhana* in the *ashrams*. As the two modes of constructing spiritual and philosophical knowledge, *shruti* and *smriti* literatures developed and preserved the foundational texts like the Vedas, the *Upanishads* and the *Bhagavad Gita*, as also the *dharmashastras, itihas, puranas, sutras, aagama* and *darsana.* Texts so developed in Sanskrit, Prakrit and Pali like the Vedas,[14] the epics,[15] the treatises[16] and the *puranas* comprising mythological writings with unknown authorship, became the hallmarks of ancient Indian sensibility and projected a predominantly Hindu view of life. Literature in Dravidian languages of the southern part of India, especially Sangam poetry in Tamil, made its own mark, as did the other linguistic clusters and the different geographical areas.

As compared with ancient Indian literature, the literature of medieval India from the eighth to the middle of the eighteenth century projected entirely new sets of discourses and created a new variety of texts which entered into dialogues with each other as well as with ancient Indian literatures. This period reflected a remarkable state of flux represented by new discourses, new sociopolitical configurations and new interactions between two major faiths, Hinduism and Islam. With the coming of the Arabs, followed by Persians, Turks, Afghans and the Mughals, India turned into a melting pot of faiths, beliefs, manners, languages, modes of perception and ways of life. The Bhakti Movement, for example, rejected intolerance in favour of harmony and an essentially pluralistic view of life. A complex web of preeminently dialogic texts emerged with those of Guru Nanak in Punjabi, Vallabhacharya and Mira Bai in Rajasthani, Kabir in Khari Boli, Tukaram in Marathi, Tulsi Das in Avadhi, and Narsinh Mehta in Gujarati. While history, culture and politics entered into the literary domain as subjects of concern, languages like Hindi, Urdu, Marathi and Bangla emerged through acquiring an extensive individual as well as collaborative vocabulary, as also due to more writers writing in these languages instead of the classical languages. As medieval India saw the development of literatures in regional languages, it also led to broadening the frontiers of literary creation and readership. This efflorescence of ideas and literary styles, produced in multiple dialogic and collaborative modes, led to the emergence of linguistic clusters and the coming together of aesthetic principles from various literary and cultural sources. This great variety multiplied in a number of ways in the establishment of cult figures like Heer and Ranjha in Punjabi, Radha and Krishna in Odia, and Sufi poetry in Kashmiri, Punjabi and Urdu. Women saints and writers like Lal Ded, Mira Bai, Akka Mahadevi and Habba Khatoon came to the fore as another set of manifestations on the literary map. Several unorthodox regional beliefs and sects, tales of chivalry and heroism, cults of Krishna and Rama, and the philosophy of Ramanuja and Madhvacharya also got a fillip, as did the Virashaiva movement which made way for the spread of Basavanna philosophy. Literature celebrating heroism and romance in all languages became yet another manifestation of the medieval literary capital. The birth of new forms and narratives, both in prose and poetry, came to be noted as the major contribution of this period. It is also remarkable to note that while literature in the pre-printing age was rather elitist in nature, it became socially and politically conscious after the advent of the printing press, by the beginning of the late eighteenth and early nineteenth centuries. The medieval period in India which came to its end by the middle of the eighteenth century is remarkable for a fine collaborative blend of the sacred, the secular and the profane. It created a curious paradigm of texts in dialogic continuity which lent themselves to much more liberal negotiations in the subsequent phase of Indian history.

The modern period in India, beginning around the middle of the eighteenth century and coming to an end with decolonisation and independence, is replete with conflicting and reconciliatory movements, manifestoes and other major hallmarks to formulate the future agenda for a nation to be.[17] This era bore the vicissitudes of social, political and economic history and it was pregnant with immense possibilities. If time and place be the text, this was the most consequential time to figure out that the texts produced during these times represented various shades of a unified literary sensibility that found its flowering in a dialogic mode. It emerged as the time for finding new ideas, discovering new literary narratives that reflected a highly complex dialogic continuity. The rise of nationalist consciousness, need for self-respect, and respect for India's heritage appeared as the important concerns, and gave birth to a literature of cosmopolitan nature that drew upon each other in a collaborative mode.

Let me take two examples, out of many others, to make a broad case regarding the impending changes in society and literary expression. The cultural, religious, and literary resurgence which emerged as a major hallmark of this era was best exemplified in the Indian Renaissance which emerged in a dialogic enterprise with history. It showed its impact in Bangla, Hindi, Urdu, and several other regional literatures that harked back to each other in a dialogic mode. It manifested itself in the intellectuals, social reformers, writers, journalists, patriots and scientists coming together to harbour a new consciousness and to underline the importance of rationalism in their texts, which were of great social and cultural relevance. It also led to the establishment of about two dozen institutions of learning. This gave a remarkable fillip to the spirit of rationalism, modernism and nationalism, along with inculcating the need for interrogating the predominant modes of perception, which were, until then, largely acquired through Western education. Literary texts in Bangla, Hindi, Urdu, Marathi and South Indian languages underlined the state of the human condition and the spirit of political morality, social reform and nationalist consciousness – all in a reciprocal and dialogic manner.

Yet another example of socio-literary resurgence in the later decades may be noticed in the Progressive Writers' Movement in Urdu and Hindi literatures. It emphasised the need for social change and a sound political order to ensure a societal structure based on the principle of economic justice. It assigned new social responsibility to the writer and urged him/her to underline the stark realities of life, like suffering and subjugation, instead of exploring themes from pure spirituality and abstract philosophy. One of the manifestos of the Association[18] underlined the need to create and translate literature with progressive bearings for the sake of social regeneration. It went well with another item on the agenda: emphasising free expression of ideas. With an ideological base in communism and anti-imperialism, this movement created an entirely new variety of texts that struck the imagination of people instantaneously and made way for liberal dialogism in the domains of art and culture.

While colonial discourse[19] found a ready space for itself, the Orientalists[20] also made a case to cut across imperial domination. In the domain of literature, various forms and genres came to acquire their individual identities. As such, literary forms and genres were exposed to new poetics of composition. Literatures in many languages like Bangla, Marathi, Odia, Gujarati, Urdu and the Dravidian languages became much more visible. With the efflorescence of English education and the receding of Persian and Sanskrit, the literary perspective underwent a major change, leading to the birth of a new sensibility and culture of writing and reading marked by dialogic reciprocity and cooperation. Individual languages and their literatures began to come into their own while the English language and literature in English kept influencing and expanding the territory of literary representation in India and re-defining the very concept of Indian literature.

As a literary site of rich variety and complexity, India entered a radically new phase in the post-independence era. As one of the largest and most diverse democracies in the world, with a plethora of issues unresolved in the domain of society, culture, politics, economy and religion, India and the Indian text have the most complex negotiations to undertake. As the Nehruvian agenda set the stage, and as the bogey of development moved on, it met with several hurdles in the form of declaration of emergency in 1975, spread of communal violence, rise of extremist parties, politics of reservation, ethnic strife, caste-class-clan differences, separatism, etc. These emerged as the major points of reference on the sociopolitical map of post-independence India, out to challenge the Nehruvian "tryst with destiny". They also emerged as texts for the writer to develop a dialogue with, and for the translator to collaborate and refigure a text in another language. This leads us to conclude that in each phase of Indian history there has been a thematic and stylistic unity and all thc phases, taken together, constitute a larger picture of a nation that has created its literature in a dialogic mode and brought the spiritual, the secular and the diversely modernist tendencies together.

Conclusion

A review of Indian religio-philosophical and sociopolitical heritage over the centuries establishes that the Indian reality is a different reality and that it creates a different text that cannot be appreciated in units, or as isolated structures of form and meaning. The Indian text must, therefore, be taken as a continuous text though authored by many, and as representing a clear sense of the Indian and reflecting a historical continuity of a civilisational site. Authoring and translating are great dialogic and collaborative engagements which the Indian author and translator undertake in relation to history and heritage. As the author develops a dialogue and composes a text, his/her translator shadows him/her all along since the translator as collaborator may not find his/her moorings in separation from his/her chosen author and his/her text. In the persona of a collaborator, the translator today is a significant entity in India; he/she draws upon the individual and collective contexts of the author and the text, only to be able to connect with a larger tradition of the past and the present. He/she is an observer of the flux of time and text, and presents them in the way the author does. He/she is a partaker of the evolutionary process of the world and the word and its materialisation in the text through the acts of collaboration. The translator takes part in historicising the nation as the author does, and also contextualising the text like him/her. He/she constructs knowledge as his/her author does but he/she shares it with a different set of readers, thus broadening the horizon of the collaborative activity.

The role of the translator as a collaborator in today's context in India is more complex than it has ever been. While the translator in the late eighteenth, nineteenth and early twentieth centuries was engaged with the translations of clearly stratified religious and secular texts, today's translator is far more seriously engaged with issues concerning historical formations, the author's knowledge and thought processes, and possible textual intent. He/she has to seek a space in a more complicated site and collaborate with a more difficult evolutionary process and literary heritage, with new paradigms of culture, politics and history. He/she is also tasked with discovering an apt form, akin to that of the original, which was born earlier in a dialogic process established by the author. We have academics, writers and literary dilettantes choosing to work as translators today but with an acute awareness that this serious vocation can only be professionally pursued.

In a country that has two thousand dialects, eight hundred distinct languages, and twenty-two official languages, one text frequently takes recourse to another, seeking a kind of sustenance to forge an individual and collective identity. Indian texts breathe in companionship; in isolation they exist feebly, and only partially. As texts in the Indian contexts have developed, both thematically and stylistically, through a dialogic process spread over centuries, the translator too can work best in a collaborative mode. Indian literature harks back and forth; it swings in time and space, and acquires its worth in this communicative relationship. In its catholicity and range, a Vedic text may bear upon a medieval one, a medieval text upon a modern one, and a modern text upon a contemporary one. Texts of immense variety – spiritual and sensual, political and apolitical, private and the public, mainstream and sub-culture – have their genealogies, the authors their legacies, and the translators their strategies for collaborating and contextualising.

As India does not have a unitary framework of cultural and literary traditions, it has developed various kinds of devotional, secular and cosmopolitan texts in the broadest possible sense.

It is not as much a case of creating many texts in many languages, as it is of creating one text in many languages. In its many texts, it constructs a sense of the "Indian". The author refigures as a collaborator–translator who delimits the original text and opens it up to a larger world. The acts of authoring, translating and reading are largely dependent on a pattern of mutual collaborations in which literary and linguistic traditions bear upon one another. Marked by inter-historicism and inter-textualities, the Indian text is better created contextually and best translated collaboratively.

While collaboration on the part of the translator happens at myriad levels, he/she approaches a text to help create a new literary condition. The linguistic vibrancy of the Indian text is rooted in the author's bilingualism or trilingualism and his/her creative capacity for linguistic intermixing. The same applies to his/her capacity to develop a dialogue with racial, communal and religious differences. These terms also apply to the translator in equal measure as he/she too negotiates with those differences to achieve his/her resolution in the text. Translation is culture based and it is through cultural interface that new knowledges can be constructed. As there are different modes of production, dissemination and reception of knowledge, the translator is a contributor to the process. The collaborative act of translation is a valuable way of negotiating with the history of social and political formations, as also of creating narratives of identity. Finally, as Indian culture is plural and diverse, collaborative engagements make them homogenous and accessible which is so central to the sustenance of a cultural and literary life.

NOTES

1. While "insemination" corresponds with the "pre-natal stage" and "delivery" with the "post-natal stage", "conception" and the "natal stage" do not correspond with one another as they are different in nature. I have used the two paradigms only as convenient metaphors to make my point regarding the stages involved in the process of writing and translation.

2. Drawing upon gynaecological metaphors (pre-natal, natal, and post-natal), one might also consider the author as a mother in whom an inseminated idea bears fruit, or as a father who causes the birth. This also brings forth a related idea concerning the author as God in Coleridgean terms, but that is a subject of a separate discourse.
3. This is reminiscent of Yeats's *spiritus mundi* as the storehouse of images and symbols that are invoked in the creative process to bring about a work of art.
4. This has been substantially theorised by Roland Barthes in "The Death of the Author". I am extending the argument here by positing that even while the author loses control over his/her text, the text engages in continuous dialogue at multiple levels.
5. The four essays written at different points of time that comprise the book are "Discourse in the Novel" (1934–35), "Forms of Time and the Chronotope in the Novel" (1937–38), "From the Prehistory of Novelistic Discourse" (1940) and "Epic and Novel' (1941).
6. This foregrounds an important question regarding the function of the translator and how he/she visualises his/her larger role *vis-a-vis* the target text and the target author. A philosophical discussion in this regard may be seen in "The Task of the Translator" in *Illuminations* by Walter Benjamin. Also see "Politics and Poetics: De Man, Benjamin, and the Task of the Translator" in *Siting Translation* by Tejaswini Niranjana.
7. The author, as the producer of a text, has been problematised in two well-known theoretical discourses by Roland Barthes ("The Death of the Author") and Michel Foucault ("What is an Author"). A precise discussion on author in relation to author function, authority, originality, the notion of the romantic author, formalism, feminism, historicism, and authorial collaboration may be seen in *The Author* by Andrew Bennett. (See works cited)
8. Text has been prioritised over the author in modern discourse on authorship and writing. A more focused engagement with the larger meaning of text may be seen in *Translation as Text* by Neubert and Shreve.
9. Most precisely, literary culture is the sum total of historical, cultural and linguistic manifestations in literature which is a repository of all human aspirations. Sheldon Pollock's (ed.) seminal work *Literary Cultures in History: Reconstructions from South Asia* may be referred to in order to appreciate its larger meaning and manifestation in relation to various South Asian sites.
10. The case of multiple translations of a text or an author would be illustrative as well as instructive in this regard. Reference may be made to the multiple translations of Rumi by both Western and Eastern translators, who represent Rumi both with uniformity and difference.

Their approaches underline the translators' broad predilections with history, text, and style.

11. The translators need to imagine their possible readers precisely because they mould and direct their work in relation to their appeal and contemporary relevance. This also explains why certain texts are translated afresh in every age and why every age needs the translation of a text in contemporary language and style.
12. Publishers and the market indirectly determine the choice of text and methodology of translation which is most often market and need based. The cases of Tagore and Premchand are relevant in this context as they sell better than others even though some of the translations of these two authors may not stand up to tough critical scrutiny.
13. This is a huge subject and has been addressed variously by literary critics and historians. References may be made to works published by the Sahitya Akademi, more particularly those by Sisir Kumar Das and K. M. George that deal with the history of Indian literature and comparative perspectives.
14. *Rig, Yajur, Sam* and *Atharva*
15. The *Ramayana* and the *Mahabharata*
16. *Vaastu Shastra, Arthashastra* and *Kama Sutra*
17. Some of the important ones include the establishment of Bengal Asiatic Society (1784), establishment of the College of Fort William (1800), the support for English education by the Governor Generals in the three presidencies of Bombay, Calcutta and Madras (1820), Macaulay's "Minutes" (1835), replacement of Persian by English as official language (1835), establishment of three universities in the three presidencies (1857), establishment of three major centres of learning: Banaras Hindu University (1915), Aligarh Muslim University (1920) and Jamia Millia Islamia (1920), founding of Progressive Writers Movement (1935), and to top them all, the beginning of the Indian Renaissance at the turn of the twentieth century.
18. Some Indian writers – Sajjad Zaheer (1905–73), Mohammad Deen Taseer (1902–50), Mulk Raj Anand (1905–2004) and Ahmed Ali (1910–94) – living in London during the 1930s, and concerned with the happenings at home, deliberated upon the need for a new sociopolitical order, and a new literary culture. This group developed a manifesto in 1936 for what came to be known as the Progressive Writers' Association. Joined by a host of writers, the Association gave a clarion call for reason against sentimentality, realism against romance, and freedom against subjugation. At the social level, it rejected feudal order and decadent morality; at the political level, it sought recourse to leftist ideology; and in the domain of literature, it made an organised effort to refute the centuries-old romanticist–spiritualist tradition. Being anti-imperialist in nature, it fostered the spirit of decolonisation, called for

India's freedom, and brought people face to face with the problems of poverty, backwardness and oppression. The movement empowered them with a new idiom to assert themselves and a new will to resist the historical legacies of overall subjugation.

19. Reference may be made to the policies and practices of Charles Grant, T. B. Macaulay, William Bentinck and Thomas Munro, among others, regarding the propagation of English education and the firmer grip of imperial power in India.
20. Important names in this connection are those of H. T. Prinsep who discovered the clues to the inscriptions of Ashoka, William Jones who founded the Bengal Asiatic Society, H. T. Colebrooke who wrote the Hindu Law of Contracts and Successions, and Gottlieb Wilhelm Leitner, William Rice Morland Holryod and Donald McLeod who fervently promoted Oriental studies.

WORKS CITED

Bakhtin, M. M. 1981. *The dialogic imagination: Four essays*, ed. Michael Holquist. Austin: University of Texas Press.

Benjamin, Walter. 1970. *Illuminations: Essays and reflections*, ed. Hannah Arendt. London: Fontana.

Bennett, Andrew. 2005. *The author*. New York: Routledge.

Neubert, Albrecht and Gregory M. Shreve. 1992. *Translation as text*. Kent: Kent State University Press.

Niranjana, Tejaswini. 1992. *Siting translation: History, post-structuralism, and the colonial context*. Berkeley and Los Angeles: University of California Press.

Pollock, Sheldon, ed. 2003. *Literary cultures in history: Reconstructions from South Asia*. Berkeley and Los Angeles: University of California Press.

FOUR

Translation as Discourse: Notes on Intent Formation

This chapter makes a case for treating translation as a mode of discourse formation and dissemination. Through a larger discussion on the nature and function of discourse and by comprehensively considering language and literature as the repositories of discourse, it has been posited that India has produced a rich variety of discourses from the ancient to the modern times that are marked by the richness of difference rather than the monotony of homogeneity.

It is posited that while translation is a hospitable and malleable site of discourse construction, the translator is a philosopher of the medium and the message. While engaging with a source language discourse he/she engages with a number of agencies involved in the act of its creation. As he/she does this in order to construct his/her own narrative, he/she enables himself/herself, through a complex process, to evolve his/her own methodology. He/she develops corresponding codes for the intended set of readers and critically intervenes to re-construct the semantics and morphology of the source text in the translated text. As he/she re-configures a certain discourse into another discourse with its own identifiers, he/she turns translation into a domain of discoursing and the act of translating into a discourse itself.

If literature is a repository of discourses, translation must be a site where they are re-negotiated by the translator for multiple readers in multiple languages. With this basic proposition in hand I would argue that while the movement of a text from one location to another authenticates the act of translation, it also turns it into a discourse. I would assert further that translation is a way of striking a balance with history, culture, language and location, both separately and together, as well as a method of discoursing and entering into serious contestations. Since both writing and translation are deeply political acts and have maintained an interminable relationship with each other over the centuries, they have created conditions for the discourse to sustain and for languages to survive.

In order to move along the trajectory laid out above, I would first discuss the nature and function of discourse itself which may be appreciated in the larger context of the agencies that construct and disseminate them. This would facilitate the evaluation of literature as a repository of discourses that the immense variety of languages and locations construct for various sets of readers. This would also help to construct my basic argument that while translation extends the frontiers of discourse it also becomes a larger agency, a kind of discourse in itself, which spells out the stages involved in the act of translating, disseminating and validating it in larger areas of reception.

NATURE AND FUNCTION OF DISCOURSE

In a variety of oral and written expressions, discourse may be appreciated as a cognisable site of knowledge that develops through a complex process of ideational and linguistic concrescence. Language and discourse implicate one another and they hold on to each other as embryo and body, as also the deliverer and the delivered. Written expressions that constitute texts of discourse are subject to structural and semantic scrutiny twice: first, when a text is composed and it projects a discourse in a given language, and second, when it is translated from one language into another. In order to examine the birth and dissemination of a text and the discourse embedded into it, I should like to underscore the implications of the three loaded terms – *discursive, discoursive* and *discourse* – to reflect upon their implicit differences, and to understand their interrelated significance towards intent formation. I would do so in order to signify the problematic of translation as a mode of multifaceted discourse on language and meaning.

Discursive, as a lexical item, has two meanings. It implies: (a) drifting, meandering, or gallivanting over a wide space, and also being aimless, indiscriminate and random, and (b) moving from one position to another in the course of rationalising or reasoning, or while creating an argument. As the first meaning extends over the other, the two meanings become inseparable and they closely reflect upon one another. The process of roaming over an undefined space brings forth certain points of contact where a fledgling reason or argument seeks its space in the domain of the discursive. This domain is infinite and its various forms stand connected at the very core. At a more complicated level, the discursive act relates with the difference between the actual and the ideal intents and utterances. The discursive practice thus approximates disseminative practice and reduces the hiatus between the real and the desired states of intent formation. Discursive practices refer to rules, norms and mental models of acceptable behaviour to receive and interpret messages. A discursive engagement of this kind, as applicable to the rooted Indian context, draws upon language, history and culture, and all of them relate with the acts of imaging and historicising. All these acts get manifested in the process of intent and textual formation and they acquire their own terms of reference in a given language.

Discoursive, on the other hand, which is supposed to be an obsolete word for "discursive", is not too removed from its replacement, as it is also identifiable with the help of reason although it goes a small step further insofar as it moves from hypothesis to thesis, or deduction to judgment. While it remains discursive in nature, it also employs the dialogic mode and develops a conversation. It becomes interjectory in its design and imparts a discoursive character to the engagement.

It is marked by communicativeness and ratiocination and makes way for the concrescence of a discourse. In this respect, discoursive harks back to discursive on the one hand, and looks forward to the emergence of a discourse on the other. It is thus intermediary in nature and plays a significant role in the formation of a text or discourse.

Discourse may thus be considered to be the end-product of the discursive–discoursive processes. As an extended expression of an idea, or a body of an organised system of knowledge, so to say, it emerges as a representation of meaning constructed in a certain order and with a certain rationale. At yet another level, discourse may be appreciated as a mode of speech between the human agencies involved in constructing and receiving it. It contains social, philosophical, political or other references at the core that constitute its frame of reference. Precisely put, discourses address, examine and interrogate language as a carrier of meaning, and meaning as a source of power and sustenance. As social systems are alterable, the structures of language and meaning too remain tentative. As such, discourses are altered and interrogated and make way for revisionist discourses. In their broader manifestation, discourses concern the domains of ideas, the cartography of imagination, the genealogy of intellect, and use of language and linguistic tools to achieve their aim.

As discourses engage with the critical use of language and the consequent production of meaning, as also the inextricability of the medium and the message, it may be argued that the formation of a text in translation rests upon the way a language is put to use, and how it engages with the creation of a possible meaning. Even though the fluidity and indeterminacy of language remains the object of interrogation, the translated text, or discourse, becomes the testament of a culture, its major characteristics and practices and its distinguishing features. While negotiating between intellectual motifs and linguistic methods, the authorial discourse represents history in terms of the agencies of power like social practices, realities, myths and fantasies. As every age creates a discourse of its own kind by drawing upon the major features and events of the times, the text of the age is also characterised by this difference. It thus creates a complex field of meaning reflecting upon the larger realities of the social and linguistic systems together – the physical image along with contemporary linguistic tropes and rhetoric. Drawing upon the above, one may develop two arguments: first, the act of translating is a discursive–discoursive act, and second, this act leads to the production of a text that constitutes a discourse. While this discursive–discoursive act can be deliberate, dialogic, or even freewheeling at different times, the discourse so created is a complex construction of language and meaning that is markedly tentative, indeterminate and alterable. Translation as discourse thus implies the simultaneous initiation of two activities that relate with (a) the process of translating a text or discourse and (b) the formation of a text or discourse in translation.

This leads me to posit that discourses, being different from subject matter, configure in multiple fields – cultural, political, religious, etc. – and are characterised by the language chosen for intent formation. They are reflected in several modes, tenors and textures as discussed by Hatim and Mason. Every mode represents the "nature of the language code" and serves as the "medium of language activity" (49). It reflects a tenor that "relays the relationship between the addresser and the addressee" (50), and represents a texture which is "one of the defining characteristics of text...which ensures that a text 'hangs together', both linguistically and conceptually" (192). Cumulatively, all these define discourse texture as something that "should be coherent (that is, have continuity and sense) and cohesive (that is, display connectivity between its surface elements), and that it should display distinct patterns of thematisation (that is, it will be arranged in such a fashion as to draw attention to those parts of its content which are deemed most important…)" (192). These issues relating to various aspects of discourse are embedded in certain interrelated questions that include, for example, how a discourse is created, who creates it, and with what aims and objectives to meet. To answer these questions, one might say that it is created through a dialogic process with the agencies involved, and it is done by one who initiates the process in order to articulate and modulate a voice. These answers also point towards a broader politics that relate with the creation of intention, dissemination of intention, and furtherance of the intention contained in the body of a discourse. There are other allied questions as to how one discourse differs from another and how one discourse can be evaluated against the other. These are complex questions that are directly concerned with the distinguishing marks of intent formation, their dissemination in a given language for a given set of consumers with a set of evaluative parameters in hand. These parameters concern the modes of discourse – verbal or written, formal or informal, and the use of a linguistic register to construct a certain kind of discourse. Discourses are ever-changing as the conditions that construct a discourse are in a constant state of flux. Language too has to keep pace with the changes through which every discourse finds its expression. The questions raised above that relate essentially with the process of intent formation and discourse construction also project a contentious issue that even while the initiators of a discourse formalise a discourse, the silent and the non-participating also construct the condition, albeit unconsciously, under which a discourse is constructed. All discourses, as such, turn political, contentious and mutable. They are born in a sociopolitical system which they interrogate and from which they seek their sustenance.

What has been posited above regarding the formation and dissemination of discourse represents a cross section of ideas on the subject. It may be noted that as a major subject of theoretical inquiry in social sciences, discourse has been approached variously in modern times, especially since the 1970s. While underlining some of the major arguments, David Howarth remarks that the "positivists and empiricists argue that discourses are best viewed as 'frames' or 'cognitive schema'...that can foster common perceptions and understanding for specific purposes..." (3). With reference to Doug McAdam, J. D. McCarthy and M. N. Zald, he accounts for an opposite view held by Realists like Rom Harré, E. H. Maden, Roy Bhaskar and Rob Stones who emphasised the ontology of discourse and for whom discourses are "particular objects with their own properties and powers, in which case it is necessary for realists 'to focus on language and as structured system in its own right…'" (Howarth, 3). He then discusses Marxists like Louis Althusser, Michel Pêecheux and Slavoj Žižek who chose to stress upon "the way discourses have to be explained by reference to the contradictory processes of economic production and reproduction…as ideological systems of meaning that obfuscate and naturalize uneven distribution of power and resources" (4). He further refers to Norman Fairclough and Ruth Wodak who drew upon a variety of other thinkers to define the contours of discourse analysis. Finally, he refers to post-structuralists and post-Marxists like Jacques Derrida, Michel Foucault, Ernesto Laclau and Chantel Mouffe who went "further than the hermeneutical emphasis on social meaning by regarding social structures as inherently ambiguous, incomplete and contingent systems of meaning" (4). With reference to these theoretical discussions which make way for our argument, I will present a case regarding discourse formation in India and its dissemination beyond time in general and the Indian space in particular in the subsequent parts of this chapter.

Language and Literature as Repositories of Discourse

Language, as a means of multiple types of communication, can be constructed with reference to a given location and its predominant beliefs and practices that lead to the formation of multiple types of discourses. However, this process becomes all the more problematic when we refer to a site like India where language, location and discourse are marked by the richness of difference rather than the monotony of homogeneity. A survey of discourse formation through different ages in India would amply substantiate the fact that each age has created its own kinds of discourses which have helped identify the age for its distinct sensibility. Some of these discourses have been carried forward and have acquired their strength by existing alongside other predominant discourses of the time. It also illustrates the fact that although India speaks differently and distinctly in different languages and ages, it remains clearly identifiable for its essential nature and sensibility in each age individually, and all ages collectively.

Compared with Western linguistic and literary traditions, India has evolved its own linguistic and literary varieties. It has appropriated revisionist tendencies to evolve new signs and gestures of language. Language, as such, has not been an end unto itself even for the sake of experimentation; it has been a means of redefining meaning and turns of expression. Psycholinguists and semanticists tell us that language is a tool that imparts concrescence to literary representations and that it helps create a form appropriate to those representations. Notwithstanding I. A. Richards's two uses of language – referential and emotive – and Roman Jakobson's extension of the same into six categories – emotive, connotative, phatic, referential, metalingual and poetic – the new literary text, and especially the new postcolonial text, has created its own paradigms of meaning. In literary theory, language has emerged as a complex site of interrogation, as it has not existed in isolation but in relation to prior conditions of living and location. Literary theory does not presuppose the existence or classification of literary and non-literary languages. It asserts that language extends its frontiers and lends itself to a variety of disciplines and discourses, and helps create various structures of discourse. It is about defining a cluster of relationships with a notion, a thought, a norm, a fantasy, a concrete experience, a scientific invention, and the likes of these. What I wish to assert here is that language links literature with discourse and imparts to it an identity of its own. Louis Althusser considered language to be a receptacle of ideologies which we may mark as being concretised as discourse. This was carried further by Pierre Macherey who considered language and ideology together to seek deeper layers of association between them which we might consider as the interplay between language and discourse. While on the one hand we may try and understand the syntactical, phonological and lexical qualities of language, on the other, we may like to consider the polyphonic nature of literary language and its multilayered ambiguity in the context of discourse formation in India with great profit. We may extend this argument further to discuss language in relation to politics and power, ethnicity and race, time and space, history and society. It is in this context that an Indian text affords a closer reading of its locational and ideological or discoursive value.

The richly ambiguous Indian context has produced a plethora of discourses in the domains of religion, philosophy, culture, literature, economy, polity and so on, which are spread over the four phases of Indian history. To illustrate my point, I should argue that while ancient India laid the foundation of religio-philosophical discourse that helped evolve a civilisational paradigm, the medieval period carved a space for secular discourses of a very wide nature with remarkable possibilities for negotiating with a variety of faiths, beliefs, languages and modes of reception. Similarly, while modern India saw the emergence of a remarkable renaissance which heralded reconfigurations of the notions of nationalism, education and a new language for a new narrative; post-independence India set a futuristic agenda for the concrescence of a new nation state, the realisation of Nehruvian ideals of development, cosmopolitanism, political economy and competitive spirit. These historical phases account for the diversity of Indian discourses that are reflected in the modes of speech and writing and mark the major contours of the larger Indian canvas.

In order to substantiate my argument, let me choose two generic examples to show the formation and extension of a certain kind of discourse through ages. These have been spread over centuries without ever becoming obsolete, or remaining in a state of suspended animation. I would draw upon the examples of what have come down to us from ancient and medieval India respectively and have been identified as the *sutras*[1] and the *malfoozat*.[2] We are aware that in literal terms sutras and malfoozat mean strings or threads, but in metaphorical terms they have evolved as the nucleus, or the fountainheads, of the larger domains of knowledge. They are incorporated in aphorisms, proverbs, sayings, maxims, sermons and teachings of the saints and the Sufis that define and validate human aspirations and actions. They bear a striking resemblance to one another in spite of the basic difference in their origins into organised systems of faith.

The history of the evolution and dissemination of *sutras* in India and outside through translations from Sanskrit and Pali to several Indian and Western languages would show that they embody larger discourses on the religious, secular, philosophical, political, legal, civil, sexual and other aspects that define human life and society in all their variety and splendour. They relate to knowledge acquired through hearing (*shruti*) and remembrance or recapitulation (*smriti*). They can be traced to a variety of sources like the ones in the Buddhist Sutras, the Jain Sutras, the laws of Manu, and the *Yog Sutra* of Patanjali, apart from many others, which serve as the bases for fuller discourses on broader issues of life. Let me draw upon some of them like those on human mind, self, world, and language, out of a huge variety of discourses, to show that there is a basic unity in all these discourses as they project a religio-philosophical vision of life and the world in general.

In a Buddhist sutra[3] called *Adanta Sutta ("Untamed")* there is a philosophical discourse on the human mind as follows:

> Monks, I know not of any other single thing so intractable as the untamed mind. The untamed mind is indeed a thing un-tractable./Monks, I know not of any other thing so tractable as the tamed mind. The tamed mind is indeed a thing tractable./Monks, I know not of any other single thing so conducive to great loss as the untamed mind. The untamed mind indeed conduces to great loss./Monks, I know not of any other single thing so conducive to great profit as the tamed mind. The tamed mind indeed conduces to great profit./Monks, I know not of any other single thing that brings such woe as the mind that is untamed, uncontrolled, unguarded and unrestrained. Such a mind indeed brings great woe./ Monks, I know not of any other single thing that brings such bliss as the mind that is tamed, controlled, guarded and restrained. Such a mind indeed brings great bliss." (Woodward, n.p.)

It may be observed that this discourse on the mind opens ways for psychological discourse on the ways in which the human mind works. This implies that while a discourse relates strictly with one subject, it also opens up a way for other discourses to emerge and broaden the frontiers of comparative knowledge. In a similar vein, there is a discourse in the "Fourth Lesson" of a Jain sutra[4] that reconciles the dichotomy between the world and the self in yet another philosophical manner:

> (Thus I say): A man should not, of his own accord, deny the world (of fire-bodies), nor should he deny the self. He who denies the world (of fire-bodies), denies the self; and he who denies the self, denies the world (of fire-bodies). He who knows that (viz. fire) through which injury is done to the long-living bodies (i.e. plants) knows also that which does no injury (i.e. control); and he who knows that which does no injury, knows also that through which no injury is done to the long-living bodies. (Jacobi, 1–2)

We may notice here the continuation of the Buddhist sutra in a Jain sutra insofar as it extends the frontiers of knowledge regarding the mind, as it deliberates upon the working of the self. Though the intended recipients have not been the same for the two discourses quoted above, they have extended and gone beyond one set of recipients to another, and have come down to us in written forms from orature. This practice continued and led to formation of multiple discourses age after age.

At a remove from the philosophical outpourings of Buddha and Mahavira, there is a discourse that classifies, defines and assigns roles to human beings. This discourse that is set forth in *Manusmriti* and rendered into English as *The Laws of Manu*,[5] has given birth to a raging debate in subsequent ages. This discourse on the *varna* system is rather authoritative and lays down a system of societal stratification leading to the principles of governance in a society:

> 31. But for the sake of prosperity of the worlds he caused the Brahmana, the Kshatriya, the Vaisya, and the Sudra to proceed from his mouth, his arms, his thighs, and his feet.

> 32. Dividing his own body, the Lord became half male and half female; with that (female) he produced Virag. (Buhler, n.p.)

Without commenting on the merit of the discourse quoted above, which does not constitute the aim of my argument in any manner, I would refer to an entirely different discourse that foreshadows the modernist preoccupation with language and theory. This may be marked in the *Yoga Sutra*[6] of Patanjali.

> I.42. In the case of the understanding reached through logic or reasoning, there is confusion on account of the discrepancies that exist between the word (description), meaning (in both connotations as the substance described and as the knowledge of the word meaning) and imagination or assumption. Hence, it is unclear and uncertain.
>
> I.43. But, when the mind-stuff is cleansed of memory, the self or personality which was nothing but the fragmentation, the conditioning or the colouring (the impurity) is wiped out as it were; and the substance or truth alone shines, without distortion, logic or reasoning which is the function of the limited personality. (14–15)

With his engagement with logic, word, meaning, imagination, truth and personality, Patanjali may be considered to be setting a discourse on these issues that preoccupy modern philosophy and theory. This implies that discourses are formed, revised and improved upon with time as they chart out the trajectory of knowledge systems. This also connects tradition with modernity and helps view the richness of discourses in a comprehensive perspective of the past and the present. These are some of the discourses that concern humankind and spell out the ways of life in general. A much more remarkable point is that even though they have their origins in the Hindu view of life, they represent the characteristic Indian ethos and embody an Indian view of life in the broadest possible sense.

Keeping in mind the general complexion of the discourses briefly discussed above, it would be extremely fascinating to trace a strikingly similar tradition in the *malfoozat* of Islamic saints which also originated in their sayings and sermons, and which concretised as comprehensive discourses on man and man's relationship with the world. Largely concerned with human obligations to the self and society, these Islamic *malfoozat*, which came into being much later, echo the *sutras* in their essential concerns. In the *malfoozat* of Moinuddin Chishti,[7] as in the sutras of Buddha and Mahavir quoted above, there are discourses on the self which are pronounced in a precise manner as follows:

> There are four cardinal virtues of the individual self:
>
> i. refraining from begging in the state of poverty;
> ii. showing the attitude of being well-fed when feeling hungry;
> iii. maintaining cheerfulness in the time of sorrow; and
> iv. befriending the enemy. (n.p.)

Saints and Sufis have ever engaged with the issue of the self in multiple ways which include primarily the problem of its purification which leads ultimately to taking pride in the self with all humility. Apart from being a religious discourse, it is also a deeply philosophical discourse. It found its extended expression in Fariduddin Ganjshakar[8] who summed up the qualities of the ideal human being from different perspectives:

> 31. Baba Farid said four questions were put to 700 saints and all of them gave the same reply. These questions were:
>
> i. Who is the wisest? "One who rejects the world," they replied.
> ii. Who is the most saintly? "One who does not get changed at everything." [sic]
> iii. Who is the richest and the wealthiest of all men? "One who is content."
> iv. Who is the most needy? "One who gives up contentment."

Considering these discourses in totality, one may clearly mark a sense of likeness and continuity in them. In all their simplicity, they sound rooted and seem to make way for other similar discourses. As such, comprehensive discourses on perseverance, contentment, renunciation, forbearance, piety, and all that concerns the spiritual development of human beings are abundantly spread out in the *malfoozat* of Nizamuddin Auliya.[9] He defined man's devotion to God in the most liberal terms:

> Devotion to God is of two kinds, *lazmi* (intransitive) and *muta'addi* (transitive). In *lazmi* devotion the benefit which accrues is confined to the devotee alone. This type of devotion includes prayers, fasting, pilgrimage to Mecca, recitation of religious formulae, turning over the beads of the rosary etc. The *muta'addi* devotion, on the contrary, brings advantage and comfort to others; it is performed by spending money on others, showing affection to people and by other means strives to help his fellow human beings. The reward of *muta'addi* devotion is endless and limitless. (n. p.)

The perennial concern with the human predicament, as well as with the world here and the world hereafter, has marked the discourses of the Sufis of all shades and types in every age. In this respect, it would be relevant to refer to Nasiruddin Mahmud Chiragh Dehlavi[10] who classified human beings as follows:

1. Common people (*awam*)
2. The elect (*khawas*)
3. Super-elect (*khas-ul-khawas*)

This classification is not based on social or intellectual differences, but on the basis of spiritual status which is more difficult for the elect to attain than the common people. What withholds the vision of God in the case of the common man is sin; in the case of the elect it is negligence or indulgence in lawful pleasure but in the case of the super-elect it is the veil of virtues he has to look beyond as there is nothing more for him to explore after that.

We may easily mark here a difference between the two discourses by Manu and Chiragh Dehlavi on the classification of man. While Manu's hierarchical order is based on the *varna* system, Dehlavi's discourse is rooted in the spiritualist tradition. With reference to the discourses preserved in the sutras and the *malfoozat* from the ancient and medieval periods of Indian history, it could be justifiably argued that while there are certain points of unity in them, there are points of variation too that make the discourses comprehensive and sustainable through the ages. Although the discourses rooted in the Hindu and the Islamic views of life represent two different religio-philosophical traditions of India, they embody what may be called the characteristically Indian worldview. This worldview, rooted in time and space, has defined the features of the Indian culture and the nature of the Indian people for several centuries.

While *sutras* and *malfoozat* are the repositories of only one kind of Indian discourse, there are many others that one may refer to from other domains of knowledge and historical periods. One might go to discourses that were established in colonial and postcolonial India. In modern and contemporary history, for example, one may locate the variety of these discourses in some of the more prominent ones like those by Raja Ram Mohan Roy, Mohandas Karamchand Gandhi, Jawaharlal Nehru, Abul Kalam Azad, and B. R. Ambedkar who figured the contours of Indian history, culture and polity. They developed a discourse on British colonialism in India, Indian nationalism and postcolonialism that reflects the modern Indian condition at large. From the literary domain, one could refer to A. K. Ramanujan who broadened the frontiers of both language and literature by initiating multiple discourses through his own poetry and prose, his translations from classical Indian languages and his collections of folktales that cumulatively underline a certain unity and redefine the Indian sensibility in a comprehensive manner. Taken on the whole, his works project a remarkable negotiation between impact and response in relation to intent formation. It may be posited that an examination of ideologies or discourses in literary texts also involves an examination of the ethos in which a text is rooted. In addition, it is an examination of the individual choice of the author with regard to his or her interpretation of the past and contemporary history. Such an exercise has never been as rewarding and interesting as it has been in the case of India, which is characterised by its historical periods, cultural configurations and political exigencies. As India is different historically, racially, linguistically and culturally, its discourses on class, gender and ethnicities, for example, have emerged differently as they are rooted in its economics, politics, sociology, history, anthropology, philosophy, and other disciplines that identify the dynamics of a nation. In modern times, it helps us see our ideologies and discourses in relation to our postmodernism, our new brands of imperialism, and post-industrialism as I have mentioned above with reference to some of the modern-day Indian intellectuals. One may quote copiously to show a variety of rooted experiences that underline the nature of various discourses a people create and by which they are identified.

A larger overview of the Indian discourse through different ages would show that the devotional, secular and literary texts of India represent a series of discourses that are united at the core. These discourses create a sense of an intriguing India. They are intertextual and inter-historicist and call upon the translator to develop an integral view of the discourse so created. The vitality of the Indian discourse is rooted in its linguistic vibrancy, its intermixing, and in its racial, communal and spiritual power. Indian discourses are the examples of multiple interfaces and consequent production of knowledge embodied in translational engagement which is akin to the production of a discourse in the ultimate analysis.

By drawing upon the above examples, it could be posited that Indian discourse is neither unitary in nature nor isolated in form and structure; it has grown organically and is complex in its intent and execution. Although configured by many and in many languages, it is an interminable discourse on the frames of historical periods and thematic clusters in which the translator emerges as a mediator–discourser who engages with linguistic tones as much as he/she does with cultural tenor. In joining the discursive–discoursive process, he/she negotiates with the evolutionary stages of the authorial text and discourse and its shifting contexts in order to concretise his/her own text and discourse. Unlike the translators of the late eighteenth, nineteenth and early twentieth centuries who developed discourses around clearly identifiable religious and secular texts, the translator today has to engage with the politics of postcolonial translation, in an entirely new role, apart from carrying forward the tradition of disseminating discourses that he/she may wish to disseminate. The new Indian discourse has emerged out of a comprehensive understanding of the new signs of culture, politics and history which needs dissemination through translation.

Translation as Discourse

Translation is a hospitable and malleable site of discourse construction. In the act of translating a text, the translator makes a deliberate choice of a text, a certain linguistic register, and a methodology in order to turn translation into a site of discourse dissemination, and by implication, into a domain of discoursing. Just as discourse relates with social meaning and social formations, translation too develops a discourse on these two subjects. Ideas and thoughts as embodiments of social experience are subject to scrutiny in discourse just as the texts themselves are open to critical inquiry as finished products of translation. Both engage with the two agencies of the social practice and their practitioners. History, politics, and their impact on people are the subjects of discourse as much as they are of translation in their ideational and aesthetic formations.

Taking a step further, let me relate it with discourse analysis. As discourse analysis facilitates the understanding of the intended message embodied in the counters of expression, as also the gaps in them, the act of translating too engages with these in a significant way to complete and convey the possible meaning. Both the acts of discourse analysis and translating thus exploit the ways of unmasking the word, be it their bare neutrality or loaded intentionality, in a context. Words, being keys to contextual meaning, annotate the world and make it accessible in the same way as translation does. Being enabling in nature, words act as agents of knowledge and help apprehend the direct and ambiguous constructions of power and their impact on society. Discourse analysis helps further in critiquing the word and identifying the discursive agencies of power as the act of translating does. Both discourse analysis and translation help understand the games of hegemonisation and victimisation, as also the possibility of disengaging from them. Both relate with a variety of social structures and cultures and engage with discursive practices which include our ways of reading, writing, speaking, listening and the broader social framework that helps create the discourse.

Translation and discourse are essentially acts of discoursing with an idea and its verbal expression. The translator creates this discourse by negotiating with structures of meaning and finding their counterparts in the structures of the target text. The discourse is born in a dialogic negotiation with the message and the word whereas the translator intervenes to reconstruct the semantics of discourse and its morphology in the target text. It entails re-visioning and rewriting of myths, motifs, signs and logos in a new discourse and situating it in a community of other discourses. The translator thus helps a discourse outgrow the boundaries of the source text and acquire a new idiom and form for its reception in a new cultural space. In this process of creating a discourse, the act of translating lends itself to the status of a discourse on the message and the medium. As such, translation becomes both an act of discoursing and a phenomenon acted upon.

This takes me to consider the agencies involved in turning translation into an act of creating discourse. The translator is a philosopher of the medium and the message who engages with various agencies of a discourse like the text and the first author of the text whom and whose text he has chosen to translate. He/she examines the possibility of setting up a discourse in his/her own text along with its overall literary culture and historical baggage. By doing this, he/she initiates a series of discourses in the reader's mind, who interrogates the verbal icons and the form. The discursive–discoursive act of translating enables the translator, in turn, to evolve a methodology in order to compose a discourse. The translator operates in new domains of the word and the meaning to develop corresponding codes which might appear different, or even alien to his/her target readers. The job of creating signs of familiarity for a new set of readers makes his/her job formidable, and at times even forbidding. The translator thus undertakes an act of problematising and rewriting a discourse in which historical, philosophical and literary equations are re-configured. Creating such a discourse is also an interrogative act where the translator addresses all the constituents of the discourse – word, meaning, and narrative strategy – and the sites of reception – geographical, political, and cultural.

This discussion also brings us to the question of the translator's participation in constructing ideological discourse and turning the act of translation into a means of discourse. In this process, the translator enters into an inevitable negotiation with notions and beliefs, values and thought patterns, and social and civil configurations. He/she vacillates between the illusion of the source text and the reality of the target text, and produces a plausible system of values for the recipients. Terry Eagleton, Antonio Gramsci and Louis Althusser theorise ideological discourse and relate it with power play. It may be argued that the translator, in turning translation into discourse, becomes a part of this ambiguous power play. Since ideological discourses relate basically to the movement of history, manifestations of culture, and human interaction within a society, they get reflected in literary and other texts that reach out to a new set of readers through translation. This is shown in the play of words and human actions and interactions, ideas and logic, beliefs and aspirations, and social and political expressions, all of which individually and collectively reflect upon the act of translation as discourse.

NOTES

1. Literally, the word *sutra* means "thread". Metaphorically, ideas, being the "threads" of knowledge, came to constitute various domains of wisdom over time. They were recorded on leaves and sewn together into an anthology of life-sustaining principles. Developing into bases of knowledge, *sutras* were memorised by students. Associated basically with Hinduism, they appeared on a huge variety of subjects like rhetoric, literature, grammar, politics, astrology, rituals, desire, sex, body, mind, justice, yoga, devotion, faith and many more, which ultimately composed a world view.
2. Literally, the word *malfoozat* (singular *malfooz*) stands for the words uttered by spiritual masters. These words, considered as threads of knowledge, are viewed with reverence and preserved and noted for use as the guiding principles of life.
3. The Buddhist *sutra* (Sanskrit), also known as *sutta* (Pali), have their origin in the sayings of Buddha. They represent the essence of Buddha's dharma that keeps the world from evils and sustains it against all odds. In more than five hundred *sutras*, Buddha's discourse can be found on every aspect of life which prominently include knowledge, desire, courage, pride, self, understanding, ignorance, justice, mind, body, sickness, fear, elements, conscience, ageing, assumption, vigilance, delight, downfall and death.
4. These *sutras*, also called *suya*, have their origins in the sayings of Mahavira. Imparted as lessons, the *Akaranga* and *Kalpa sutras* are the most prominent of the Jaina sutras. The *Akaranga sutras* deal with the overall behaviour expected of the monks and emphasise caution, austerity, restraint, humility, culinary preferences, manners of speech, denial of ego, carnal desires and worldly passions, as well as abstinence from the acts of destroying the lives of even the most minute organisms. The *Kalpa sutras* develops a discourse on the life of Mahavira and others who propounded and followed Jainism.
5. An ancient and generic discourse on Hinduism, *Manusmriti* took shape as answers on the origin of the universe, social structure, the *varna* system, state, polity, and the judicial system, among others. These came to be recognised as the words of Brahma himself through his son Manu who passed it on to his disciple Bhrigu, who in turn, narrated them to his own students. The elements of drama, story frames, characters and dialogues characterise the discourse and impart to it a unique place among the ancient Brahminical texts. It received extraordinary attention both in terms of warm appreciation and severe criticism during both colonial and postcolonial times.
6. An ancient Indian classic that passed through phases of obscurity and prominence along with controversies regarding more than one Patanjali

as its author, is a collection of one hundred and ninety-six yoga sutras that helped achieve tranquillity through meditation. It was developed upon preceding sutras and was anthologised around 400 CE. It is divided into four sections that include *samadhi* (state of blissfulness), *sadhana* (discipline), *vibhuti* (power), and *kaivalya* (isolation). The ethical codes prescribed include abstinence from violence, falsehood, stealing, sexuality, and resisting temptation. He prescribed rules, postures, modes of reflection, and methods of achieving inwardness to achieve the aims of yoga.

7. Moinuddin Chishti (1141–1236), orphaned early in his life, relinquished his home in the Siestan region of Eastern Persia in the quest for divine knowledge. He travelled through innumerable centres of religious learning in Samarkand, Bukhara, the Middle East, and several others. He found his spiritual master in Usman Harooni whom he attended upon for nearly two decades, and performed Hajj with him before setting out for India after a sign from the prophet of Islam, as has been generally narrated in the accounts of Moinuddin's life. Traversing a long distance and staying at several places, he finally landed in Ajmer in his early 50s where he established the Chishti order, one of the four major orders of Islamic Sufism. He practised and preached, as all Chishti Sufis did after him, the observance of discipline and liberalism, disengagement from worldly riches and seats of power, and need for spiritual rejuvenation and larger human catholicity. His major *malfoozat* are included in *Dalil-ul-Aarefeen*.
8. Fariduddin Ganjshakar (1173–1266), born in a village near Multan, emerged as a prominent Sufi saint of the Chishti order. He received his education in Multan where he met Qutbuddin Bhakhtiar Kaki, who happened to pass through that place and who accepted him as his valued disciple. On the advice of his venerable master, he travelled far and wide in many Islamic countries and met Sufis and saints to gain greater ground in spirituality. He became his master's successor after his death and left Delhi to settle in Ajodhan, now known as Pakpattan in Pakistan. He was also a poet of high spiritual order in Punjabi whose hymns form a part of the Guru Granth Sahib, the holy book of Sikhs. He is popularly known as Baba Farid and there are many miracles associated with him that make him an iconic figure with places and institutions named after him. His *malfoozat* are collected in *Rahat-ul Quloob* and *Asrar-ul-Auliya*.
9. Nizamuddin Auliya (1238–1325) was born in Badayun but made Delhi his spiritual seat. He was a distinguished Sufi saint of the Chishti order. He was the fourth Sufi of the order to follow the great lineage of Moinuddin Chishti, Bakhtiar Kaki and Fariduddin Ganjshakar, who chose him as his disciple and successor. He also had a distinguished line of his disciples among whom Nasiruddin Chiragh Dehlavi and Amir Khusro are the most prominent ones. Nizamuddin's *malfoozat* are

collected in his *Fawaid-ul Fawad*, apart from four others that stand as testimonies of his great spiritual wisdom.

10. Nasiruddin Mahmud Chiragh Dehlavi (1274–1356), a distinguished disciple and successor of Nizamuddin Auliya, was born in Ayodhya. He left Ayodhya in his forties to be with his master for the rest of his life. As the fifth and the last of the Sufi saints of the Chishti order in Delhi, he distinguished himself both as a Sufi and a Persian poet of high order. Uniquely endowed with the power of negotiating with pain and exercise forgiveness, he is said to have pardoned a lunatic who attacked him with a knife. He has been assigned the title of "Chirag Dehlavi" which means the "Lamp of Delhi". His *malfoozat* are included in *Khair-ul- Majalis* and *Miftah-ul-Aashequeen.*

WORKS CITED

Buhler, G., trans. The laws of Manu, c. 1500 BCE. In *Internet Indian History Sourcebook.* http://legacy.fordham.edu/halsall/india/manu-full.asp (accessed on 31 Jan 2018).

Howarth, David. 2000. *Discourse.* Buckingham: Open University Press.

Fariduddin Ganjshakar. http://www.sufiwiki.com/Fariduddin_Ganjshakar (accessed on 31 Jan 2018).

Hatim, Basil and Ian Mason. 1990. *Discourse and the translator.* London: Longman.

http://www.buddhasutra.com/profile.html (accessed on 31 Jan 2018).

http://www.sacredtexts.com/jai/sbe22/sbe2206.htm (accessed on 28 June 2015)

Jacobi, Hermann, trans. 1990. *Jaina sutras.* New Delhi: Atlantic Publishers and Distributors.

Nasiruddin Chiragh Dehlavi. http://www.sufiwiki.com/Nasiruddin_Chiragh_Dehlavi (accessed on 31 Jan 2018).

Nizamuddin Auliya. http://www.sufiwiki.com/Nizamuddin_Auliya (accessed on 31 Jan 2018).

Sayings of Hazrat Khwaja Mu'inuddin Hasan Chishti. https://wahiduddin.net/sufi/muinuddin_sayings.htm (accessed on 31 Jan 2018).

Sayings of Hazrat Khwaja Mu'inuddin Hasan Chishti. https://wahiduddin.net/sufi/muinuddin_sayings.htm (accessed on 31 Jan 2018)

Venkatesanand, Swami. 1975. *Enlightened living: A new interpretative translation of the yoga sutra of Maharsi Patanjali.* Cape Province: The Chiltern Yoga Trust. (Electronic edition 2008).

Woodward, F. L., trans. *Adanta suttas: Untamed.* https://www.accesstoinsight.org/tipitaka/an/an01/an01.031-040x.wood.html (accessed on 31 Jan 2018).

FIVE

Broadening the Frontier: Towards a Poetics of Painting and Architecture

This chapter posits that discourses on translation are best located in time, place, history and culture. With reference to some of the ancient sites of translation which created conditions for the construction and dissemination of knowledge systems through translation, it has been posited that unlike earlier times, translation today has no empire, although it survives and flourishes along with divergent and convergent ideologies and theories.

In trying to develop a new paradigm for the practice and evaluation of translation, an effort has been made to draw upon the poetics of painting and architecture as there are close parallels between these arts and that of translation. It has been argued that the act of translating is an act of placing the right words in a verbal structure , just as the act of painting is an act of creating the right shade on the canvas, and the act of creating building structures is an act of evolving the right architectural design. Superior works of painting, architecture and translation are similar, in that they commonly exhibit a balance of language, grammar, density and design. These propositions have been tested in relation to select texts in translation to show that the poetics of the three arts converge and make way for a new translation poetics.

Translation, as a primordial human activity, has collected a huge amount of material around itself in terms of theoretical discourses and personal narratives, apart from a large variety of material in undefined categories. Revisiting this site for all its massive capital of theory and practice in the twenty-first century is like moving through seven continents, wondering at the uniqueness of each one of them, but arriving at some unspecified space, a kind of nowhere. One arrives ultimately, if one does, at one's own site of belonging in this postmodern and postcolonial world, where meaning is constructed along different lines, with particular emphasis on location and identity. I have used this metaphor of a long and arduous voyage through seven continents to underline that all acts of translation and theorisation are rooted in specific cultural and linguistic spaces, and that there can be no general discourse on translation unless it is contextualised in time, place, history and culture.

OLD AND NEW CANONS

In order to construct my argument regarding the old and the new canons of literary translation and translation poetics, let me go back in history and refer to some of the ancient institutions that laid the foundation of what we call Translation Studies today. As they created conditions for the construction and dissemination of knowledge systems through translation, they also made way for future advancement in this domain of mutual acquisition of knowledge. When I say this, I have in mind Chang'an School in China,[1] the great library of Alexandria in Egypt,[2] the academy of Gundishapur in Persia,[3] Bait al-Hikma in Iraq[4] and the School of Toledo in Spain.[5] In constructing a great variety of knowledge systems through translation, these institutions laid down the classical tradition of developing contiguities with peoples, faiths, and languages. These seats of comprehensive learning emerged as empires of knowledge, and as seminal sites of negotiation among people from locations as divergent as Greece, Persia, Arabia, India, China, Japan and Europe; faiths as different as Islam, Hinduism,

Christianity, Judaism and Buddhism; and languages as varied as Greek, Arabic, Latin, Hebrew and English. While knowledge systems pertaining to various domains of philosophy, grammar, mathematics and sciences flourished in these locations, translation too grew into an art while interacting with peoples, languages and scholastic traditions. Unlike today, translation was then an intra-communal, intra-national and intra-religious engagement. As scholars and translators travelled beyond boundaries and created a condition of larger mutuality, they evolved as makers and disseminators of knowledge, and also helped others to evolve on their own. From ancient India, for example, we have the case of an individual like Kumarajiva (350–410 BCE), a Kashmir-born Buddhist monk, who travelled all the way to China and translated Sanskrit sutras there, as did many others like him in other places. With the passage of time, and with the altered conditions of history, such interactions between different groups of people shrunk from being cosmopolitan to being restricted at the national level. For instance, the advent of the Portuguese, Dutch and British, followed by the coming of the Jesuit missionaries, travellers, and political emissaries, created vastly different conditions for the construction and dissemination of new knowledge in India as compared with those created in the empires of knowledge in the ancient world, as mentioned above. This trend continued in the modern times, as can be seen in the establishment of the College of Fort William in Calcutta in the year 1800, which opened up newer territories of production and dissemination of knowledge through translation within a much more limited space. Today, translational activities continue at smaller and individual levels in the postcolonial period of Indian history, as they do in literary sites everywhere else. In sum, over the successive phases of history, translational activities started shrinking from the macro to the micro level all over the world, even though translational activities grew phenomenally and translation theory kept consolidating in volume and value over time.

Drawing upon the above, I should like to propose that there is a Translational Drift today, much like the Continental

Drift. In its engagement with postcolonial theory and practice, translation has moved towards, as well as drawn away from, in a richly ambiguous way, traditional norms of writing and reading. It has developed as a formidable site of intense discourses on race and history. At the new sites of literary production, translation is subject to contestations in the spheres of society, politics, identity and the larger configuration of the nation state. Even though these nation states pretend to move together with each other for the sake of political expediency, correctness or necessity, they have, in fact, drawn apart to safeguard their hidden and proclaimed agenda. Acts of literary production and translation are, therefore, required to chart a way of difference for themselves in order to deny their belonging to a universal order of mixed or blurred identities. Unlike earlier times, translation today has no empire; there are instead sites of divergent and convergent ideologies where dominant and subaltern constructions regarding language, textual formation, history and cultural configurations are hotly debated. In this postcolonial and postmodern world, translation survives as a severely contested domain of knowledge where the figure of the author, the persona of the translator and the nature of the text are frequently and variously interrogated with reference to history, politics, ideology, identity and location.

Let me extend the case laid out here in another direction by putting forward a question: did the translators in the past choose their texts only for transferring them from one language to another, or did they also have in hand a method or a theory to do so? To answer this, we would have to consider their individual or combined practices of translation which would show that during the process of translation, they also actively developed their methodologies. This may be testified to with reference to the practice of translation pursued in those empires of knowledge construction which underlines the fact that their theories emerged out of their practice, and not vice versa. This brings a critical truism to the fore that in the domain of translation, practice has ever generated theory, and this has often led to serious contestations leading to the enrichment of theoretical knowledge. In our times, translational engagements have made way for the emergence of translation theory in a more organised way, and we have today a new domain of knowledge to engage with much more seriously than ever before.

I would posit further that translation theory has now drawn upon many other theories associated with disciplines like literary theory, linguistics, and culture, each one of which has branched out in several directions and helped translation theory also to move in many concourses. In the subsequent part of this chapter, I would like to draw upon a different field of human creativity and seek parallels with the poetics of painting and architecture to see if they may bear upon translation theory in any possible way.

Towards Fine Art and Architecture

Let me begin by reiterating that the act of translating is an act of placing the right words in a verbal structure on the part of the translator, just as the act of painting is an act of creating the right shade on the canvas on the part of the painter, and the act of creating building structures is an act of evolving the right design in the case of the architect. The translator's text, the painter's painting and the architect's structure acquire their own languages and speak eloquently through them. I might also propose that just as a translator brings language to text, and text to language, the painter brings colour to canvas, and canvas to colour, and the architect bricks to the building, and the building to bricks. In putting their counters of expression together, all three of them, create their own artefacts – their own configurations of language, shades and structures.

Just as every building follows certain structural principles, every translation follows a set of rules to construct a text. And just as an architect appropriates different strategies for different building types, a translator does so for different text types. This implies that every literary form like fiction, poetry, drama or prose, and their different genres like romance or picaresque, epic or lyric, melodrama or burlesque, essay or memoir, calls for different strategies of translation. Similarly, every building type, like theatre or amphitheatre, tower or skyscraper, gymnasium or stadium, needs a different set of principles to be employed. In the same manner, just as a good text has to stand out and turn canonical, good architecture too has to prove sustainable and qualify to be a classic in the course of time. Let me take this argument in yet another direction and think of structural elements that distinguish a literary text and architecture. No literary text, or text in translation, can ever be structured without its base in figures of speech like simile or metaphor; myth, symbol or allegory; allusion, antithesis or irony; metonymy, personification or hyperbole; oxymoron, paradox, or pun. Extending this analogy further, I would posit that no architecture, which in itself is a text of another kind, can ever be composed without making use of and choosing between elements like beams, columns or span; aisle, arcade or pathway; dome, arch or tower; labyrinth, basement or attic; porch, portico or balcony. Furthermore, literary texts as configured in translation, and a structural design as translated into a building, need a primary mind mapping, and concept mapping, as the bases of their structures. Once the two structures – the text and the building – are complete in their external form, they need chiselling. A work in translation goes through several revisions in order to pass as a final product of a certain merit. Similarly, a building achieves perfection with molding, tattooing, festooning or etching, as the facade may demand. As the translated text acquires its own voice and maintains its acoustics, an architectural text too reverberates with its own sounds and echoes. In the ultimate analysis, both of them approximate a condition of architectural mythology, which may be considered to be the height of achieving artistic excellence. Both the works of art – the text in translation, and the building in execution – acquire their culmination when they are presented as pleasantly readable and comfortably habitable spaces.

Drawing upon another analogy to substantiate my argument further, let me consider the poetics of painting to consider its applicability on the aesthetics of translation. Just as the painter chooses a certain colour from his/her colour wheel to enliven a canvas, the translator chooses a certain idiom, or figure of speech to energise his/her text. Both the painter and the translator have at their disposal a large variety of the primary, secondary or tertiary; complimentary, neutral or fugitive colours and words to choose from. The painter has to decide on colour permanence and colour scheme; colour separation and colour space; colour temperature and colour quality for his/her text in the process of painting a canvas. The translator goes through a similar process while determining which words to use, and in what combination.

The processes of translation, painting and architecture, then, complement one another. In the ultimate analysis, the translated text, the finished painting, and the completed building bear upon one another in their accomplished forms. Standing in unison, they erase the distinction between the forms of writing, painting and architecture. The reflective, the imaginative and the discursive in literary texts merge with the impressionistic, the surrealistic and the concrete in paintings, and they in turn, merge with the Gothic, the Romantic and the Modernist in building structures. The natural, the real and the abstract in all of them bear upon one another in creating their aesthetic appeal, and in exploring the possibility of their canonisation.

A Pattern Language

Extending the above argument further with reference to the argument that translation is a cultural engagement with language, I would like to dwell upon the concept of "pattern language" put forth by Christopher Alexander, Sara Ishikawa and Murray Silverstein in their pioneering work entitled *A Pattern Language: Towns Buildings Construction* (1977).[6] In this book, they engage with the basic idea of how certain tools and techniques help create good architectural designs. They argue that even common people are capable of creating architectural patterns, a process which is quite akin to the creation of linguistic patterns. Drawing upon the basic composition of language, they advocate that pattern language, as used in architecture, is also composed of vocabulary, syntax and grammar, and these three elements configure themselves in complex ways to create designs. Pattern language, they believe, offers solutions to problems that help the structure grow into good design. An architect, in other words, is one who solves problems by creating designs, with the help of vocabulary, syntax and grammar. As words embody meaning, and work through grammar, meaning and grammar become inseparable in order to play their combined role to create designs. As such, a collection of words put together creates a structure and all the components of this structure are logically fused into each other to evolve a language which the finished piece of architecture ultimately speaks. Since this architecture, based on pattern language, is a thing of utility for the user, it also turns into an empowering agent. Another significant part of the pattern language is the context, which makes it meaningful. It works through the principle of striking balance amidst divergent elements. It acquires its strength or character in relation to another design within and outside the architecture, imparting it value in comparative terms. There is also a hierarchical relationship in the pattern language which is a complex web of many languages, and which ultimately writes the text of a given architecture and constitutes a philosophy of its construction.

In a sub-section of this book entitled "The poetry of the language", they put forward a thesis that brings verbal and architectural expressions together and explains how they bear upon one another. In order to bring forth their thesis directly, let me quote the lines that I would like to apply in the case of literary translation to show how the acts of translating a literary text and constructing a building are identical at the very basic level:

> The difference between prose and poetry is not that different languages are used, but that the same language is used, differently. In an ordinary English sentence, each word has one meaning, and the sentence too, has one simple meaning. In a poem, the meaning, the meaning is

> far more dense. Each word carries several meanings; and the sentence as a whole carries an enormous density of interlocking meanings which together illuminate the whole.
>
> The same is true for pattern language. It is possible to make buildings by striking together patterns, in a rather loose way. A building made like this, is an assembly of patterns. It is not dense. It is not profound. But it is also possible to put patterns together in such a way that many many patterns overlap in the same physical space: the building is very dense; it has many meanings captured in a small space; and through this density, it becomes profound.
>
> In a poem, this kind of density creates illumination, by making identities between words, and meanings, whose identity we have not understood before. In 'O Rose thou art sick,' the rose is identified with many greater, and more personal things than any rose—and the poem illuminates the person, and the rose, because of this connection. The connection not only illuminates the words, but also illuminates our actual lives.
>
> O Rose thou art sick.
> The invisible worm,
> That flies in the night
> In the howling storm:
>
> Has found out thy bed
> Of crimson joy:
> And his dark secret love
> Does thy life destroy.
>
> William Blake
>
> (xli–xlii)

They posit that a similar thing happens in the case of buildings. In a broader perspective, it would appear that the key issues in pattern language are vocabulary, syntax, and grammar; problem, solution, and context; balance, empowerment, and design. The architect identifies a project, finds out its context in terms of the intended users, understands the problem in relation to balancing his/her act, and finds a solution in terms of how best the project may be used with maximum utility and pleasure accruing to the user.

In relation to this thesis, I propose that a translator too is a writer of pattern language who works with his/her own vocabulary and syntax, and knows his/her context in terms of his/her readers, as the architect knows his/her own in relation to his/her users. Both of them balance their acts of languaging their problem, and both work towards achieving pleasure and empowering their users and readers. Developing a multidisciplinary approach and drawing upon the three domains of literature, biology and geometry, I further suggest that translation is a symbolic, metabolic and parabolic activity. As a symbolic act, translation is a source of cultural empowerment; a sign of comparative growth of a people. As a metabolic act, it is a process of acquiring energy; multiplying new cells for better survival. If not done properly, translation may result in a parabolic activity in which an object, thrown into the air, falls back on the ground in a parabola.

Examples

Finally, I would like to examine the above propositions in relation to some of the translation practices. I have chosen examples from such translators who deliberate upon their work in a critical manner. Good translators, like good authors, are the first and the most incisive critics of their work. This statement would remain unqualified unless I sought an answer to a basic question: how do we know a good translator from a bad one? In order to seek an answer, I would discuss a few translations of poetry and fiction from pre-modern and modern literatures in order to exemplify good translations.

In his preface to *Selected Poems from the Divani Shamsi Tabriz*,[7] Reynold A. Nicholson[8] has outlined his major concerns as follows:

> My translation seeks to reconcile the claims of accuracy and art: it is therefore in prose. Obviously English verse cannot convey the full verbal sense of oriental poetry without lapsing into grotesque doggerel; the translation

> must either profess a general adherence to his author's meaning…or, rising above letter, he must catch the elusive spirit of his original and reproduce it in a worthy frame. Of this, the highest and rarest kind of translation, Fitzgerald's *Omar Khayyam* is a classic example. I have done my best to avoid gratuitous banalities, when no misapprehension was possible. (ix)

Nicholson's major concerns are (a) achieving accuracy, (b) attaining artistic excellence and (c) capturing the meaning and spirit of the Oriental poetry as represented in the ghazals of Jalaluddin Mohammad Rumi.[9] Let me quote an example where Nicholson succeeds in achieving his professed aim:

> He said: 'Who is at the door?' Said I: 'Thy humble slave.'
> He said: 'What business have you?' Said I: 'Lord, to greet thee.'
> He said: 'How long will you push?' Said I: 'Till thou call.'
> He said: 'How long will you glow?' Said I: 'Till resurrection.' (55)

This dialogue with the divine continues in a few more couplets and concludes as follows:

> He said: 'What do you intend?' Said I: 'Constancy and friendship.'
> He said: 'What do you want of me?' Said I: 'Thy universal grace.'
> He said: 'Who was your companion?' Said I: 'Thoughts of thee, O King.'
> He said: 'Who called you here?' Said I: 'The odour of thy cup.' (55)

It may be observed that Nicholson has been able to develop a dialogic mode in imitation of the original and has acquired a tone and tenor that characterises Rumi's couplets. Thus, his strategy lies in selecting a particular kind of diction, like a painter selects a particular colour for his painting, or an architect, a particular design for her architecture. Rumi, thus, charges his work with contextual meaning, as do the painter and the architect with their own engagements. This act on the part of Rumi may also be considered akin to the act of discovering a pattern language which is characterised by density, and which prioritises a stronger text over the weaker one.

My next example comes from the translations of Kabir[10] by Arvind Krishna Mehrotra.[11] In his introduction to *Songs of Kabir*, he sums up his methodology after engaging with various other methodologies employed earlier for translating Kabir. He writes,

> As with [the] Kabir text, so with this Kabir translation; it is made keeping the text's inclusive genius in mind. (xxxi) ... *Songs of Kabir* is both a work of translation based on the best available critical editions and...a further elaboration of Kabir corpus, taking its place alongside those that have already been in existence for hundreds of years. (xxxiv)

To accomplish his task, Mehrotra seeks a comparative methodology to (a) assess Kabir's text, (b) evaluate its translation and (c) place it in a historical perspective. He develops an inclusive approach to negotiate with his text. It is a case of recasting Kabir both with certain freedoms and certain constraints, which ultimately results in rewriting a Kabir poem:

> The mind's a shortchanging
> Huckster with a crafty
> Wife and five
> Scoundrel children.
> I won't change its ways.
> The mind's a knot, says Kabir,
> Not easy to untie. (13)

It may be easily noticed that this is a poet's translation. Mehrotra, the poet–translator has chosen an acutely contemporary form and language to represent Kabir, as the painter and architect would do in their work to match the contemporary canon. Mehrotra's translation may be read as part of a larger whole rather than in isolation. He too has tried to discover a pattern language to represent Kabir to a readership that may appreciate the value of a text which has its roots in the larger tradition of humanism, and which discards the constraints of narrow religiosity.

I have now an example from a fictional text to illustrate how the translator defines his methodology. In translating *Samskara* by U. R. Ananthamurthy,[12] A. K. Ramanujan[13] has spelt out his aim in the "Translator's Note" as follows:

> I have tried to make the translation self-contained, faithful yet readable. But 'the best of this kind are but shadows; and the worst are no worse, if imagination amend them'. A translator hopes not only to translate a text, but hopes (against all odds) to translate a non-native reader into a native one. (not paginated)

Ramanujan's basic concerns relate with achieving (a) inclusiveness, (b) faithfulness and (c) readability of the text. More importantly, he aspires to bring the text to a new readership that may identify with the spirit of a text conceived differently at the religious level. The most poignant moment, as represented in the last lines of the novel may be considered from this point of view:

> The sky was full of stars, the moon, a silver. A perfectly clear constellation of the Seven Sages. A sudden noise of drum beats. Here and there, the flames of a torch. The hard breathing of the bullocks climbing the hillock. The sound of cow-bells round their necks. He will travel, for another four or five hours. Then, after that, what? Praneshacharya waited, anxious, expectant. (138)

Precision is the hallmark of this passage. It comes from the linguistic register chosen for the purpose and from breaking the regular sentence structure. Being a poet and a linguist with a deep understanding of language and culture patterns, Ramanujan has been able to fill his language with density and poetic precision, as we have seen earlier, and evolve a pattern language for his translation. This helps him bring the text closer to his readers who may be aware of the native and religious elements involved in the story, or even to those who may be entirely alien to the total spirit of the story but may appreciate the same through the linguistic vitality with which he fills his text and makes the passage work in its entirety.

Considering the choice of words to charge a language, it would be pertinent to refer to "Translator's Foreword" by Gayatri Chakravorty Spivak[14] who translated *Chotti Munda and His Arrow* by Mahasweta Devi.[15] Spivak has made a basic statement about her way of approaching the text at a primary level to produce her thoroughly competent translation. She writes, "To my great delight, among the first things Mahasweta Devi said to me…'Gayatri, what I am really enjoying in your translation is how you've shown that dialect can be dignified'" (viii). Spivak is a theoretician and her engagement with language and postcolonialism equip her well enough to engage with this text at a more pragmatic level. I would extend this case of critical engagement with language still further with reference to a unique negotiation with language that Ahmed Ali[16] chooses to perform in his novel *Twilight in Delhi*. Interestingly, this is not a work of translation; it is written originally in the English language but it manipulates the English language in such a manner that it comes very close to the rhythm of the Urdu language which happens to be Ali's mother tongue. Ali empowers his English in the novel to bear the beat of the Urdu idiom as well as the rhythm of life lived at a certain point of time in the history of India by a certain community. In his introduction to the novel he writes,

> Many who have read only the translation tell me they cannot believe it could have been written originally in English; and some have even said that I must have written it in Urdu and then translated it into English. On the other hand, some have refused to read the Urdu version because, they say, the English original is untranslatable. (vii)

Ali's major achievement lies in his ability to blur the distinction between two languages – English and Urdu – and obliterate the distinction between them insofar as he transfers the rhythm of the Urdu language, which is his mother tongue, into the English language which is his acquired second language. This may be exemplified by the way Ali writes two languages

– one directly and the other indirectly – and preserves two cultures simultaneously. This may be amply seen in a particular sequence when he chooses to construct his story through verse. He describes a scene where he dramatises the movement of the *fakir*'s song as follows:

> They stood before the doors and sang a verse or just shouted for bread or pice or, tinkling their bowls together, they waved their heads in frenzy, beating time with their feet, singing for all they were worth:
>
> Dhum! Qalandar, God will give,
> Dhum! Qalandar, God alone;
> Milk and sugar, God will give,
> Dhum! Qalandar, God alone… (17)

I am not aware of the exact verse in Urdu that the fakirs in Ali's days must be singing, nor do I know as to how it could form a part of his memory. The important point is that he chooses to preserve a cultural condition and record that condition in another language. I may only guess that what the *fakir* sang could have been something like this which I back-translate here to illustrate my point:

> *Dhum Qalandar, Allah dega*
> *Dhum Qalandar, Allah hi Allah*
> *Doodh aur shakkar, Allah dega*
> *Dhum Qalandar, Allah hi Allah*

I quote one more example in this connection to show how Ali recreates the rhythm of the Urdu language and its poetry in English which does not correspond with the oral–aural systems of the Urdu language:

> Betake your way, O breeze of the Spring,
> Frolic not with me:
> You are in a playful mood,
> But I in none of ecstasy. (32)

Those who have an exposure to Urdu language and its literary culture would immediately recognise this well-known *shair* from a ghazal of Insha Allah Khan Insha:

Na chhed ai nikhat-e baad-e bahaari raah lag apni
Tujhe atkheliyan soojhi hain, hum bezar baithe hain

The fictional plot is lit up brightly in the way Ali chooses to appropriate the rhythmic ambience of one language into another. This is also the quality that distinguishes the text in the company of texts developed around this kind of experience. I may elaborate upon this point by referring to another work of Ali. In his "Note on the Translations" of Meer and Ghalib included in *The Golden Tradition: An Anthology of Urdu Poetry*, he reflects upon this issue in yet another way. There, he chooses to abandon rhyme as he notes that the "retention of rhyme would have meant either sacrificing sense or faithfulness to the originals, or distortion of syntax, or both" (106). He explains his technique further:

> If I had allowed my interpretations to enter, the translated poems would not have remained Ghalib, as Fitzgerald's translations are not Omar Khayyam. So, I have left the translations, like the originals, unexplained, so that each reader can interpret the poet in accordance with his sensibility, as he does the poetry of T. S. Eliot. (107)

It may be observed that in both the cases it is rhythm, not the rhyme, that Ali chooses to recreate. Even though he interferes with the formal structure of the original text, he retains the spirit and the density of the text which are also the aims that the painter and the architect keep in mind to achieve their excellence.

The examples quoted above substantiate that all these translators have tried to evolve their own versions of pattern language, find their own structures of meaning, and their own shades and tones of voice, as the painters and the architects do in their own contexts. All of them have negotiated with their own vocabulary, syntax and grammar; context, problem, and solution, design, balance and empowerment. All of them have done so in their cultural contexts as all texts, all architecture and all paintings exist in their cultural time and a cultural space.

An analysis of the translators' intention and methodology as mentioned above would show that all these translators have been essentially concerned with the problematic of language. These include their concern with measuring the density of language in order to create new identities and relationships between word and meaning in order to develop new associations and identifications with a set of new readers. This is akin to finding the right colour in the case of the painter, and discovering a pattern language in the case of the architect. All the three – the translator, the painter and the architect – reconstruct their spaces into a meaningful text, or canvas, or architecture, as the case may be. Once they succeed in finding their equivalences, they naturally take care of other issues of accuracy and fidelity in creating a verbal text; tonality and texture in creating a canvas; and pattern and design in creating a structure. This is what happens generally with every translation, and this is what happened with those in the ancient past who constructed various domains of knowledge in their translations but always with reference to time, place, history, and culture, and with attention to language, grammar density and design.

NOTES

1. The Chang'an School was established by Dao An in 379 CE with state support to carry out translational activities. Although the history of translation in China is traced back to the eleventh century BCE, it was this school in Chang'an (now known as Xi'an) which emerged as a major centre of translation with the influx of migrant monks from Kashmir who chose to translate their native texts into Chinese. With the coming of the Arabs, yet another trend of translation of scientific texts from Arabic and European languages started there. Along with promoting actual translations, the school also saw the emergence of a debate on translation methodology. While Dao An supported literal translation and the Indian scholar Kumarajiva favoured free translation, the Chinese Buddhist scholar Xuanzang saw greater merit in a reconciliation between the two approaches. This proves that the practice of translation also made way for the emergence of its theory which emerged later as a major concern in different locations and places.
2. The great library of Alexandria in Roman Egypt was founded in 300 BCE by Pharaoh Ptolemy I Soter at a strategic location connecting Asia, Africa and Europe. It was a fruition of Alexander's dream to consolidate the world into a whole. The library emerged as the earliest and the

greatest site in terms of written knowledge preservation from various languages and lands apart from Greece and Egypt. Aristotle's student Demetrius, also its first librarian, was assigned the job of promoting translations of works from other languages into Greek. His massive and contemporaneously relevant job included the translation of the Old Testament from Hebrew into Greek for which he is said to have engaged seventy-two rabbis. Later, many texts from the collections of this library were translated into Arabic and Hebrew, which turned the library into a centre where knowledge could be preserved both in original and in translation for posterity.

3. The Academy of Gundishapur reached its greatest height in sixth-century Persia with the Sasanian King Khusraw Anushirawan promoting the collection of Greek, Syriac, Roman, Jewish and Sanskrit texts and their translation into Pahlavi. As it became a sanctuary for the scholars who had fled Plato's Academy after its closure by Justinian, the atmosphere was charged with the spirit to produce and translate knowledge texts in the fields of philosophy, medicine, sciences, and mathematics. With the translation of a vast body of texts into Pahlavi by the end of the tenth century, the Academy distinguished itself as a great centre of culture and scholarship in ancient Persia and came to be known as the meeting point of Greek, Indian, Persian and Aramaic knowledge systems.
4. Bait al-Hikmah, founded by Caliph Haroon al-Rasheed, was instituted and given formal shape by his son Caliph al-Mamoon in 830 CE in Baghdad. He welcomed scholars from Islamic, Christian, and Jewish affiliations and promoted it as a major centre for the production and translation of texts from a great variety of subjects in the domains of natural sciences, medicine, and humanities. As a liberal site that did not discriminate between cultures and languages, translations from Christian, Jewish, Greek and Hindu sources were promoted which transformed this institution into the biggest storehouse of various kinds of knowledge within six decades of its existence.
5. The School of Toledo, which emerged following the taking over of Spain from the Muslims by the Christians in 1085, flourished under its founder, the French Archbishop Raymond in the twelfth century and King Alfonso X in the thirteenth century who promoted translations in Latin and Castilian respectively. While the Christian conquerors of Spain inherited a vast amount of literature in original and in translation into Arabic from the Greek, Latin, Hebrew, Persian and Sanskrit sources, they also brought translators from all over Europe to undertake new translations of philosophical and scientific texts into Greek and Hebrew. By transferring the wealth of knowledge accumulated over thousands of years to communities of new readership in the Christian world, Toledo became the gateway for Europe to enter into a grand

capital of classical knowledge systems. Apart from encouraging actual translations, Toledo also became a place for experiments in translation as a collaborative activity and came to distinguish itself as the first full-fledged centre given entirely to translational activities.

6. The authors have explained the nature of this book in relation to a companion volume called the *Timeless Way of Building* as follows: "Volume I, *The Timeless Way of Building* and Volume 2, *A Pattern Language*, are two halves of a single work. This book provides a language, for building and planning; the other book provides the theory and instructions for the use of language. This book describes the detailed patterns for towns and neighbourhoods, houses, gardens, and rooms. The other book explains the discipline which makes it possible to use these patterns to create a building or town. This book is the sourcebook of the timeless way; the other book is its practice and its origin" (ix).
7. In order to appreciate the curious relationship between Jalaluddin Rumi, the poet, and Shams Tabriz, the spiritual master, in whose name the work is assigned, let me quote Reynold A. Nicholson, the translator, who wrote a brief note in his "Introduction" as follows: "In a certain mystical sense Shams Tabriz may be regarded as a *takhallus*. Jalaluddin asserts the identity of subject and object: to him Shams Tabriz represents the divine Beloved, the one Being in whom all individual names are manifested and ultimately merged" (xv).
8. Reynold A. Nicholson (1868–1945), a Cambridge alumnus and a scholar extraordinaire of Arabic and Persian, is a highly regarded Orientalist. He translated Rumi's *Divani Shamsi Tabriz* and his *Mathnawi* in eight volumes during 1925–1940, which is considered to be a work of monumental stature. He also translated the works of Hujwairi, Ibn al-Arabi, Shah Abdul Lateef Bhitai, Mohammad Iqbal and many other poets and writers. In addition, he authored highly valued books like *A Literary History of the Arabs* (1907), *The Mystics of Islam* (1914), *Studies in Islamic Poetry* (1921) and *Translations of Eastern Poetry and Prose* (1922).
9. Jalaluddin Mohammad Rumi (1207–1273), popularly known as Jalaluddin Rumi, Maulana, Mevlana and Rumi, was a canonical Farsi poet, Sufi, scholar, and jurist. As a poet, he is best known for the two most celebrated works *Divani Shamsi Tabriz* and *Mathnawi*, his prose discourses *Fihi ma Fihi*, sermons *Majalis-e Sab'a*, and letters to his disciples called *Makatib*. Rumi is one of the most widely translated and read poets across the globe.
10. There is no general agreement about the dates of birth and death of Kabir but he is supposed to have lived in fifteenth-century India. Similarly, there is no consensus about his parentage; some believe he was born to a Brahmin widow and abandoned thereafter to be adopted by a Muslim couple; others consider him to be born to Muslim parents. An untutored genius, Kabir developed a direct communion with the

divine and emerged as a major Bhakti poet who uttered poetry rather naturally in the vernacular Hindi which drew upon the Avadhi, Braj and Bhojpuri dialects. His poems have been collected in different volumes and editions through the ages and widely translated into English.

11. Arvind Krishna Mehrotra (b. 1947) is an influential Indian English poet, translator, critic, essayist, anthologist and editor with valuable publications in each of these areas. An academic by profession, he emerged as one of the canon makers of Indian English literature and made a mark as a poet and writer with an intriguingly individual stamp of his own.
12. U. R. Ananthamurthy (1932–2014), associated with the Modernist movement in literature called *navya*, was a noted Kannada fiction writer, poet, playwright and literary critic. He was an iconoclast in his social, political and religious understanding. The elements of acute sociopolitical realism and keen psychological understanding mark his fictional work, of which *Samskara* is a good example, apart from others like *Bhava, Bharatipura* and *Avasthe.*
13. A. K. Ramanujan (1929–1993) was a major poet, folklorist, translator, philologist and a critic of Indian literary and intellectual heritage. He is remarkable for his understanding of the linguistic and cultural varieties of India. His translation of *Samskara*, and other writings, as also his writings on translation, spell out a poetics that is characterised by a keen understanding of linguistic and cultural traditions of the sites in which the texts are rooted.
14. Gayatri Chakravorty Spivak (b. 1942), one of the pioneering postcolonial theorists, is also a translator of Jacques Derrida and Mahasweta Devi. Known for discoursing on complex postcolonial issues but in no less complex terms, her translation has to be assessed in the light of her theoretical postulations in relation to the overall subaltern categories of people in the postcolonial sites.
15. Mahasweta Devi (1926–2016) has the unique distinction of being a fiction writer and an activist. Both her vocations are inextricably linked as she discourses on issues concerning tribals, dalits and women and around whom her stories revolve and from whose world they seek their power. Some of her well-known fictional works have also been made into contemporaneously relevant films.
16. Ahmed Ali (1910–1994) was a fiction writer, critic, diplomat and translator of literary texts and the Holy Quran. He is remembered as one of the pillars of the Progressive Writers' Movement since its inception and is best known for his acclaimed novel *Twilight in Delhi* and some epoch-making short stories in Urdu.

WORKS CITED

Alexander, Christopher, Sara Ishikawa, Murray Silverstein with Max Jacobson, Ingrid Fiksdahl-King and Shlomo Angel. 1977. *A pattern language: Towns, buildings, construction.* New York: Oxford University Press.

Ali, Ahmed. 1966. *Twilight in Delhi.* Bombay: Oxford University Press.

———, trans. and ed. 1973. *The golden tradition: An anthology of Urdu poetry.* New York: Columbia University Press.

Ananthamurthy, U. R. 2009. *Samskara.* Trans. A. K. Ramanujan. Delhi: Cambridge University Press.

Devi, Mahasweta. 2002. *Chotti Munda and his arrow.* Trans. Gayatri Chakravorty Spivak. Calcutta: Seagull Books.

Mehrotra, Arvind Krishna, trans. 2011. *Songs of Kabir.* Delhi: Hachette.

Nicholson, Reynold A. 1898. *Selected Poems from the Divani Shamsi Tabriz.* Cambridge: Cambridge University Press.

Paradigms

SIX

Translation as Empowerment: The College of Fort William

By drawing upon the theories and paradigms of power and empowerment, this chapter examines the role played by the College of Fort William towards educating the Company's junior civil servants to help them gain political control. A case has been made to establish how, in this curious process, a double advantage accrued both in favour of the empire as well as the natives. It has been argued that as it came through a fine balancing of the Imperialist and the Orientalist logic, several other aspects also acquired significance. These included the changing dynamics of cultural domination by consent and the construction of knowledge on a wide variety of subjects in several Indian languages.

In discussing how the college tried to meet its aim, it has been proposed that one of the major contributions the college made was in the domain of translation which defined the parameters of textual preference and translational negotiation. It is proposed that as this politico-scholastic engagement matured, an Indian literary tradition too came into being which defined language, text, readership and translation as a serious vocation. These propositions have been examined with reference to the texts, translators, policies and politics involved in the entire process that marked the preoccupations of the colonial power through the College of Fort William.

Translation is an empowering agency in general but when pursued with a purpose, it empowers a people in particular both directly and by proxy. As the purposes of translational undertaking vary, the results also keep pace with the purpose. Sometimes, these undertakings chasten the language and define the form; at other times they construct the domains of knowledge and contribute towards sociocultural advancement. In the case of the College of Fort William, translation played multiple roles – of constructing knowledge in a formal manner, disseminating it with a defined aim, and finally projecting a far-reaching discourse of domination by the colonial power and the subjection of the complaisant colonised people. In addition, these undertakings defined the contours of Orientalism in terms of defining a people and their culture, and also in relation to redefining the nature of the text, translator and the intended reader. These arguments may be studied appropriately in relation to the paradigms of empowerment created, and the assigned and accepted roles of the creators and recipients of knowledge systems.

PARADIGMS OF EMPOWERMENT

Paradigms of empowerment are created by time and place, regulated by conditions around, and marked for evolving a sociopolitical praxis for a people. They can be liberating and constraining, even authoritative and arbitrary, as power can be appropriated towards achieving any of these ends. Of the various paradigms available, we have one of the already powerful acquiring even more power; another of the powerless gathering courage to sustain. One paradigm may relate to a culture, another to a society; one to an economy, another to a polity. Similarly, one may refer to a person, another to a class; one to a tradition, another to a canon. It may be acquired in one or multiple areas, and may operate as such, according to its own dynamics.

Considering these broad paradigms of empowerment in general, one may proceed to consider the sources of empowerment themselves, which are as varied as the paradigms. One of them may relate to knowledge, another to the agencies of power, and this power–knowledge nexus may take us to other areas of deep philosophical dimensions. We may thus recognise the will to truth (Schopenhauer)[1] in order to distinguish the truth from untruth, and then identify the truth with our will to power (Nietzsche).[2] Further, we come across base and superstructure, and the idea of knowledge related to the base (Marx).[3] Various shades of these thoughts are represented in the ideas of coercion and consent/state and civil society (Gramsci),[4] consent to exploitation and repression (Althusser),[5] and repressive and generative power (Foucault).[6] This complex power structure is known to have controlled knowledge, as also generated certain bodies of knowledge, especially in colonial times.

In the Indian context, the colonial power generated a body of discourse which found its expression in two different ways. It empowered the empire; in a different way, it empowered the natives as well. While this power-play sought and found various sites of operation, translation emerged as an extremely important one with the transfer of Oriental texts into the so-called "language of power" and vice versa. Translation as a generative mode of empowerment thus found many sites for its operation; it empowered the translator, the source text, the reader, the target language, and the two traditions of the East and the West simultaneously. In the given context, it could help both the translator and the recipient of the translation to acquire newer areas of their relevance and that of their literary baggage. This context offers a fresh perspective for looking at the new power equations between the coloniser and the colonised from a postcolonial angle today. The following sections examine the aspects involved in this curious process of dual power acquisition with respect to both the coloniser and the colonised, which is curiously marked as partly literary and partly political.

Whose Empowerment/Whose Education?

Even though the story of the British connection with India goes much deeper into the past, it was with the British victory in the Battle of Plassey (1757) that the East India Company decided to rule over India. This virtually made the Company the master of Bengal, the bastion of much consequential political, cultural and literary activities in the following decades. The hundred years from the Battle of Plassey to the First War of Indian Independence (1857) saw the imperial power acquiring roots, evolving policies and getting them implemented. These decades also witnessed the emergence and establishment of two strands of thought and action rather clearly. Persons like Sir William Jones, in founding the Bengal Asiatic Society (1784); H. T. Colebrooke, in bringing out *Digest of Hindu Law of Contracts and Succession* (1797–98); James Prinsep, in discovering the clue to the Ashokan inscription; and later, the Company's officials, in discussing the holy Quran with Maulana Mohammad Ali, and *Puranas* with Viswanath Sastri, both individually and collectively, underlined the British interest towards discovering and appropriating the genius and spirit of India. However, the imperial policy to educate Indians took two different directions to keep pace with the changing conditions. The pressing need for qualified Maulvis and Pundits to help the judges in the administration of justice led to the strengthening of Persian and Sanskrit. The establishment of a *madrasa* in Calcutta by Warren Hastings (1781) and a Sanskrit College in Benaras by Jonathan Duncan (1792) were steps in this direction. There was yet another need equally pressing. Young Indians were required to know English and help the officials by working as their clerks and translators and assist in running their offices. The best that they could aspire for was to become teachers and translate useful books for the benefit of the Company's officials. The Charter Act of 1813 contributed favourably towards this end by spelling a new role for the empire towards the education of the natives, and by relaxing control over the missionary activities in India. The Orientalists and the Anglicists pursued their own interests with vigour though they were uncomfortably conscious of each other's policy. Finally, Lord Thomas Babington Macaulay gave the final call with his *Minute on Education* (1835) as Lord William Bentinck yielded and cleared the way for English education in India. Later, Sir Charles Wood took it to a definite end by evolving his own imperial logic and proclaiming the use of English for higher education, and vernaculars for all other intercourses by the masses (1854). These moves, representing a certain power structure, divided languages, cities and people, and helped the empire in achieving its aim. The theory of filtration worked only too well even though it left behind a large body of intellectual evidence to work out another theory that Oriental learning, different from the one championed by William Jones, was also seeking its own sites of existence.

The case of cultural domination working by consent, thus, came to be testified in no uncertain terms. The production of knowledge being one of the intentions, was further qualified as "objective knowledge" in the process of selectively delivering it to the colonised people. The Anglicists and Orientalists worked together towards finding new ways of governance. For the former, it was a resort to defence mechanisms, while for the latter, it was a much more sophisticated way of negotiating with their predicament. The project of Orientalism, different from Jones's, calls for a closer examination as it may afford a different perspective to the understanding of power-play at several different levels.

Orientalism: A Different Project

Every language and every tradition is decidedly different from the other, just as a culture and its varied manifestations are different from those of the other. The colonial masters needed to understand this difference by exploring the genius and the spirit of this land. This could give them a sure way of evolving their administrative mechanism. It is only natural to talk of Sir William Jones in this context, whose reputation as a major British Orientalist rested upon his mastery over the Arabic and Persian languages, his being a poet, a jurist, and above all, a classicist. He took up a position with the East India Company and was impelled by his need and desire to know India in depth. In his "Objects of Enquiry During My Residence in Asia" (1806), as quoted by Edward Said, he has enumerated a number of areas[7] that he should have liked to explore in order to familiarise himself and others, and also to imbibe the spirit of the land with all its grand variety and dimension. It is rather customary to recall, along with Jones, other Orientalists like H. T. Colebrooke, the founder of the Royal Asiatic Society in 1823, and Charles Wilkins who learnt Sanskrit well enough to translate *Shakuntala*, the *Manusmriti*, and produce the first English translation of the *Bhagavad Gita.* These engagements underlined Hastings's plea that the codes of governance were to be found only in Sanskrit, which were available in Persian translations, and as such there was a need to know the Sanskrit language to reach the source texts.

In this whole Orientalist project, at least one institution has not received the kind of attention it deserved in the Oriental and English literary accounts. References to the College of Fort William are not quite encouraging[8] except in the books of history and the works discussing the growth and development of Urdu, Hindi, Bangla and certain other literatures during the early nineteenth century. The College of Fort William, however, is an important site of inquiry not only because it provided a fillip to Indian languages, literatures and translation, but also because it helped the Anglicist project of knowing India in order to rule over it. Critics and historians have assigned to it a secondary place in the hierarchy of the Orientalist project, considering it to be concerned merely with the teaching of language, writing of grammar, and such other preoccupations considered of lesser value compared with the serious Orientalist concerns of exploring the spirit of the land. As such, they took it to be an agency of service rather than an institution of any consequential value yielding remarkable results. Such an attitude is not quite justifiable and does not hold well. The first objectives and the final accomplishments of the college provide ample evidence for taking it much more seriously than we have.

THE COLLEGE OF FORT WILLIAM

The purpose behind the establishment of the College of Fort William was indeed a curious one. This may be amply substantiated with reference to two significant contemporary imperial sources that vividly spelt out the obvious and the latent intentions rather differently from each other. Let me first mention Thomas Roebuck's *The Annals of the College of Fort William* (1819), a vivid account of the establishment, growth and achievements of the college during its first eighteen years. Roebuck, who had been a Captain in the Madras Navy Infantry, and served the College of Fort William as a Public Examiner in the Hindoostanee, Braj Bhasha, Persian and Arabic languages, apart from being an Assistant Secretary to the Council of the college, had access to Lord Wellesley, the Governor General (1798–1805) and founder of the college, and played a major role in realising the cherished goals of this institution. While referring to the Minutes of the College Council, he recorded how Wellesley reasoned out the establishment of this institution:

> A college is hereby founded at Fort William in Bengal, for the better instruction of the Junior Civil Servants of the Company in such branches of literature, science, and knowledge as may be deemed necessary to qualify them for the discharge of the duties of the different offices constituted for the administration of the government of the British possession in the East Indies. (xvi)

While spelling out his expectations from the British civil servants, Wellesley wrote that they "can no longer be considered as the agents of a commercial concern; they are in fact the ministers and officers of a powerful sovereign..." (iv). He clarified his point still further:

> Their education should be founded in a general knowledge of those branches of literature and science which form the basis of their education of persons destined to similar occupation in Europe. To this foundation should be added an intimate acquaintance with the history, languages,

> customs, and manners of the people of India, with the Moohummadan and Hindoo codes of law and religion, and with the political and commercial interests and relations of Great Britain in Asia. (iv)

Roebuck justified the imperial aspirations with great satisfaction and pride in his "Preface" when he underlined that equal advantages would accrue to both the parties: the Europeans would acquire the knowledge which they could only "seek in vain from other sources" and the native subject with "the enjoyment of those means of intellectual gratification, of which, the perishable nature of his manuscripts and the neglect of his rulers, would shortly have deprived him" (viii). This is amply borne out by the themes of the Public Disputations which Roebuck recorded in his book from where relevant extracts are quoted below:

> Motion: 'An Academical Institution in India is advantageous to the Natives, and to the British Nation.' First public disputation in Persian, February 11, 1802. (15)
>
> Motion: 'The Natives of India under the British Government enjoy a greater degree of tranquillity, security and happiness, than any other former government.' Second public disputation in Persian, July 25, 1803. (31)
>
> Motion: 'The interests of general knowledge would be promoted by encouraging men of education and learning in Europe and India to study the works of science and literature which both countries have produced.' Ninth public disputation in Hindoostani, September 15, 1810. (224)
>
> Motion: 'The Arts, Sciences and general Literature are better cultivated and more widely diffused throughout Hindoostan, than in any other Asiatic state.' Twelfth public disputation in Hindoostani, September 20, 1813. (344)
>
> Motion: 'The science of general or philosophical Grammar, is more successfully cultivated, and better understood, by the Eastern, than by the Western Grammarians.' Sixteenth public disputation in Persian, June 30, 1817. (528)

This practice of public disputations which continued till 1814 in these three languages, and sometimes in other languages like Arabic, Marathi and Sanskrit, was one of many such practices meant to strengthen and to realise the aim of the College with the help of the living languages of the time. A glance through the motions over the years would reveal that the College kept itself concerned mostly with issues involved in the learning of Oriental languages and literatures, and other aspects broadly related to social customs, governance, and the bipolarities of the East and the West. The motions struck an unmistakably sympathetic chord with the natives and their educational and cultural life even though the imperial policy in this regard had to pass through several phases in the succeeding generations.

Even though it may be easily noticed that the motions selected for disputation were essentially condescending in tone and tenor, the college was emerging essentially as a strong agency to strengthen British rule by teaching Indian languages and literatures in original and in translation. This scheme was well propounded by Wellesley when he mentioned the institution of professorship in Indian languages that were as varied as "Arabic, Persian, Sunskrit, Hindoostanee, Bengalee, Telinga, Muhratta, Tamool, Kunura"; in European languages as diverse as "Greek and Latin"; and subject as varied as "Moohammudan law, Hindoo law, English law, Ethics, Civil Jurisprudence, the law of nations, political economy, English classics, Greek history, Indian history, natural history, botany, chemistry, and astronomy" (xvii). The college planned its curricula in a meticulous manner befitting an educational institution established with a clear purpose, as Roebuck outlined, by combining the European and Asiatic modes of governance with the base laid in England and superstructure created in India, which interestingly enough, meets, in retrospect, with the Marxist idea on the subject.

A very different view of this dispensation emerges in Hugh Pearson's *Memoirs of the Life and Writings of the Rev. Claudius Buchanan* (1817). Like Roebuck, Buchanan too had the advantage of access to the imperial power and was appointed the Vice Provost and Professor of Classics at the establishment of the college. While Roebuck laid emphasis on the policy of educational dispensation, Buchanan was preoccupied with the propagation of Christianity among the natives of India. As it constitutes the core of the book, Pearson has made direct references to his intention towards meeting this aim. Pearson wrote in his preface that the "foundation of our Episcopal Establishment has indeed been lain in India: but it requires to be strengthened and enlarged, and a more goodly and majestic superstructure to be erected upon it." (xi). This is once again prophetically Marxist as it is borne out by the impassioned plea Buchanan made to the Archbishop of Canterbury in his letter to him in which he pleaded for the appointment of an Archbishop in India who would be a man of "sacred and exalted character…of ample revenue and extensive sway; a venerable personage whose name shall be greater than that of the transitory governors of the land; and whose fame for piety, and for the will and power to do good, may pass throughout every region". While he looked forward to Nietzsche's will to power as can be marked here, he clearly made an impassioned plea for the sway of Christianity in India which should be "something royal in spiritual or temporal sense for the abject subjects of this great eastern empire to look up to" as the Indians were incapable of realising themselves "without a Sultan or a Maha Rajah", a role which the Archbishop alone would appropriately fill. He also said that the natives were superstitious and unable to enjoy freedom, and that they were a "mixed multitude" with no idea "of truth or falsehood, of right or wrong" (370–71).

These sentiments found their ultimate expression in the following letter that Buchanan wrote to the Archbishop of Canterbury in 1805:

> I have the honour to present to your Grace, for the archiepiscopal library at Lambeth Palace, in the name of the College of Fort William, and with the permission of Marquis Wellesley, a valuable copy of the Mohammedan Koran in folio, beautifully ornamented with paintings and

> oriental enamel, and written by the pen of the Sultan of Allavuddeen Siljuky, about four hundred years ago. It has descended to these times in the line of emperors; and was found in the library of Tippoo Sultan at Seringapatnam, after the reduction of that capital by the British armies.
>
> By depositing the most valuable Koran of Asia in the ancient library of the Archbishop of Canterbury, the College of Fort William would intimate, that the sway of the East, once usurped by the Arabian imposter, has now reverted to a Christian power; and would express the hope that, in return for this volume of emblazoned delusion, the Church of England will exhibit to all nations the dutiful act so long expected, and send forth to the inhabitants of Asia the true revelation of God. (373–74)

With the two projections of the College of Fort William by Roebuck and Pearson, we come across a dual design that these benefactors of the college had in mind regarding the role that the college could and did play in the Indian context. As an extension of the latent imperial design it would be interesting to note that even though the college was formally founded on 18 August 1800, the day of its inception was declared as 4 May 1800. This marked the first anniversary of the British victory over Tipu Sultan at Seringapatnam. It seems symbolic that the day of Tipu's defeat should have been the day of launching an institution to study the Orient in order to be able to rule over it. A special medal, minted for the occasion, bore the engravings of Tipu Sultan's capital on one side and the date of his defeat on the other. The two engravings bring out the double intent of declaring one power dead and another taking birth. This was a declaration of a will to rule and to construct a new capital of power.

Irrespective of the two positions projected by Roebuck and Buchanan, the College of Fort William functioned for three decades with great success and delivered, by proxy, a huge amount of scholarship to the Indian scholastic tradition. The college did not have the lofty aims of the Asiatic Society; it followed the pragmatic objectives of Hastings and Cornwallis, which were given a practical shape by Wellesley. A notification of the Public Department in January 1799 made it compulsory for Company officials to know Persian, Hindustani and Bangla if they had to hold important offices after 1 January 1801. The College appointed only Europeans to the rank of professors and teachers at a fabulous salary of Rs 1500 and Rs 1000 respectively. Indians were appointed only as Munshis. They were designated as Chief Munshi, Second Munshis and Subordinate Munshis and were paid a vastly different salary of Rs 200, Rs 100, and Rs 40. These Munshis, who were scholars of different languages, were drawn from various parts of the country and were attached to the departments of Arabic, Persian, Hindustani, Sanskrit and Bangla. They represented a variety of linguistic, cultural and geographical backgrounds; came to live and work together as teachers and translators; and create, thereby, a rich literary capital in the city of Calcutta, producing knowledge in the contemporary languages of India.

During the thirty years of its existence, the College survived threats of closure and conflicts of purpose on account of the reservations the empire had regarding its very existence. Objections were raised regarding its utility and the huge expenditure involved. Lord Wellesley, who had established the College without prior approval from the Court of Directors of the East India Company, made a strong case on each occasion and saved it from all threats as long as he held the office of the Governor General. Even as controversies raged, the College kept doing its job, which suited both the British and the Indians, though not always in the manner as the company might have wished. It is remarkable to note that the College produced textbooks in translation that dwelt on readings of history, biography, tales, letters, dialogues, proverbs, grammar and lexicon in several Indian languages. It educated 691 officers in different languages and subjects during the period of its existence. It published 130 books;[9] collected 2990 manuscripts on a large number of subjects including science, philosophy and divinity; regulated punctuation and the Perso-Arabic script; and organised printing in a scientific manner. The College owed its reputation largely to its faculty, which had, over the years, thirty

Europeans and 157 Munshis of various categories in various departments. It had a rather marginal presence of non-Indian languages, which included Pushtu, Nepali, Bhutani, Burmese, Malaya, Turkish and Chinese. While assessing the contribution of the college, it would only be proper to take note of other institutions like the Serampore Mission, Asiatic Society, Calcutta Madrasa, Oriental Seminary, and School Book Society, which made their respective contributions towards the dissemination of Oriental knowledge in a manner different from Jones, even though they have remained rather eclipsed in literary accounts.

TEXTS/AUTHORS/TRANSLATORS

In discussing texts, authors and translators, it should be relevant to mention the two sources referred to above once again with respect to the tradition of public disputations where some of the motions proposed underlined the need for translation and the way for translational activities in a significant way. There are at least three motions mentioned in Roebuck's work that made a case for translation:

> Motion: 'The translations of the best works extant in Sunskrit into the popular languages of India, would promote the extension of science and civilisation.' Third public disputation in Oriental languages, September 20, 1804. (60)
>
> Motion: 'The difficulties of translation between the English and Persian languages are far greater than between the former and any of the other languages of Europe.' Tenth public disputation in Persian language, August 07, 1811. (272)
>
> Motion: 'It is easier to diffuse the literature and science of Western nations among the Natives of India, by translating European Books into their own Tongue, than by instructing them in the European Languages.' Sixteenth public disputation in Hindoostani, June 30, 1817. (529)

There was a concerted effort to promote translation so that knowledge from a variety of sources, subjects and languages could be disseminated both amongst the British and natives. It is also clear that a case was being made in a critical framework to translate from an extant language to a modern language, as also to sort out the problems involved in translating from languages as different as English and Persian. Further, the disputations also made way for the dissemination of knowledge from the domains of literature and science in order to extend the frontiers of the two cultures involved in the process. Significantly, these are the issues that have emerged as the points of debate in Translation Studies today.

This argument may be extended further with reference to Pearson's *Memoirs of the Life and Writings of the Rev. Claudius Buchanan* where a strong argument has been made for the translations of scriptures and tracts into the languages of the Orient. This was reiterated, rather differently, in Buchanan's letter to the Archbishop of Canterbury where he engaged with the idea of promoting Christian knowledge and lamented over the opposition to the continuance of the College, without which it could not have made way for the dissemination of the Christian faith at a larger scale. He wrote: "Had the College of Fort William been cherished at home with the same ardour with which it was opposed, it might in the period of ten years have produced translations of scriptures into all the languages from the borders of the Caspian to the sea of Japan." (368). This idea came up with greater force of logic in the lines quoted below:

> It will be a satisfaction to your grace, to know that the translations of Scriptures into the oriental languages still proceed with spirit, though many do not smile on our labours. A few individuals have devoted their slender means to the furtherance of this great work. But these private resources will soon fail. A commencement, however, in the translations is of vast importance. They are begun 'in faith'; and we trust to the divine Author to bring to a happy termination (though not perhaps in our time) the versions of his own most holy word. (372)

Both Roebuck and Pearson projected the logic for translational engagements within the precincts of the College although their narratives did not necessarily project the reason and purpose of translations in the same manner. It may also be noted that even though the contribution of the college has generally been underlined in a discursive manner, the translation project promoted by the College has not received the critical attention it deserved. The fact remains that even a casual glance through the galaxy of authors, translators and texts would prominently bring out the contributions of the College within a brief period of thirty years in spite of all odds, and the departure of Wellesley, its most ardent supporter. The prominent scholars associated with the College were James Atkinson (Professor of Arabic and Persian), Rev. C. Buchanan (Professor of Greek and Latin), William Carey (Teacher of Bangla, Marathi, and Sanskrit and later, Professor of Sanskrit), H. T. Colebrooke (Professor of Sanskrit), John Gilchrist (Professor of Hindustani), M. Lumsden (Teacher of Persian, then Professor), and T. Roebuck (Assistant Professor of Hindustani) from the European establishment; and Mir Amman (Munshi, Hindustani), Mir Hyder Bukhsh (Munshi, Hindustani), Mrityunjay Vidyalankar (Munshi, Bangla-Sanskrit), Ramram Basu (Munshi, Bangla-Sanskrit), Tarini Charan Mitra (Munshi, Hindustani), Lallujilal (Munshi, Bhakha[10]), Mir Sher Ali Afsos (Chief Munshi, Hindustani), from the native establishment. As the contribution of these scholars cannot be discussed here in detail, reference is being made here to only two of them – John Borthwick Gilchrist and Mir Amman – who played a significant role in the development of Oriental studies and the complex power structure that evolved between the coloniser and the colonised. These two scholars, one of them a Professor and the other a Munshi, are remarkable for their seminal contributions to the development of Hindustani language, literature and translation.

Gilchrist's contributions are manifold; he distinguished himself most remarkably as a lexicographer, philologist, grammarian, teacher, translator, editor, printer, supervisor of projects, and a definition giver of Urdu, Hindi, and Hindustani. He started learning the Urdu language after he landed in

Bombay in 1782. A medical doctor from Edinburgh, Gilchrist reached the Indian shore via the West Indies where he was engaged in the business of indigo. He served the Company during his postings at Fatehgarh and Farrukhabad in Uttar Pradesh but took greater interest in learning the Urdu language. He continued this process of language acquisition by touring the land, observing the local people, talking to them, and taking notes concerning the lexical and grammatical nuances. While he learnt the language, he also collected material for his grammar and lexicon, which underwent revision after revision as he always kept improving upon his previous work. In his introduction to *The Oriental Fabulist* (1803), a polyglot translation of Aesop's and other ancient fables from English to various Indian languages in Roman characters by diverse hands, he mentioned two modes of language learning – from theory to practice, or from practice to theory. While he contemplated upon and practised the two methods, he also drew upon the models of Latin grammar, which served as the basis for learning European languages. He considered grammar to be an integral part of linguistic empowerment and thought that Urdu grammar might also be developed along the same scientific lines. *A Grammar of Hindoostanee Language* (1796), *The Oriental Linguist* (1798), *The Anti Jargonist* (1800), *The Stranger's East India Guide to Hindoostanee* (1802), *The Hindoostanee Principles* (1802), and *The Hindee-Roman Orthoepigraphical Ultimatum* (1804) bore the results of his researches into philology, vocabulary, sounds and the principles of language. Gilchrist's interest in language quite logically led him towards lexicography. *A Dictionary of English and Hindoostanee* (1810), and *The Hindi Dictionary or Students' Introductor to the Hindoostanee Language* (1802) are his attempts at giving the language a sound basis for written and verbal expression with emphasis on meaning and orthography. These two kinds of attempts at compiling grammatical principles and dictionaries were further strengthened by works like *The Oriental Fabulist* (1803), *The Hindi Manual, or the Casket of India* (1806), and *The Hindi Story Teller or Naqaliat-e Hindi* (1806), where he evolved his own language to express himself and also to see if it worked with the set of readers he intended to communicate with. Gilchrist was so passionate about language learning and the expressive power of diction that he wished to develop it as an art based on the principles of sound and auditory appeal.

It must be taken as wise and remarkable on the part of Gilchrist to have eschewed any possible controversy between Hindi and Urdu even though he incessantly worked for a language that was Urdu by his own admission. As he did not wish to create any linguistic barriers, he preferred to call it Hindustani, which included other dialects and styles from Braj Bhasha, Arabic and Persian. Hindustani was "the grand language of India", as he wrote in *The Oriental Fabulist*, and this was the language that the British officers found to be the most useful for their purposes. For Gilchrist and all others, it was the common language, that kept all linguistic chauvinism apart. Even though Hindustani meant Urdu for him and the Urdu language was well noticed and mentioned as *Urdu-e-mu'alla* in Meer Taqi Meer's *Nukat-us-shuara* (1752), he did not mention it as such, and preferred to write and speak a language that derived its strength from an admixture of Persianised Urdu and Khari Boli which later became the source of a new prose style in Urdu.

Gilchrist's efforts at evolving a scientific system of transliteration; Romanisation of Perso-Arabic and Devanagari script; innovations in the Perso-Arabic script, especially regarding certain sounds, punctuation and diacritics; and the establishment of Hindoostanee Press for the publication of texts aimed at preserving and disseminating this knowledge are his major contributions towards the refinement and establishment of a language which he took very seriously. All these, taken together, also created a context for translational activities which he promoted and supervised personally in order to evolve a condition that could contribute towards the making of a truly Hindustani tradition of literary translation. Gilchrist's passionate involvement with language cannot be understood fully without reference to Mir Amman of Delhi who was appointed a Subordinate Munshi in 1801 in the Hindustani Department under Gilchrist. Mir Amman has a very special place in the history of modern Urdu prose, which he developed in the College while doing his *Bagh-o-Bahar*, which has been rendered into English as *A Tale of Four Dervishes* for the modern reader by Mohammad Zakir.[11] This oral tale, ascribed to Amir Khusrau, has had a unique history. From oral narration in Hindi, it went on to be recorded in Persian, before being translated into Urdu by Zarrin and Tehseen. Mir Amman referred to the Persian version as well as the Urdu version by Tehseen. As Amman wrote this tale in an entirely new Urdu idiom, far removed from the ornate prose of Tehseen, it was supervised by Gilchrist and revised by another Munshi, Sher Ali Afsos. Mir Amman's *Bagh-o-Bahar*[12] set new parameters of prose, narrative structure, sequence of causality and naturalistic fictionalisation. For a modern literary reader, this text poses several important questions about its authorship and the contexts of reading. The reader may like to examine it as an oral tale, a written story or even as a genre. It can also be taken as a canonical text, and the starting point of a major literary controversy regarding its Urdu and prose style. At yet another level, it may be approached as a bold experiment in adaptation, or as a text of pedagogical value. It could also be read as an exercise in helping to start a conversation with Indians, as Amman himself clarified in his prologue to *Bagh-o-Bahar*. Emerging as a culture text, it exercised control through a language that was not the language of power itself. The text might also pose another important question as to whether one was listening to a story, or reading it, and whether one was reading a story or reading a language. Further, it could also be appreciated as a way of knowing a language and a people to be able to rule over them as the text also addressed questions regarding governance and statecraft. *Bagh-o-Bahar* seems to meet a number of aims by proxy. Amman shows his concern with a language that should be simple and able to communicate with those for whom it was essentially written and for the natives who were scattered far and wide and were living through a plethora of linguistic influences. While this language went against the literary norms of the day, it created a new taste and found a new readership both among the colonisers and the colonised. The simple language of this text in translation became, in turn, the language of the day even though it was severely criticised by the literary establishment of Lucknow for corrupting the taste and language of the readers.

The Munshis of the College, belonging mainly to the Departments of Hindustani, Persian, Sanskrit and Arabic, were interested in translating from prose works. Although prose got the major chunk of attention, poetry was not altogether neglected. Books on law, religion, administration, and literature in older languages were adapted and translated both for scholarly interest as also for use in the classrooms as aids and insights into administration. These translations were done both from European languages to Indian languages, and from Indian languages to English. Even while a passionate case was made for the translation of Christian texts, the college developed a huge storehouse of translations of both religious and secular texts. It would be pertinent to argue in a larger context that translation became a major preoccupation with those who charted the way for the college and recruited scholars to translate both religious and secular texts of astounding variety. The list of published translations has been variously compiled by literary historians. Thomas Roebuck, Hugh Pearson, R. W. Frazer, T. Grahame Bailey, Ram Babu Saksena, Mohammad Sadiq, Ralph Russell, S. K. Das, S. R. Kidwai and Saleem Akhtar mention names that do not necessarily agree in terms of numbers as translators worked in various languages and chose to translate texts from various sources that are not always uniformly recorded. In *The Annals of the College of Fort William*, Roebuck provides a catalogue of Oriental and other works that were published under the patronage of the college since its inception in 1800 to 1818. He also records the contribution of the college with admiration and categorically mentions the benefits that accrued to British India with these scholastic and translational activities. Some of the important works translated both individually and jointly, and many of them from Hindoostanee Press that emerged as a major institution of knowledge production, included works on subjects like grammar, ethics, history, literature, religion, jurisprudence, fables and politics that contributed to a wholesome construction of knowledge systems.[13] The aim laid out by Buchanan was fittingly carried forward by William Carey who translated the Bible into Bangla, Odia, Marathi, Hindi, Assamese and Sanskrit. He also published parts of it in twenty-nine other languages and dialects. He and his assistant Joshua Marshman also translated the *Ramayana.* Carey's accomplishment of this feat may also be appreciated in the context of the role he played as the founder of the English Baptist Missionary Society (1792) and as an ardent missionary while based in Serampore, Bengal.

Conclusion

The European scholars and the Indian Munshis of the College of Fort William, with their writings and translations, help us draw several important conclusions. The texts made available in translation constructed knowledge by bringing in additional power to the already powerful. For acquiring this power, the coloniser chose to develop a synchronous relationship with the language and the experience of the colonised which was, in a case like this, a political act of consensual negotiation. This was a power-game played in subterfuge by the powerful, as they could enter a new language zone and reach out to a new literary tradition. They thus acquired a supplementary power in this process which enabled them to engage with the cultural condition and intellectual discourse of the colonised. Conversely, this process brought another kind of empowerment to the colonised as it empowered the language of the colonised, their authors, their texts and their literary traditions. It also empowered them by getting them a whole new range of readership. In this process, the colonised translator too empowered himself by entering the aesthetic act of translating and rediscovering himself and his language. In all, the entire engagement was essentially political in nature as it delivered with one hand and received with another which may justifiably be considered an exercise in negotiation of power in favour of the self as well as the other. The most remarkable feature of the College, however, remains that it initiated a discourse on the power–knowledge nexus as it created domains of knowledge in fields as varied as grammar, lexicography, history, biography, dialogues, proverbs, tales, fables, epics – representing both the religious and cultural markers of a people and their modes of expression. In meeting these larger aims, the translation projects of the College revived classical languages like Sanskrit and Persian, and also redefined the so-called vernaculars like Urdu, Hindustani and Bangla. In addition, and by proxy, the college emerged as a site that enriched the tradition of scholarship in the Indian languages over a period of thirty years. While the new domains of knowledge were configured over a period of time, translation developed both as art and craft apart from being recognised as an ideological apparatus. As an agency and an instrument, the College embodied the imperial will to acquire power and exemplified the relationship between the imperial base and the correspondent superstructure. It underlined a curious relationship between state and civil society that generated power in terms of setting up a vital discourse over the construction and dissemination of knowledge.

NOTES

1. Schopenhauer underscores man's "will to live" which impels the universe and defines the reality of this universe. This imparts man with a power to deny the inescapable death and perishing. This argument is presented in *The World as Will and Representation* (1819) and *On the Freedom of the Will* (1839).
2. Nietzsche takes the "will to live" further and qualifies it with ambition which brings in its wake a desire to acquire power over the other. This philosophy found its earliest manifestation in his *The Wanderer and His Shadow* (1880) and *The Daybreak* (1881).
3. In our context, "base" may be taken as the force/condition that determines an action and "superstructure" as the power equation. In this paradigm, the base determines the superstructure. See Marx's "Preface" to *A Contribution to the Critique of Political Economy* (1859).
4. "State" represents the agencies of power operation and "civil society" remains a subsidiary, a recipient conglomeration of men and women as subject. This implies that the state uses coercion/force and the civil society submits in consent through hegemony. See *Prison Notebooks*, Volume 3 (2007).

5. In discussing dual state apparatuses as "repressive" and "ideological", Althusser distinguishes between the public and private domains of power operation as unified and plural. While repressive state ideology works primarily through repression and only secondarily through ideology, ideological state apparatus works just the other way. This is theorised in "Ideology and Ideological State Apparatuses" (1970).
6. Foucault argues that "power" is both "repressive" and "generative" as imprisonment is restrictive while discipline is generative. See full discourse in *Discipline and Punish* (1975) in the context of penal system in modern age.
7. Some of these include "the laws of the Hindus and the Mohammedans, Modern Politics, and Geography of Hindustan, Best Mode of Governing Bengal, Arithmetic and Geography, and Mixed Sciences of the Asiaticks, Medicine, Chemistry, Surgery, and Anatomy of the Indians, Natural Productions of India, Poetry, Rhetoric and Morality of Asia, Music of the Eastern Nations, Trade, Manufacture, Agriculture, and Commerce of India" (78).
8. While Sir William Jones and his Bengal Asiatic Society find mentions in all accounts (as in Edward Said's *Orientalism*), there is not enough discussion of an important institution like the College of Fort William and those associated with it, especially during the first few years after its establishment in 1800 when the College and its scholars were asserting themselves against several odds. Although D. Kopf's *British Orientalism and the Bengal Renaissance* (Calcutta: 1964) and Raymond Schwab's *Oriental Renaissance* (New York: 1984) mention this institution, full-length studies may only be seen in S. R. Kidwai's *Gilchrist and 'The Language of Hindoostan'* (New Delhi: 1968) and S. K. Das's *Sahibs and Munshis: An Account of the College of Fort William* (New Delhi: 1978).
9. Arabic: 20, Bangla: 18, Burmese: 1, Chinese: 2, Hindustani: 37, Kannada: 1, Marathi: 6, Oriya: 1, Punjabi: 1, Persian: 18, Sanskrit: 24 and Telugu: 1
10. "Bhakha" refers to a language, speech or *bhasha.* In its earlier usage it referred to a dialect or a vernacular. "Bhakha" has now become obsolete and has made way for what is now known as "bhasha".
11. Mir Amman wrote in the "Prologue": "The noble and high officials became interested in learning the Urdu language to be able to converse with Indians and carry out the administration of the country more effectively. As such, many books were compiled the same year at his instance" (Zakir 1994, xiii).
12. I am indebted to Professor C. M. Naim and his seven lectures on this text, which he delivered to the students of English, Hindi, and Urdu literatures in the Department of English, Jamia Millia Islamia, New

Delhi, in February 2002. He discussed various contexts of reading this text from where I drew my idea of approaching the text and the whole phenomenon of the College of Fort William.

13. Recording the translations into Hindustani, he mentioned texts like *Bagh-e Urdu* (1802), a translation of Shaikh Saadi's *Gulsitan* by Sher Ali Afsos; *Ataleeq-e Hindi* (1803), a moral preceptor and Persian scholars' guide to Hindustani language jointly translated by the natives; *Hidayat-ul Islam* (1804), a collection of forms and ceremonies of Islamic faith jointly translated by the natives; *Akhlaq-e Hindi* (1803), a translation from a Persian version of *Hitopadesh* by Meer Bahadur Ali; *Gul Bakawali* (1804) a tale translated from Persian by Munshi Nihal Chand; *Tota Kahani* (1804) a translation of a popular Persian tale called *Tooti Nama* by Haider Bakhsh Haidri (1804); *Bagh-o-Bahar* (1804, 1813) a Persian tale translated into Hindustani and titled *Qissa-i-Chahar Darwesh* by Meer Amman; *Baitaal Pacheesi* (1805) a collection of twenty-five highly interesting stories from Braj Bhasha told by a demon to King Vikramajeet by Mazhar Ali Khan, Lallulal and the Munshis; *Singhasan Batteesi* (1805), the anecdotes of celebrated Vikramajeet, from Braj Bhasha by Mirza Kazim Ali Jawan, Lallulal and other Munshis; *Ikhwan-us-Safa* (1811) translated from the Arabic original by Maulvi Ikram Ali, and *Khirad Afroz* (1815) translated from Hindustani by Maulvi Hafeezuddin Ahmed from *Ayyar-e Danish* by Abul Fazl of Emperor Akbar's court. Roebuck also mentioned the translation from English into Hindustani of the New Testament (1805) and into Persian, Arabic, Braj Bhasha, Bangla and Sanskrit, apart from the Hindustani translation of *Aesop's Fables* (1803) by various hands. Among others, Roebuck also mentioned *Rajneeti* (1809), a Sanskrit text of Narayan Dutt highlighting moral precepts along with the Hindu way of civil and military administration translated into Braj Bhasha by Lallulal; *Prem Sagar* (1810), the story of Hindu deity Sri Krishna from Braj Bhasha of Chaturbhuj Mishra into Hindavi by Lallulal; *The Megha Duta* (1813), a Sanskrit classic of Kalidasa translated by Horace Hayman Wilson; *Majmua Shamsi* (1807), a text on the Copernican system of astronomy translated from English into Hindustani; and *Sirajeeya* (1811) and *Kitab-ul-Junayaat-o-Hudood* (1813), texts on jurisprudence from Arabic, into Hindustani. Some other works of distinction mentioned variously include the translations of texts like *Satsai* (1811), *Ramcharitmanas* (1811), *Gul-i-Maghfirat* (1812), *Ramayana* (1806) *Meghdootam* (1813), *Naladay* (1814), *Megha Kavya* (1815) and *Kiratarjuniya* (1815). Most of the translations were done by the Hindustani, Persian, Sanskrit and Arabic departments.

WORKS CITED

Akhtar, Saleem. 2005. *Urdu adab ki ukhtasar tareen tareekh* (Urdu). Delhi: Kitabi Duniya.

Bailey, T. Grahame. 1932. *A history of Urdu literature*. London: Oxford University Press.

Das, Sisir Kumar. 1978. *Sahibs and munshis*. New Delhi: Orion Publications.

Frazer, R. W. 1898. *A literary history of India*. London: T. Fisher Unwin.

Gilchrist J. B. 1803. *The oriental fabulist*. Calcutta: Printed at the Hirakaru Office.

Kidwai, Sadiqur Rahman. *Gilchrist and the language of Hindoostan*. 1968. Delhi: Rachna Prakashan.

Pearson, Hugh. 1817. *Memoirs of the life and writings of the Rev. Claudius Buchanan*. Vol I. Oxford: Oxford University Press.

Roebuck, Thomas. 1819. *The annals of the College of Fort William*. Calcutta: Hindoostanee Press.

Russell, Ralph. 1992. *The pursuit of Urdu literature*. London: Zed Books.

Sadiq, Mohammad. 1964. *A history of Urdu literature*. London: Oxford University Press.

Said, Edward. 2001. *Orientalism*. New Delhi: Penguin Books.

Saksena, Ram Babu. 1927. *A history of Urdu literature*. Allahabad: Ram Narain Lal.

Zakir, Mohammad, trans. 1994. *A tale of four dervishes*. New Delhi: Penguin Books.

SEVEN

Translating Representation: The Problematic of Indian Literature

The concept of representation in general, and literature as representation in particular, is necessary in order to understand the translation of Indian literature in a historical perspective with all its literary and political implications.

An effort is made here to develop the idea of literature as representation and translation as re-representation. This involves a remapping of the socio-political conditions that determine the possibility of representation and re-representation. In examining this idea in the context of Indian literature and its essential markers, a number of considerations involving text, tradition and history have come to the fore. In trying to examine how India was represented in the past both by Western and Indian translators, I have tried to underline the politics of translation and also examine the different ways through which it has defined and disseminated the idea of India and Indian literature. While tracing this trajectory of translation, this chapter also traces how the strategy of translating India in the postcolonial period has undergone a transformation. As translating India is now a serious academic engagement, the chapter retraces the conditions that cause resistance and facilitate representation in the postcolonial period, which draws upon the colonial time in certain ways but registers a marked difference in comparative and contrastive terms.

The title of this chapter invokes a question. How can one translate representation, one might ask, especially when translation is by itself a representation of one kind or the other? An appropriate answer to this question could be found if we tried to appreciate that the act of translating, which is an act of reconfiguring a text, is an act of representing the representable in several ways, which is by implication an act of translating representation. Furthermore, as a text is re-carved in the process of translation, one might argue, it acquires a representational value and by this virtue, a translation turns out to be representative in nature like the text it represents in translation. The question may further be addressed with a little more effort directed towards examining the various shades of expressions such as "presentation", "re-presentation", "representation" and "re-representation". The following sections examine these aspects in theoretical terms and try to implicate them in the understanding of Indian literature which has been translated as representation through the ages, with varying intentions, and by appropriating varying methodologies.

LITERATURE AS REPRESENTATION

Let me assert, to begin with, that life as lived and portrayed is not a material for literature; it is at best a presentation of life in non-literary terms. This implies that all sustainable literatures and arts are not presentations or re-presentations by repetition, but creative/imaginative representations[1] of one kind or the other. This further implies that in their varied forms literatures and the arts are representations of semblances between the signifier as verbal expression and signified as mental images. Representations re-contextualise the phenomenal world and validate semiotic and aesthetic manifestations in a work of art. Signs and language join together in a literary representation and configure in different forms by calling literary devices to use. These representations are determined by their contexts which characterise them as personal, communal, metaphoric and mythic in nature. As literary representations materialise in this manner, they acquire a cognitive value and assert reckonable truths with reference to their location and their sociocultural markers. In their varied expressions through ages, they acquire newer references of their identification while shedding the older ones in order to save stereotyping or essentialisation. As vibrant linguistic constructions that qualify to become part of the canon over a period of time, literatures emerge as representations of the timeless as well as of the temporal. While they subscribe to and reiterate given positions, they also open avenues for contestations, and through that, make way for comprehensive cultural growth and civilisational advancements.

I would extend these basic ideas further to say that while literature produced in a language is a representation of one kind, its translation into another language is the extension of that representation to newer areas of reception which I should like to call a re-representation. This implies that since texts written originally in one language and translated into another are two separate examples of representation and re-representation, they also open possibilities of multiple representations at two different levels. This implicates the parameters of representation in two directions: in one way it relates with the representation of message, and in another with the representation of medium. Translation, being a site of manifold negotiations with language, content and form, is also a medium through which thematic and stylistic representations are interrogated in order to be accepted or contested. As all literary representations in a given language are subject to multiple responses within the framework of the same time, same place and same set of readers, they also get exposed to a set of new conditions and responses in translation. It may, thus, be justifiably asserted that literatures in translation extend the frontiers of representation in numerous ways and are differently authenticated in this process of inter-lingual and inter-cultural interaction.

With the arguments made above, it seems appropriate to point out that the idea of literature as an expression of human condition, which has been a popular and universally acceptable approach for long, is now being redefined in a theoretical way by developing newer parameters in the larger contexts of time and place. This implies that literature is no longer considered to be holding a mirror to life; it is being redefined now as representation which is different from just holding a mirror and reflecting an image. As such, representation, in theoretical terms, having its conceptual roots in Aristotle and Plato, became a serious subject of discourse in modern times. Contemporary engagements with representation in the domains of literary criticism and theory, apart from other disciplines, make way for me to say that never before in the past has the word representation been used in such a variety of contexts, and with such a wide range of meanings, as in the present time. It is a focal point of reference in diverse disciplines, such as literature and the arts, media and popular culture, pure and applied sciences, social and behavioural sciences, and many more. In fact, it has been appropriated in all areas that concern broad human perception, action and experience. Interestingly, the basic intent in all the usages of the word *representation* almost always draws closer to its general lexical meaning, but in specific disciplines it refers to much more complicated areas of human knowledge and knowledge systems.

To situate this argument in precise terms, I would argue further that a question regarding the types of representation in Indian literature does not yield a single and simple answer. As a major site of knowledge construction ever since ancient times, India's literary representations, in the broadest possible terms, are as varied as the historical periods and conditions they have passed through. In a historical sequence, some of its representations are religio-philosophical, while others are sociocultural. In yet another way, they may be designated as mundane and materialistic, as well as peripheral and perishable, as they are judged variously while keeping close to the defining conditions of the ages in which they are produced. While at one time the representations are ethical or inspirational, at others they are ritualistic or mechanistic. They are judged on the Classical, Romantic or Modernist parameters of critical reading and acquire their place in the canon accordingly. The contemporary postcolonial representations of Indian literatures, for example, are more complex and multifaceted than those in any other period of Indian literary history. They raise complex issues concerning history, identity, power, language, resistance, ethnicity, indigeneity, nationalism and hybridism, etc., which characterise Indian postcolonial literature. These representations are read in contrast with the colonial discourse alongside postcolonial theory.

Since translated texts as re-representations have now become an integral part of the larger literary capital in India and they, along with literatures written in various languages, constitute a remarkable literary collective, the broader questions of representation and re-representation have acquired yet another dimension and have imparted further complexity to this issue. One may thus assert that just as the pre-colonial, colonial and postcolonial source-language literatures raise a variety of issues concerning representation, the target-language literatures in translation add further complexity to the literary capital and make the critical discourse more complex. This complexity is more clearly noticeable in a multifaceted site like India than other postcolonial sites in the world that represent unitary patterns of history and culture. These arguments may be carried further with reference to Indian literature, its translation into the English language for historical reasons, and its academic credibility.

The Case of Indian Literature

Having reflected upon literature as representation, it should be appropriate to consider the case of Indian literature and raise specific questions with reference to Indian literary representations which are remarkably different from other literary representations. One might ask, for example, what does Indian literature represent? Drawing upon the literary representations of the ancient times, one could ask if, directly or indirectly, it represents the spiritualist–secularist traditions of the land, or moves beyond it to evolve an inclusive representation of the cumulative spirit of the land in its multiple manifestations. Moving further in time, one may extend this question to find out if it represents multiple nations within a single nation, or myriad paradigms of living within a larger paradigm of life marked by racial hopes and fears, or even the personal desires and dilemmas of the people in their individual locations and contexts. Broadly speaking, one could also try and find out if Indian literature is a representation of India's complex sociocultural paradigms, or if it is a representation of the deep-rooted concern for constructing a definite kind of knowledge, a certain longing for a form, or even a quest for a contemporary idiom to create a contemporaneously relevant and meaningful literature. It would be difficult to formulate even a broad answer, as there is none that could hold for sure, and underline the problems of India's multifaceted existence. One answer that may be appropriate to a considerable extent is that typically, Indian creative aspirations are directed towards creating a literature that is characteristically rooted in historical time and physical space. It is diverse in terms of racial, historical, cultural and individual representations and it is this multifaceted representational variety that distinguishes Indian literature from other literatures.

In order to make a point regarding Indian literary representations in translation, one would need to understand the very nature of the Indian text. It must be added here that the Indian quest for an individual expression has produced a characteristically different kind of literature. This literature, whether produced in a certain language, or translated from that, is neither an isolated nor a wholly independent entity; it takes birth, sustains and survives in a collaborative process with other literary traditions, linguistic norms and canonical formulations, as also other texts, genres, ages and milieu. This literature acquires its vitality in the way it identifies its curious readership and calls for scholastic or critical interventions. In major parts, these collaborations are neither noted nor acknowledged as they naturally grow upon co-texts and sub-texts to create a text. Thus, the characteristic Indian literature which draws both upon the local and the general ethos of the land qualifies well to be identified as archetypal Indian literature which is sharply different in spirit and substance compared with literatures of other locations. While other literatures are the literatures of unitary representation, Indian literature is one of holistic representation incorporating a larger body of references within itself. As Indian literature is one larger body of writing, although written in many Indian languages, it is also a huge paradigm of literary representations in which each representation, being different from the other, is both an image of its own, as well as a reflection of the whole.

To elaborate upon the case of Indian literary representation, let me posit further that the nature of every literary representation, like that of Indian representation, is quite precisely determined by the constituents of that representation. It relates with how the language conducts an experience and how the literary tradition conditions a representation within a piece of literary writing. As Indian literature has evolved and matured through a long historical process spread over thousands of years in different locations, languages and cultures, its microcosmic and macrocosmic representations are replete with intricacies. In spite of being diverse and disparate, and in spite of maintaining textual and contextual peculiarities, Indian literary representations have reached out to larger areas of readership only through translational negotiation. Translating Indian representations in English and other languages has been, since the sixteenth century, a preoccupation of a political and acutely critical nature. The literary representations produced over all these centuries in original, and their re-representation in translation, have accumulated into a comprehensive body and call for newer theoretical apparatuses to study them in relation to their multiple contexts. The following section tries to locate Indian literature written in many languages and translated into English in order to understand the problematic of representation and re-representation.

Indian Literature, English Translation

We are aware that a great tradition of translating literary representations from Sanskrit, Arabic and Turkish languages into the Persian language was initiated in India in the late sixteenth century. As it continued further with a shift in emphasis on texts and authors, this tradition was carried forward in Western locations where such translations were undertaken in the English language in the eighteenth century; a project which continued in future years. What makes this entire engagement with translational activities in and outside India intellectually sustaining and critically tenable is that there is a visible pattern in the way certain kinds of literary representations were chosen for translation and dissemination. Another important point to consider is that since the Orient has always appealed to the West, India, which represents the Orient with marked difference, also interested Western translators who chose to translate Indian literary representations, sometimes condescendingly and at other times, with curious cultural concern. A brief survey of the reception of Indian literature in the West during the colonial period would show that the very phrase "Indian literature" has long held for the Western world two contradictory and conflicting meanings. It has traditionally served as a major signifier of literature that is either "sacred" or "profane" rather than secular and all-inclusive. Drawing upon Emile Durkheim, it may be argued that while the category of "sacred" related to faith and belief, that of "profane" did not necessarily relate to evil, which implies that the Indian literature which did not strictly fall in the category of the religious was not necessarily malevolent but represented a larger body of literature that was largely inclusive and secular. The typical Western notion of Indian literature has quite naturally conditioned readers' responses and created stereotypes regarding Indian literature, which the West thought would be sacred if not profane, and vice versa. With reference to the Western response to Indian literature, it may be said that such simplistic perceptions regarding the straightjacketing of Indian literature over a period of time led to the mystification and mythicisation of this literary harvest. Such reiterations generated essentialist positions and narrowed the space for an alternative representation or discourse till the advent of postcolonialism. It may be justifiably argued that stereotypes, once created, take long to get revised and make space for new perceptions to appear. It must also be added here that representing essentialisms is easier than resisting them by calling for yet another kind of representation. Essentialist representations, thus, survive longer than even a period, or periods of history, as they are politically motivated and are made to appear crucial, critical and even fundamental to the body it holds. Resistance in order to project another kind of representation, on the other hand, presupposes conflict, confrontation and long struggle. Even a quick and non-detailed review of Indian literary representations in English translation during the colonialist, nationalist and post-independence, or in other words, pre-modern, modern, and postmodern phases of India's history, would strengthen this argument. They would tell the story of how an essentialist representation came to gain ground and how, in the course of time, that position came to be questioned, making space for newer representations.

Considering the stereotypical notions regarding Indian literature, it should not surprise us that several British and Indian translators also pursued the pre-defined line of textual classification and chose only such texts to translate that fell into the two categories mentioned above. Even Akbar, the great Mughal emperor, with the intention of promoting dialogue and bringing the followers of various religious and cultural communities together, got texts of religious and philosophical significance translated from the classical Sanskrit, Turkish and Arabic, into Persian by the end of the sixteenth century.

This pursuit was carried further by another Mughal descendant, Dara Shikoh, an icon of religious tolerance and holistic approach towards faiths and peoples, who extended this great tradition and had the *Upanishads* translated as *Sirr-i Asrar* or *Sirr-i Akbar.* As these texts were considered to be iconic representations of the Indian ethos, they found favour with Western translators and readers by the end of the eighteenth and early nineteenth centuries. In translating the *Bhagavad Gita*, for example, Charles Wilkins, the first European translator to have translated from the Sanskrit original, made the first sacred text available to English readers. Similarly, in translating Kalidasa's *Abhijnanasakuntalam*, Sir William Jones, the celebrated philologist, jurist and Indologist, made the first literary text available to the English readers towards the end of the eighteenth century which also ran into several editions. This tradition was carried forward by Nathaniel Brassey Halhed who learnt Arabic, Persian and Sanskrit and chose to translate a sacred text, the *Upanishads*, and a non-sacred text concerned with laws and legality, *Vivadarnavasetu* as *A Code of Gentoo Laws*. However, a major attempt was made in the early nineteenth century by Ram Mohan Roy in translating sacred texts like Sankara's *Vedanta* as *An Abridgement of Vedanta*, *Kena* and *Isa Upanishads*. This was followed by Michael Madhusudan Dutt's translation of Ishwarchandra Vidyasagar's literary and dramatic text called *Sermista*. Interestingly, an anonymous translation of Dinabandhu Mitra's *Nil Darpan*, a play of socio-political intent concerning indigo planters that went into several editions for its controversial nature, also appeared around the same time. Horace Hayman Wilson translated a literary masterpiece, Kalidasa's *The Megha Duta*, in order to make a different kind of representation to the recipients. It would be interesting to consider what he aimed at in making his choice. An extract from the preface of this translation quoted in *An Illustrated History of Indian Literature in English* (2003) would be of interest:

> The dramas of Sacontala and the songs of Jaydeva have prepared the readers of the West, for the character of Sanscrit poetry…the profane poetry of the Hindus affords better specimens of style and taste, than are to be found in the poems which are considered by them as sacred: such as the Puranas, the Mahabharata and the Ramayana, the portions of these works therefore, which on various occasions have appeared before the public, cannot be

> allowed to detract from the general merits of Sanscrit composition, even though it should appear that they have more charms in the eye of literary curiosity, than of public taste... (369)

As the tradition matured, the late-nineteenth century saw the translations of the *Bhagavad Gita* by Mohini Chatterjee, *Ramayana* by Romesh Chunder Dutt, Manmatha Nath Dutt and Ralph T. H. Griffith, who also chose to translate the four Vedas. It would be instructive to refer to another extract quoted in *An Illustrated History of Indian Literature in English* where Dutt made a humble submission about his work in his epilogue:

> Ancient India, like ancient Greece boasts of two great epics. The *Mahabharata,* based on the legends and tradition of a historical war, is the *Iliad* of India. The *Ramayana*, describing the wanderings and adventures of a prince banished from his country, has something in common with the *Odyssey*. Having placed before the English readers a condensed translation of the Indian *Iliad,* I have thought it necessary to prepare the present condensed translation of the Indian Odyssey to complete the work. (Sattar 2003, 370)

It may be noticed that both Wilson and Dutt were trying to hand over the literary curiosities of India to the West. While Wilson acknowledged the character of Sanskrit poetry, Dutt went a step beyond in venerating the *Mahabharata* and the *Ramayana* as the *Iliad* and *Odyssey* of India which was a way of venerating the East in terms of the West, a stance that does not hold value in today's postcolonial condition.

These translators of the eighteenth and the nineteenth centuries, as may be seen, were not given to translating the Hindu sacred texts alone; they chose to work on non-religious texts as well which were considered profane but could justifiably be termed as the secular representations of India. It would be instructive to note that although they made a distinction between the so-called sacred and profane literatures, they chose to consider both as worthy of attention and fit to be translated for English readers into English. For them, these Indian representations had both literary merit and spiritual worth. W. Franklin's choice of translating a Braj text of the eighteenth century called the *The Love of Kamarupa and Camalata* in the late eighteenth century and C. A. Elliot's choice of translating a collection of Urdu-Hindi ballads of the early eighteenth century called *Chronicles of Oonao* in the mid-nineteenth century fall in this category. One would also like to place in this category Michael Madhusudan Dutt's translations of his own Bengali plays in the mid-nineteenth century and Romesh Chunder Dutt's translation of his own novel *The Lake of Palms* at the beginning of the twentieth century. This period also saw Sri Aurobindo emerging as a prolific translator from Sanskrit and other Indian languages like Tamil, Gujarati, and Bangla into English.

With regard to the translation of a wider variety of texts, relevant references may be made here to Lord Wellesley and his College of Fort William, Sir William Jones and his Bengal Asiatic Society, and H. T. Colebrooke and his Royal Asiatic Society, which emerged as the most powerful centres of knowledge construction and played a major role towards creating holistic representations of the Indian ethos. Orientalists like William Jones, John Gilchrist, J. T. Platts and Duncan Forbes translated literatures from both Persian and Sanskrit for the English readership. Alongside, Persian literary masterpieces like Sheikh Sadi's *Gulsitan,* Mir Amman's *Bagh-o-Bahar,* and archetypal narratives like *Dastan-e Amir Hamza* and the *Qissa-i-Alif Laila* were rendered into simple Urdu under the patronage of Gilchrist at the College of Fort William for the colonialists who had come to rule over India, and for which they needed to know the life and letters of the land. It was with this purpose in mind that the British administration encouraged the translation of novels into English for the British officers. The translations of Nazir Ahmad's Urdu novel *Taubat-un-Nasuh* by M. Kempson as *Repentence of Nusooh*, Bankim Chandra Chatterjee's Bangla novel *Kapalkundala* by H. A. D. Phillips as *Kopal-Kundala: A Tale of Bengali Life* and Chandu Menon's Malayalam novel *Indulekha* by W. Dumorgue with the same title came up towards the end of the nineteenth century. Through the later phases of colonial India, this tradition of translating

Indian literary representations into English continued at a regular pace alongside the translations of Indian literatures in several Indian languages for both a British and Indian readership. These engagements, dating back to the late eighteenth century, helped create a rich harvest of Indian literary representations to the West on the one hand and bring them to a cross section of readership across time and place on the other.

In the late nineteenth and early twentieth centuries, we have the examples of self-translations by Michael Madhusudan Dutt, Romesh Chunder Dutt and Rabindranath Tagore followed by a Maharashtrian monk, Purohit Swami's unique experiment of translating *Ten Principal Upanishads* in association with W. B. Yeats. Let me refer here to a letter W. B. Yeats wrote to a fellow poet and close friend Dorothy Wellesley, regarding this translation by Swami. The letter dated 21 December 1935 says:

> … I help Purohit Swami to translate the *Upanishads*. It is amusing to see his delighted astonishment when he discovers that he can call a goddess, 'this handsome girl' or even 'a pretty girl' instead of a 'maiden of surpassing loveliness'. I say to him 'think like a wise man but express yourself like the common people' and the result is that he will make the first great translation of the *Upanishads*. (44)

Interestingly, this book which Yeats helped to get published states "put into English by Purohit Swami and W. B. Yeats" on the title page, and not "translated into English by Purohit Swami and W. B. Yeats". While this tells us something about the methodology they adopted to put this volume together into English, it also raises certain other questions regarding the structuring of the representation, the identification of the context, and the possible emergence of a credo.

All these efforts at translating Indian literatures clearly underline the desire for representing India to the English reader as a land of spiritualism on the one hand, and of exotica, romance, grandeur and larger secular preoccupations on the other. Quite simply, it established that the West mattered and the translators needed to seek acceptance from Western quarters. The postcolonial critic would look at this phenomenon as yet another move towards the acceptance of a colonial hegemonic power which was favoured, quite often, by writers of Indian origin themselves. In his essay "Indian Traditions and the Western Imagination", Amartya Sen says that western attempts to interpret India fall into three distinct categories: exoticist, magisterial and curatorial. The exoticist approach, he says, underlined the "wondrous aspect of India", (141) the magisterial approach looked at India as "a subject territory", and the curatorial approach included "various attempts at noting, classifying, and exhibiting diverse aspects of Indian culture" (142). In spite of the fact that we may place many of these efforts at understanding the Indian context by translating the Indian text in the curatorial category, they still reiterate a certain image of India and represent the land as the interesting other.

The mid- and the late-twentieth centuries offer more complicated contexts of translation. The major difference lies in the fact that now the translator no longer translates principally for the Western reader but for a larger readership within India itself. Translational efforts are homebound now and have taken on a trajectory quite different from the one followed during the colonial period. The need to create a sense and a definition of Indian Literature and Indian representation has been a major factor behind the works by conscious and informed translators. They are given to creating a post-independence and pan-Indian identity in order to voice postcolonial concerns that include questions of universality and difference, representation and resistance, nationalism and hybridism, and ethnicity and indigeneity. As such, the translation of Indian literatures in English, with a view to disseminate broader Indian representations, has turned out to be a serious engagement with young academics, established writers and translation experts who have joined hands, sometimes even unconsciously, to create a new literary culture. A. K. Ramanujan, Gayatri Chakravorty Spivak, William Radice, Ralph Russell, Qurratulain Hyder, Agyeya, C. M. Naim, Mohammad Umer Memon, Girish Karnad, Dilip Chitre, R. Parthasarthy, Arvind Krishna Mehrotra, Vinay Dharwadker and a number of others figure in the formidable list of translators. This is only a random list but it tells us how creative writers, critics and academics have chosen to work as translators and potential agents of representation to disseminate a poetics characterised by the typical postcolonial concerns mentioned above. In his *Poems of Love and War* (1985), Ramanujan chose to revive and represent an ancient Tamil poetic tradition and assert his conviction in the "Translator's Note":

> These poems are 'classical,' i.e., early, ancient; they are also 'classics,' i.e. works that have stood the test of time, the founding works of a whole tradition. Not to know them is not to know a unique and major poetic achievement of the Indian civilization. (ix)

His other anthologies *The Interior Landscape* (1967), *Speaking of Siva* (1993), *Hymns for the Drowning* (1981) and *Folktales from India* (1992) also bear witness to his desire to revive Indian literary heritage through select representations of the Indian ethos. Similarly, when Dilip Chitre chose to translate Tuka Ram (*Says Tuka*) or Linda Hess and Arvind Krishna Mehrotra chose Kabir's verses (*The Bijak of Kabir* and *Songs of Kabir,* respectively), they made a confident choice of retrieval and revival for a certain kind of representation that had acute relevance for the contemporary reader. These efforts are much more than mere efforts at translating texts; they are valuable efforts at revisiting the classics to re-contextualise them for their larger representational value in modern times. These are also efforts at reliving a tradition, and reinventing a form for the modern reader. Spivak's translation of Mahasweta Devi falls in an entirely different category. When she chose to translate Devi's "Stanadayini" ("Breast Giver"), she did not only translate a story; she also evolved a theoretical framework to deliberate upon its representational value in her essay entitled "A Literary Representation of the Subaltern: Mahasweta Devi's 'Stanadayini'". Spivak's translations and studies are efforts at representing a political agenda and constructing a discourse on resistance and representation. A number of examples representing the variety of Indian texts and their translations may be quoted and it may be argued that this activity of conscious translating is now well defined, both in aim and manner for creating a new literary tradition for India. Considering this scenario, it would be quite possible to go beyond the three categories proposed by Amartya Sen and suggest that Indian literature in English translation may be appreciated with reference to three other categories. These categories, I would suggest, could be (i) philosophical and mythical (ii) cultural and multicultural, and (ii) socio-economic and political. One could locate Indian representations in these categories and be able to contextualise, theorise and canonise them for a better construction of the broader Indian reality. This India, or this Indian literature, that eludes neat categorisations, or sometimes even a holistic definition, may be seen in terms of these identities that are strikingly representational, relevant and contemporary. The new Indian nation and its new literary representations, at the two levels of the original writing and their translation, concern new cultural icons, new socio-economic equations, and new adjustments that the nation state is negotiating in the present moment in history.

These translational engagements at representing Indian literatures would have proved futile if publishers in India had not taken the entire phenomenon with such remarkable seriousness.[2] An analysis of the pool of writers, translators, languages and genres would yield interesting results and would establish that translation is fast formulating its canon and posing an alternative discourse on the problematic of representation. Dharwadker and Ramanujan, the editors of *The Oxford Anthology of Modern Indian Poetry* (1997) rightly recorded in their preface that their attempts are "attempts at transmission—and more than transmission" and "if they succeed, they change emphasis, attack old biases and introduce new ones, even remake…a reader's sense of his or her literary tradition" (vii). Behl and Nicholls in their introduction to the special issue on "Contemporary Indian Literatures" of *Chicago Review* also underlined yet another facet of this phenomenon: "What has emerged in this collection is an 'India' whose literary scene is vital, diverse, and changing" (6). To follow this line of argument, one more reference may be made here regarding the validity of the translated text which is drawn from Amit Chaudhuri's introduction to *The Picador Book of Modern Indian Literature* (2001). It says,

> If there is anything this anthology says, it is that it is possible, in this time of postcolonial theory on the one hand, and trivial curiosity on the other, to place authors and their texts at the centre, rather than on the margins, of a discussion and a reassessment of how we think about India. (xxxiv)

Considering the points made above regarding the intents and contents of translational representation through various phases of history, it may be safely asserted that in sharp contrast to the past, the theory and practice of translation, especially with reference to Indian literature have emerged as the major areas of academic engagement in India in the recent past. The complexion of curricula in the departments of languages and literatures has changed of late. Today, the author, the translator and the reader have entered into a new relationship, and together are trying to engage with some vital questions like why represent, what to represent and how to represent.

An Academic Engagement

The huge amount of translational engagement undertaken in the past and its proliferation in the present times amply demonstrates its cognitive value. It may be justifiably posited that that the intents and methods of translation have undergone a drastic transformation during the past three centuries. While the earlier translators were principally engaged with the transference of message, modern translators are concerned with both the representation of message and the method of representation.

In at least two brilliant studies – Rita Kothari's *Translating India* (2003) and Tejaswini Niranjana's *Siting Translation* (1992) – we come across a comprehensive study of the contexts and theoretical positioning of Indian literatures in English translation. In her chapter "Recalling: English Translations in Colonial India", Kothari traces the history of translation during the colonial period and remarks how India has been made accessible to the West as well to Indians from various Indian language traditions through translation, and how nineteenth-century colonial India registered a decline of Orientalist activities, especially among British scholars, even as the Germans carried this activity at a greater pace. She also comments on nineteenth-century missionary activities which put Hinduism on a confrontational path with Christianity and prioritised English as the language of power at the cost of the Sanskrit language and its literature. Even while this went on and English emerged as the repository of new knowledge, Indian intervention towards constructing new bases of knowledge about India continued. As translation emerged as a mode of retrieval and re-assertion, images of India were reiterated in different ways. While Kothari draws attention to the various roles translation played, she also traces this trajectory through modern times with reference to mother tongue, other tongue, academia, English studies, postcolonialism, readership, market, institutionalisation of translation in our times, and the example of a particular location as a certain kind of paradigm with regard to translational activity. This concise study affords us a chance to consider the case of translating India in a larger historical framework of the past and the present with all the attendant issues involved.

Viewed from the vantage point of the present time I should like to argue that the act of translating India has ever been (a) a historical necessity, (b) a political inevitability, (c) an administrative exigency and (d) a cultural imperative. All these major aspects that underline the significance of the entire undertaking also point towards other issues that relate with the problems of thematic representation, stylistic negotiation and methodological conciliation involved in the process of extending the frontiers of knowledge through translation.

Locating the entire undertaking of translation through the colonial period from a theoretical perspective is an area that has been developed in Niranjana's study. In her "Introduction: History in Translation" which includes sections on "Situating

Translation", "Translation as Interpellation" and the "Question of History", Niranjana advances several arguments that contextualise these translations quite differently. She considers translation to be playing a key role towards interpellating India which implies that it was supposedly inferior and thus liable to subjection. She discusses the relationship between translation and colonialism, and drawing upon post-structuralism, she argues that translation is not merely a matter of finding linguistic equivalences but playing a political role. Speaking from the vantage point of being a postcolonial writer, she posits that translation is a site to engage with the problematic of representation, power and historicity, which implies that the colonised subject is projected in a manner that justifies colonial domination. She goes on to elaborate further upon this by problematising reality as the given, knowledge as representation of the given reality, and representation as a direct mode of reaching out to that given reality. She engages with the idea of reality and representation in relation to a wilful construction of the colonised while overlooking the violence it perpetrates in the process. Translation, as such, evolves methods by which the coloniser may privilege himself over his colonised subject by representing him as the other and controlling him through a process of perpetual suppression. The colonised is thus represented as languishing in a state of stasis without a history of his own. Such representations are perpetuated across a complex of literary and extra-literary discourses comprising a variety of disciplines and subjects. She extends this argument to the postcolonial moment which is still conditioned by the shadows of colonialism but may be subverted in a decolonised moment of living through assigning a new role of representation to translation. She traces the operation of this hegemonic strategy through the works of Friedrich Hegel, the philosopher; James Mill, the historian; and William Jones, the Orientalist, who perpetuate the strategy of interpellation and the tactic of othering.

The translations produced by the British colonisers during the eighteenth and nineteenth centuries may be generally assessed in the light of these arguments put forward by Niranjana. With reference to them, she seems to suggest that they chose to translate Indian texts because Indians lacked the capacity to interpret their own texts reliably, which meant that they had to act as their interpreters and hand over their own texts to them in purified, or sanitised forms as representations of their culture. She refers to the well-orchestrated translational practices of persons of various affiliations like William Jones, William Carey, William Ward, John Wilkins and others to substantiate her idea that their translational activities were aimed at interpellating the colonised people. This leads her to conclude that translation and historiography are interlinked activities.

These two studies critically and theoretically engage with major issues concerning the problematic of representation in the larger contexts of history, colonial power and image-making of the colonised people and their world. The re-representations of India through translation both by Indian and Western translators during the earlier phases did not engage directly and consciously with methods of translation as they did in the later phases. Today's translators are acutely concerned with the poetics of translation as is borne out by the growing number of scholastic engagements with translation as a linguistic and cultural undertaking. This is further strengthened by the growing number of works in English translation as has been mentioned above. Both translation theorists and practitioners have engaged with the problematic of representation in a larger framework that broadly includes their concern with the selection of texts and strategies of translation. They are also concerned with the problem of dealing with the ambiguity of the Indian text, its contemporary relevance and its cognitive value. The issues of cohesion, comprehensibility and disambiguation in order to represent the discourse embodied in the text also form parts of this engagement. These include, in turn, the possibility of reaching out to the ideational meaning and recreating a form and a genre that represent the essential Indian ethos. Translating representation, as such, has now become an undertaking of a critical, theoretical and practical nature that defines and disseminates the images of India to readers both in and outside India.

NOTES

1. The concept of "representation" has been discussed variously in literature and the arts. Apart from the basic and broader discussion on the subject in Aristotle's *Poetics*, some contemporary discussion may be seen in Erich Auerbach's *Mimesis: The Representation of Reality in Western Literature* (1953); Umberto Eco's *A Theory of Semiotics* (1978); W. J. T. Mitchell's *Picture Theory: Essays on Verbal and Visual Representation* (1994) and Stuart Hall's (ed.) *Cultural Representation and Signifying Practices* (1997).
2. Penguin India, Oxford University Press India, Macmillan India, Orient Blackswan, Permanent Black, Ravi Dayal, Stree, Seagull, Hachette, Katha, Kali for Women, Writers Workshop and Manas are some of the best sites for the new generation of translators today. This may be traced back to the pioneering role Asia Publishing House, Jaico, Hind Kitab, Orient Paperbacks and Arnold Heinemann played in this direction in the 1960s. A significant move was made in 1996 by Macmillan India who published a series of modern Indian novels translated into English. By 2003, they had published eighty novels of repute from almost all Indian languages. Sahitya Akademi, the national academy of letters, which promotes translation activities in a major way, has played a role in a much more planned manner. Apart from publishing translations in its journal called *Indian Literature*, it has published individual and award-winning authors in translation and put together several volumes where noted Indian writers find their space in English translation.

WORKS CITED

Behl, Aditya and David Nicholls, eds. 1992. Introduction. *Chicago Review 38* (Vol. 38, Numbers 1 & 2).

Chaudhuri, Amit , ed. 2001. *The Picador book of modern Indian literature.* London: Picador.

Dharwadker, Vinay and A. K. Ramanujan, eds. 1997. *The Oxford anthology of modern Indian poetry*. New Delhi: Oxford University Press.

Guha, Ranajit, ed. 2005. *Subaltern studies v.* New Delhi: Oxford University Press.

Kothari, Rita. 2014. *Translating India: The cultural politics of English.* 2014. London and NY: Routledge. (St. Jerome, 2003).

Niranjana, Tejaswini. 1992. *Siting translation: History, post-structuralism, and the colonial context.* Berkeley: University of California Press.

Ramanujan, A. K., ed. 1985. *Poems of love and war.* New Delhi: Oxford University Press.

Sattar, Arshia. 2003. Translations into English. In *An illustrated history of Indian literature in English*, ed. Arvind Krishna Mehrotra. New Delhi: Permanent Black.

Sen, Amartya. 2005. Indian traditions and the western imagination. In *The argumentative Indian: Writings on Indian history, culture and identity*. London: Allen Lane.

Yeats, W. B. 1964. *Letters on poetry from W. B. Yeats to Dorothy Wellesley*. London: Oxford University Press.

EIGHT

Translating the Urdu Ghazal: The Classical Contexts of Meer and Ghalib

Ghazal is the most quintessential form of Urdu poetry, and has its roots in the larger tradition of the early Arabic and Persian poetry. As it has its own terms of reference and is unlike any other kind of poetry in any of the European traditions, it makes severe demands upon the translator with reference to form, content, diction and metaphor.

This chapter engages with some of the broad principles of translation that are directly relevant to the translation of the Urdu ghazal. Some of the major issues discussed in this chapter relate with the idea of "primary" and "secondary" translation, types of translation, extinction of the translator's personality, and the intriguingly individual form of the Urdu ghazal. It has been emphasised that the translator needs to enter into a tough critical negotiation at multiple levels in the process of translating a uniquely endowed text like the ghazal from one system of language to another, and from one cultural domain to another.

All these issues have been discussed with reference to the translations of Meer Taqi Meer and Asadullah Khan Ghalib, the two canonical poets representing the grand classical tradition of Urdu poetry in general and the ghazal in particular. An effort has been made to assess some translations of their ghazals in a comparative frame with emphasis on verbal analysis.

Literary texts evolve their own form; they find their own language and discover their own literary devices. It may be easily testified that of all the literary forms in the Perso-Arabic tradition, it is the ghazal[1] that has engrossed the attention of the poets the most, compared with any other poetical form. It may be argued further that the ghazal has not engrossed the attention of the poets alone; it has also been the most favoured form of poetry for readers as well through all the ages. It might appear baffling that a set of a few couplets, better called *sheyrs*,[2] that constitute a ghazal, which every Urdu poet takes to naturally, should pose a curious set of problems when chosen for translation into another language. Even a brief survey of the translations of Urdu ghazals into English would show that a number of problems have either remained unattended, or unresolved if attended, which is not the case with the translation of other poetical forms. It may be justifiably argued that the seeming simplicity of the ghazal is rather deceptive as it makes tough demands upon the translator with respect to his ability to negotiate with the constraints of the form on the one hand, and the most ambiguous thematic concerns on the other. Let us examine these propositions in the following sections with reference to the principles and practices of translation, the nature of the text in question, and the methodology chosen by various translators of Meer Taqi Meer (1722–1810) and Asadullah Khan Ghalib (1796–1869) to negotiate with their ghazals.

TRANSLATION: PRIMARY AND SECONDARY

Let us begin with two basic assumptions even at the risk of denying any role to translation theory and its usual preponderance in any discussion of translation as a vocation and the translated text as a finished product of certain cognisable merit. These assumptions spring from a practical realisation that (a) every expression is an act of translation[3] and (b) the principles of every translation are quite often the same.[4] One might wonder as to what different principles and practices could possibly be discussed here but there would appear many a point of discussion as one moves forward with the two statements in mind. It could be argued that the act of creating a source language text on the part of the author is the act of translating one's basic material – one's idea and image – into a form of one's own making in one's own language. For the sake of making a point here, let the act of creating a text in the source language be designated as an act of "primary" translation. When this primary translation reaches the translator, he/she re-negotiates with the constituents of what we have called primary translation and produces a text which we may like to designate as "secondary" translation. In the hands of a translator, the source-language text, which we have called primary translation, becomes his/her basic material, model and source, and in his/her endeavour to transmute it into another language, what he/she delivers is the secondary translation of the primary translation. This process of translation and re-translation, as proposed above, is akin to translating one system's thematics and stylistics into another system. It may, therefore, be interpreted as an exercise executed at a certain remove which may hopefully be transformed into a redeeming exercise, for the art of the translator, it may be argued, lies in concealing the distance he/she has traversed from the primary experience and revealing, in turn, the proximity he/she has achieved with it. We should, thus, like to approach this idea, first, with a brief analysis of the principles of translation relevant to our concern here and, second, try to examine them in the context of Urdu ghazals and, finally, illustrate with examples to show, in consequence, the causes of their failure or success as models of excellence.

Principles and Practices

It is the translator's first business to determine what he/she wants to do – to translate a language or register, intent or style, form or cultural oeuvre; or pursue his/her vocation rather differently by simply rewording or paraphrasing the text, or configuring it to one's own understanding, or even transfiguring or transcreating it by taking a greater risk. His/her choice would very naturally show the type of work he/she wishes to do, for these different methods are chosen for different purposes and effects and are applicable to works ranging from purely scientific texts to simple prose, and from plain and narrative verse to highly emotive and allusive poetry like that of the ghazal. In the context of poetry in general and the constraining form of the ghazal in particular, the translator may not like to choose the methods suited to referential texts, for poetry may run the risk of breathing too feebly and being buried in a cemetery of dead words. A translator of the ghazal for example, acutely conscious of the constraints the text invariably poses, may also disapprove of "paraphrasing" and weigh between "metaphrasing" and "imitation",[5] or what has been creatively called "transcreation". He/she may reconcile with metaphrasing but may also be tempted by the methods of imitation due to the liberties it naturally affords. The latter, it may be arguably posited, is a dangerous zone with too many allowances. Herein, the translator is liable to lose touch with the source text and discover a new kind of freedom which may easily make his effort prone to deprecation. The translation of the ghazal, an alien form in English, may therefore naturally require a keen understanding of the form, the basic nature of the idiom, and the cultural aspect of the idea and the experience represented, apart from the innumerable demands that the translation of the ghazal into the English language would entail. For a more discerning translator the act of translating a ghazal may be a matter of developing a possible correspondence with the primary experience, the literary predilections of the poet, his personality, and the text to be recreated[6] into his/her own language. This takes us to a brief discussion of how far the translator may need to disengage from his/her own personality in order to represent the chosen poet/text in a cognitive frame of reference.

We need to remind ourselves here that the translator of a ghazal is decidedly different from the translator of any other poetical form, as the ghazal, in spite of being a distinct poetical form, is clearly different from all other poetical forms found in world literature. As such, the translator's business in this case may not only be to apprehend the form of the source text, that is the ghazal, with all its attendant identifiers but also to configure her own self to engage with the poet's, and evolve his/her own strategy to negotiate with the poet's strategy at the multiple levels of language, culture, and literary devices peculiar to the ghazal. This is purely an aesthetic problem, for the translator's success may lie, to a considerable extent, in identifying the literary condition of the source text and discovering his/her own counters to approximate in his/her own text. The translator, thus, may move beyond one condition of socio-literary belonging to another, in order to acquire impersonality of a greater sort by being one with the personality of the source language poet. He/she may succeed in this difficult exercise as he/she may possibly develop an affinity with the poet and ultimately translate himself/herself into his/her self, and his/her work into his/her own language.

After the translator may choose to sacrifice his/her personality, the next preoccupation for him/her may be to assess as to how far he/she has been able to let the text emerge as a text on its own and impart to it a form and value of its own kind, and shape it into an organic whole, so to say. The translated text, in spite of being a secondary creation, as we have called it earlier, must appeal ultimately as an independent creation reflecting fully the nuances of the original – its feeling, tone, possible meaning and rhythm. It may be rightly argued here that synonyms do not simply exist, for words always have a life and a clime of their own; yet the translator may try to find their equivalents, howsoever deeply rooted they might be in their history, culture, society and aesthetics. This becomes a problem when the translator is at the most allusive of the poems that represent great imaginative vitality in terms of perception and expression. It might appear in certain cases that only an "inspired" translation has saved the translator from many a pitfall involved in this arduous undertaking, and this alone has imparted an organic structure, a form to the Urdu ghazal in English translation. The form is a mode of poetic apprehension and the translator establishes a communion with the source language poet in order to get the best out of his/her effort. He/she may enquire of himself/herself whether he/she has been able to impart to his/her work a form which emerges from subterranean fountains of the source-language text and becomes entwined with its thematic burden. It also includes the inner design and the external appearance of the poem – the text as a pattern of properly modulated sounds, a visual configuration, a dramatic entity, and an organic whole where the poet's ingenuity, his imaginative skill and the intensity of his experience interact, and form a consortium. The translator, it would appear, can hardly keep pace with so many rules in translating (for rules emerge out of practice) which implies that his/her basic understanding of the text may help him/her through the demanding exercise of translating a text entirely alien to the target language's literary tradition. We may now profitably try and examine these basic principles along with those of immediate relevance in translating the Urdu ghazal.

GHAZAL: NATURE AND FORM

An attempt at translating the Urdu ghazal into English or any of the European languages is an attempt at initiating a curious reader into an alien zone of strange mysteries and rare delights. Translating from Urdu into English is not the same thing as translating from one European language into another. The only proximity it has, if at all, is with the Persian, not even fully so with Arabic. Every act of translating the ghazal must, therefore, present greater problems, and also of a very different nature.

A closer reading of the Urdu ghazal would reveal that it has always been more difficult to translate the classical poets than the modern poets. This is more or less true of all poetry. However, the case with Urdu is a little different because its classical tradition has rightly been called a "golden tradition" characterised by the "cry of the gazelle," "the anguished heart" and the "molten flame".[7] The ghazal has been both, the most liked and the most disliked form of poetry. Some critics are of the opinion that it is a rigid, semi-savage form of poetry and that it should unhesitatingly be throttled to death while some others consider it to be the pride of poetry, a series of climaxes, and reading it to be akin to a journey through a culture.[8] The ghazal, in fact, does not merely reflect the varied facets of a culture; it has its own rich and varied culture as well. It has reached its apex in the hands of the two canonical poets, Meer and Ghalib. Translating the ghazal, modern or classical, is by far the most difficult of all the poetical forms in Urdu. It demands a rare sensitivity to words and nuances, myths and metaphors, motifs and symbols. It calls for an awareness of the Perso-Arabic culture, the Indo-Pak Muslim mind and the Muslim society in South Asia in general.[9] It has, moreover, no model in English or any of the European languages, whereby the translator may have an idea of this form in his/her own language. This need for a pre-knowledge of a model is not so intense when the translator approaches the other poetic forms in Urdu as there is the panegyric for *qasida*, elegy for *marsiya*, satire or repartee for *hajw*, romance for *masnawi* and forms like the haiku for *rubai* and *qita*. Each *sheyr* composed of two lines in a ghazal stands independent of the other and is complete in itself. The *sheyrs* are, however, put together under a certain rhyme scheme and follow a pattern of *qafia* and *radeef*.[10] The ghazal is quite peculiarly suited to a particular people and their sensibility, and the translator has to face many a challenge in translating its form and essence for a different people with entirely different set of literary and cultural markers.

The greatest challenge for a translator of Urdu ghazal emerges when he/she has to look for the cultural equivalents. It always remains a practical problem to search for exact equivalents for the romantic-cum-mystical concepts like *firaq, wisal,* and *ishq*, or institutionalised concepts like *naseh, zahid*, or *saqi*.[11] The translator's failure upon such arduous grounds explains why there always remains something untranslatable in poetry, more so in Urdu poetry in general and the ghazal in particular. A part of all great poetry often remains ambiguous and that also explains, in a way, the causes of the failure of primary translation. Translating the ghazal offers greater difficulties, for it presents the problem of deciphering personal allusions, esoteric symbolism, indigenous myth, and above all, that which communicates beyond and above words.

Much of the classical Urdu ghazal has traditionally been associated with a romantic world. The wine cup and the beloved are its most favoured images and symbols while rhythm and rhyme constitute its basic capital. In the hands of poets like Meer and Ghalib, the ghazal acquires a rare complexity of form and value as they transcend the mundane into magical, the real into eerie, and vice versa. While working on such ghazals, the translator may at one place be worried over the question of understanding the poet's world of imagination and at the other be engaged over the problem of transferring the favoured images and symbols as well as the metrical effects in the target language. It is true that the rhythms of Urdu and English are quite different from each other; yet they have to be communicated well to the speakers and listeners of each other's language. In dealing with the rhythm and rhyme, the inner ear may surely be the safest guide and it may be an extreme view to hold that the rhythms of Urdu cannot be truly apprehended by the English and those of English, by Urdu readers.[12] The Perso-Arabic culture, of which Urdu culture is a part, is quite often prone to a facile auditory scheme and its poetry very aptly assimilates the rhythms of its life. The oral–aural system of English poetry, being very different, assimilates the subtle rhythm of that life in a manner that would appear alien to the Urdu system.[13] In the absence of a true rhythmic feel it is not a happy choice to imitate the effect created by the subtly differentiable sounds and subject the effort to interrogation. With this essential background of the process involved and the practical difficulties faced in translating the Urdu ghazal, we may now choose to examine some translations of the ghazals of Meer and Ghalib to assess their worth as literary translations.

Translating Meer and Ghalib

Translating the classical ghazals of Meer and Ghalib is singularly difficult for various reasons; either because of their belonging to a different age and tradition, or exhibiting complex poetic configurations that are intensely individual, rooted in time, place, and culture, and therefore inimitable. They exhibit an admixture of the sensuous and the Sufistic, the timeless and the temporal, and have many strange cultural exhibits in store for non-Urdu readers. Meer, generally known as a poet of despair, is more widely concerned with existential issues and the world beyond the pragmatic and the physical. He views man and his universe in totality and expresses himself with an amount of confidence hitherto unknown. His identification with the physical world is both real and illusory and he exhibits a rare skill to turn his intellect into feeling and vice versa, as he apprehends concrete universals and makes them cognisable. Ghalib, the most difficult of the ghazal poets to translate, has been the most popular choice to translate, just as *Hamlet*, the most baffling of Shakespeare's plays, has been the most fascinating text for critics. Ghalib expresses a seemingly casual attitude towards the universe but his commitment to it has deeper roots. His awareness of the historical process and his perception of change attribute a philosophical dimension to his poetry. The other remarkable features of his poetry are the amazing swiftness and fertility of his imagination that yields him his metaphors. He is most distinguishable for the element of unexpectedness in his expression and ambiguity in his diction, as much as for his precision, wit and wry humour which he appropriates to create a kind of poetry that is playful yet serious, close by yet remote, and acutely physical yet metaphysical in nature and appeal.

Let us now consider some examples from these poets and examine their translations for their worth. We may begin with examining the translation of a *qita*[14] by Meer rather than a ghazal, to demonstrate that a *qita* composed of four lines approximates the form of a ghazal which also carries forward an idea from one *sheyr* to another to complete the cycle of meaning. Furthermore, a *qita* shares the rhyming and rhythmic pattern of the ghazal as can be seen here:

Kal paon aik kasa-i-sar pe jo aa gaya
Yaksar wo istkhwan shikaston se choor tha
Kahney laga ke daikh ke chal raah bekhabar
Main bhi kabho kisi ka sar-e pur ghuroor tha

J. D. Matthews and C. Shackle translate the four lines as follows:

> Yesterday when my foot trod upon a skull, that bone had entirely crumbled into dust—
> It began to say, Look as you walk, O heedless one! I too was once someone's proud head. (60)

Another rendering by Ahmed Ali reads thus:

> Yesterday I chanced to step
> Upon a skull that lay
> Broken and shattered in dust
> With despair and decay.
> 'Walk with open eyes and see
> O heedless,' it said
> 'I too was once upon a time
> A proud and haughty head.' (139)

The obvious formal difference between the two translations is that the first translator has chosen to paraphrase each line as distinct from the other but does not create a simulacrum of the precision and continuity of ideas the source text exhibits from one line to another. Although he has followed the meaning closely and accurately, he has not been able to create the appeal characteristic of a poetical composition. Rendered in simple prose, the first translation replicates the meaning but does not recreate the impact the meaning might have created rendered differently. One may not call it a translation in the true sense of the word as it qualifies more appropriately to be called a paraphrase of the source text. The second translator has also violated the four-line structure of the source text and chosen to translate the idea in eight lines. He has allowed himself space enough to be expository and assimilate all that the four lines of the source text contain by doubling the number of lines from four to eight. He has followed a rhyme scheme in order to give it the semblance of the ghazal form and also of the Urdu rhythm. The key words in the first line – *aa gaya* – are faithfully and poetically represented in the second translation as "chanced to step" for it suggests stepping as an act of mere chance or accident. The first translation being a prosaic one, fails to represent this feeling in "trod". This practice is but reversed in the other lines where the first translator rather poetically translates *dekh ke chal* into "look as you walk" whereas the second translator renders it purely prosaic in "walk with open eyes and see". Meer recreates the sense of brokenness of the skull and its bones with two words – *shikast* and *choor* – which, in spite of being repetitive, make the lines intensely suggestive. The second translator captures this feeling by using two words – "broken" and "shattered" – which appears befitting whereas the first translator uses only one word "crumble" for this effect which fails to accumulate the sense contained in the source text. Another remarkable point is that both the translators use the word "dust" in their renderings even though it does not occur in the source text. It simply goes to show, although it is not necessarily justifiable, that the translator enjoys the freedom of recreating effects even though they are not squarely stated but obliquely suggested.

We may now take an example to show how the translator's choice of inversions, his penchant for the musical, and his effort at imparting the formal effect of the ghazal may sometimes prove unworthy. The example is from Meer again.

Ahd-e jawani ro ro kata, peeri mein leen aankhein moond
Yaani raat bahut they jaagey, subha huwi aaram kiya

In Matthews and Shackle, the paraphrase reads as follows:

> I passed the time of my youth in weeping; and in old age I closed my eyes. In other words, I spent my nights awake and when the morning came, I rested. (62)

Ahmed Ali's poetic rendition follows a different scheme altogether:

My youth I spent in grief and tears,
And in old age I closed my eyes

As though I kept awake all night
And when the morning came I could not rise. (140)

The most remarkable quality of the source text may be seen in its rhythmic design. This design is created by inversions, the sound of the individual words, their arrangement in the lines, and their cumulative impact in the sheyr. The two inversions – *leen aankhein moond* and *bahut they jaagey* – create a certain musical tinge. It is further intensified in the repetitive sound *ro ro* which corresponds well with *kaata* and the nasal sounds *mein, leen, aankhein* and *moond* which perfectly synchronise with each other. If we divide the first line in two parts – *ahd-e jawani ro ro kaata* and *peeri mein leen aankhein moond* – the pattern of sounds and ideas emerge clearly. The time of youth has been spent in misery, so the sounds are repetitively raucous (*ro ro kaata*) and old age, the time to sleep, has accordingly been represented by milder nasal sounds (*mein, leen, aankhein, moond*) as if they are invoking sleep. All these words are so arranged in the *sheyr* that one reaches unto the other as if in a swift musical rush and the lines thus read like this: *ahde-e jawaani—ro ro kaata—peeri mein leen—aankhein moond—yaani raat—bahut they jaagey—subha huwi—aaram kiya.* It may not be quite fair to demand of the translator the exact reproduction of the rhythmic design, or the prosodic patterns as in the source text, yet he would do better in recreating an illusion of this predominant rhythmic rush. Since the first translation is only an attempt at paraphrasing, we need not look for its poetic qualities but the other translation is to be taken seriously. It appears to be quite close to the original and the diction exhibits a poetic ring to it. It may be realised better in contrast with the first translation where *ahd-e jawani* has been simply translated as the "time of youth" and *yaani* as "in other words". The second translation encapsulates the sense of the first phrase better in "youth" and the second phrase in "as though". He also succeeds well in representing the sense of *ro ro kaata* in "spent in grief and tears" and not in "weeping" as has been done in the first example. The second translator, however, falters in the first phrase. The phrase – *subha huwi aaram kiya* – does not mean "when the morning came I could not rise" but implies just the opposite, that is, "when the morning came, I went to sleep". The translator has resorted to a poetic method of inversion and he appears to have been misled by the need of the rhyme as he provides a musical correspondence of the "eyes" with "rise". This improper poetic license leads to misdirection and the sense appears to be sacrificed to sound for no poetic gain. We have another example of about the same nature in the *maqta* of the same ghazals translated by Ahmed Ali:

Meer ke deen-o-mazhab ko ab poocchtey kya ho un ney to
Qashqa khaincha, dair mein baithha, kab ka tark Islam kiya

Why do you ask the faith of Meer?
He sits in the temple, it is said,
A caste marked on his brow, having lost,
None knows when, the faith of Mohammad. (140)

We should not insist upon the translator imitating the sound effects of *ke, ko, kya, ho, un, ne, to* and *qashqa, khaincha, baithha, ka* and *kiya* but it must be said in all fairness that the translation lacks fire and does not recreate either its music or its sense in proportion to the source language text. He, moreover, takes unwarranted poetic license in translating Islam as "the faith of Mohammad" whereas it could have been retained as such with better effect. Similarly, "it is said" in the second line is an addition from his side and it is neither stated nor implied in the original. The first line in the source text does not pose a question; it is only a suggestion of the poet's loss of certain faith but the translator has turned it into a question in the first line. It reads, on these accounts, as a purely prosaic rendition of a highly suggestive *sheyr* as the translator fails to meet the demands of his art. There are several other examples where poetry loses its tone and touch in translation. Even in simple gestures of language, or where language turns itself into a gesture or a half expression, the problem emerges quite naturally. Let us examine the following two examples by Ahmed Ali:

Shaam hi se bujha sa rehta hai
Dil hua hai chiragh muflis ka

Right from the evening it burns
Low and dim
My poor heart has become
A pauper's lamp. (141)

Hum huwey, tum huwey, ke Meer huwey
Sab usi zulf ke aseer huwey

May it be you or I
Or Meer, each one is held
Captive by her ringlets. (171)

The first one reads like a poor translation as the source language text suggests a lamp which, though burning, is as good as already burnt out but the translator misreads it as a lamp which burns low and dim. He has not been able to represent the image of a lamp which, in burning low and dim, does not burn at all, as a pauper living his life does not live it but is, in fact, himself lived and consumed by life. Moreover, the image of *chiragh* is untranslatable on account of its being rooted in a particular culture. This is not so much a matter of the inefficiency of a synonym as it is a question of relating to two cultures wherein their images, metaphors and symbols stand apart and communicate alone to its people fully, rather than with those falling outside the cultural domain. Another problem in translating this *sheyr* is that of finding out an equivalent for *sa* which is but only a half-expression, although rich and subtle and endowed with full meaning. In the next *sheyr*, simplicity deceives the translator and it is inimitable on this account as also for the rhythm embodied in the repetition of the word *huwey* in double meaning. This translation also, like the first one, is at best a paraphrase of the source language *sheyr* and it does not represent any of its qualities. It would be fit to mention that *zulf* can hardly be translated here as "ringlets" and *aseer* as "captive". These are also rooted in culture and do not mean the same to those of an alien culture. Its translation, therefore, is bound to lose much of its significance. The meaning of the *sheyr* could somehow be communicated but not its spirit.

As opposed to these examples, we have another example where Ahmed Ali succeeds to a great extent in negotiating with the source language *sheyr:*

Faqeeraana aaye sada kar chaley
Mian khush raho hum dua kar chaley

A beggar I came and cried my say
May you live happy and happy stay. (173)

Simplicity is again the poet's challenge to the translator. He could save himself by imitating the tone as well as by exploring a corresponding diction for his purpose. We may agree that the translator is successful in doing it as also in imparting to his *sheyr* a form and value of its own. Even though the word *faqeerana, mian* and *dua* have not been literally translated, they communicate the ideas embodied in these words with almost the same exactness. The expression – *sada kar chaley* – which is clearly indicative of a different tradition with Sufistic connotations, is well reflected in "cried my say". Since the *sheyr* corresponds well with the tone and the mood of the next line along with rhyme of "say" and "stay", it seems to acquire its value as an independent creation. The translator succeeds here in becoming one with the primary experience and imparting to his *sheyr* a tone and tenor which is much like the one in the source text.

After these examples representing certain practical problems in translating from the ghazals of Meer, we now examine some examples from the translations of Ghalib. Since Ghalib has been the most widely translated poet, it should not be of much use to pick up his *sheyrs* for illustrating problems of more or less the same nature as discussed above. We would do better to try and examine two experiments in translating from Ghalib in order to be able to look at this problem from a different angle. In the example quoted below we may observe how Ahmed Ali makes an attempt at creating the English ghazal while translating Ghalib:

Dil-e nadaan tujhey hua kya hai
Aakhir is dard ki dawa kya hai

Jab ke tujh bin nahin koyi maujood
Phir ye hangama ai Khuda kya hai

Ye pari chehra log kaise hain
Ghamza-o-ushwa-o-ada kya hai

Sabza-o-gul kahan se aaye hain
Abr kya cheez hai, hawa kya hai

Jaan tum par nisar karta hoon
Main naheen janata dua kya hai

My foolish heart, what is ailing thee
What is thy sorrow's remedy?

Wherefore all this tumult, O Lord,
When nothing exists without thee?

Who are these beguiling ones? What is
This winking, ogling, coquetry?

Where has the cloud come from? What is
The air, the rose, the greenery?

Devoted to you with all my heart
I know not prayer or piety. (153–54)

It would appear that the translator has artfully manipulated the last syllables of these *sheyrs* and made them rhyme with each other under the rhyme scheme of "thee," "remedy," "greenery," and "piety". The two lines in the first *sheyr* rhyme together with "thee" and "remedy" in the same way as a *matla* does in a ghazal. We may argue that the last syllables act as the *radeef* in this example of the English ghazal. Apart from this kind of experiment, there is not much that could make it unique in other ways.

In yet another effort at translating Ghalib, we come across a radical approach in translating this poet.[15] Reproduced below are the samples of translation of the same *sheyr* attempted by diverse hands:

Ishrat-e qatra hai darya mein fana ho jana
Dard ka hud se guzarna hai dawa ho jana

Thomas Fitzsimmons in Aijaz Ahmad's anthology *Ghazals of Ghalib* (1971) has translated it as follows:

Waterbred ecstasy: dying in a stream
Too strong a pain brings its own balm. (26)

W. S. Merwin treats it thus:

The drop dies in the river
Of its joy
Pain goes so far it cures itself. (26)

In a different strain altogether, here is how Ahmed Ali translates:

The joy of every drop
Is to merge into the sea:
When pain exceeds all bounds
It becomes its remedy. (230)

In the first two examples we have two poet-translators trying to appreciate the poet's possible intent in their own ways while in the third example we have a translator trying to work within the limits, yet with enough freedom to interpret. He has, in addition, tried to keep close to the rhythm of the ghazal while it is absent in the former examples. The first rendition is purely creative while the second is a case of misreading the original. It is the joy of the drop to merge with the sea while in the second example the drop does not merge with the sea but dies in the river of its joy. It should be possible to evaluate the last translation as the best of the three translations quoted above. Let us illustrate this diversity of approach by referring to yet another example:

Bazeecha-i-atfaal hai duniya merey aagey
Hota hai shab-o-roze tamasha merey aagey

W. S. Merwin renders it as follows:

To me this world is a children's playground. (163)

David Ray treats it quite differently:

Since I began ogling colors in dime stores
all manners of toys and bubbles

> I have been ecstatic. It is like
> Other habits I learned slowly, then sped up. (164)

Ahmed Ali has translated by finding an intermediary way between the two translations quoted above:

> The world is for me but child's play
> I watch its whirling both day and night. (257)

Here again, in the first two cases we have examples of poor or no translation at all. The first one is too trite and turns a metaphysical proposition into a direct and mundane statement. It does not open to readers the same world of rare combinations as does the source language *sheyr*. The second translation is so removed from the original that one wonders whether it is a translation of the same *sheyr*. The only translation which is close to the source is the third one where the translator has not lost touch with the original and worked with greater catholicity and discipline. It captures the sense and also, to an extent, the music of the *sheyr* and its cumulative impact.

In these translations of Ghalib we find that the level of secondary translation is rather poor. The translators, being unaware of the form of ghazal, its tradition and also of the poet they have translated, fail to conceal the distance they have traversed from the primary experience. They are, therefore, unable to show any proximity with the source material. Their attempt, however, reveals an interesting aspect of literary translations and establishes rather well the impossibility of any poetic translation unless the translator is fully aware of the manifold aspects of the source material. These may, at best, be called free transcreations which might also have been, incidentally, the aim of the translators. In such a case, it may not be quite proper to look for establishing links between the remote ends of the source and the target material. It is only rarely that a creative flash corresponds so well with the original that the translation emerges successful.[16]

The problems in translating the classical Urdu ghazals of Meer and Ghalib may be examined and discussed rather endlessly. Every *sheyr* has its own parameters of excellence and sometimes the *sheyrs* are much more ambiguous than the translator can comprehend. This, at times, might explain the causes of the failure of secondary translation. One could explore many more aspects of this practical art but it is almost certain that one might read a ghazal in translation with a mixed sense of doubt and despair, though a good translation may still catch one unawares, exposing one to two experiences at a time – the delight of reading a good poetic composition and the pleasant shock of recognising something entirely different.

NOTES

1. A ghazal is a collection of at least four independent *sheyrs*; it is written in a single metrical frame and it uses the same rhyme scheme preceding a refrain throughout the composition. The first *sheyr*, called *matla*, has a given scheme of rhyme and refrain in both the lines but the subsequent *sheyrs* do not have the rhyming phrase in the first line.
2. A couplet is a two-line poetic composition which may not follow a given structure or discipline of rhyme, rhythm or line length, as exemplified by the *doha*, whereas a *sheyr* is characterised by a given metrical pattern, a rhyme scheme and a rhythmic design.
3. This is a basic assumption which includes all the written, oral, physical expressions, efforts, behaviours or action of human beings and animals including their reflex actions. Think, for instance, of a child crying or smiling which suggests that there must be something that the child needs to translate/communicate.
4. A broad survey of practical issues involved in translation would show that irrespective of their individual affiliations and intentions, translators have been engaged usually with the problem of translating the specificities of language, the supposed meaning, and the organic form of the source text, apart from various other issues that relate with the peculiarities of a culture that configure a text in a certain time–place framework.
5. John Dryden, in his *Epistles,* writes of "metaphrasing," "paraphrasing", and "imitation". He is of the opinion that imitation may not be translation at all.
6. It reminds one of an old proverb – "faithful ugliness and faithless beauty". It has been often used in the context of literary translation.
7. Ahmed Ali's anthology of classical Urdu poetry is rightly titled as *The Golden Tradition* and its chapters are most aptly named to suit the tradition.

8. Azmatullah Khan, one of the proponents of Modernism in Urdu poetry, said that the ghazal should be throttled to death without hesitation for it has spoiled the taste of the people. Noted Urdu critic Kalimuddin Ahmad rejected it as a semi-savage form of poetry. Well-known poet Firaq Gorakhpuri, himself a major poet of ghazal, made a case for ghazals and treated them as a form where each *sheyr* contributed towards creating a series of climaxes.
9. For a broad survey see C. M. Naim "Traditional Symbolism in the Modern Urdu Ghazal," *Language and Areas Studies* presented to George V. Borbrinskoy, Chicago: University of Chicago, 1967, pp. 105–11; Frances W. Pritchett "Conventions in the Classical Urdu Ghazal," *Journal of South Asian and Middle Eastern Studies III* (Fall, 179), pp. 60–77; Saleem Ahmed "The Ghazal, A Muffler and India," *Annual of Urdu Studies 2* (Chicago, 1982), pp. 53–83; Shamsur Rehman Faruqi "Expression of the Indo-Muslim Mind in the Urdu Ghazal" and Gilani Kamran "The Urdu Ghazal as Material for the Study of Muslim Society in South Asia," *Studies in the Urdu Ghazal and Prose Fiction* (ed.) Mohammad Umar Memon, Madison, South Asian Studies, University of Wisconsin Publication No. 5, pp. 1–23 and 24–43.
10. In the famous ghazal of Ghalib – *Dil-e naadan tujhey huaa kya hai/ Aakhir is dard ki dawaa kya hai* – the rhyming words, *huaa, dawaa, wafaa* are called *qafia* and the recurrent phrase *kya hai* is called *radeef.*
11. There are a number of words, images, metaphors, concepts rooted in myth, history, culture, religion, etc. that are often used in the classical ghazal that are difficult to translate. A random selection of such words would illustrate the point: *ishq, husn, qafas, chaman, bijli, ashian, gul, bulbul, maikhana, paimana, hijr, wasl, garebaan, naz, neyaz, raqeeb, saqi, qasid, qatil, sheikh, bismil, Brahman, zulaikha, majnun, laila, mehmil, ghaznavi, ayaz, khizr, yusuf, yaqub, dhaj, angya,* etc.
12. V. G. Kiernan in his "Preface" to his *Poems of Faiz* (London: George Allen and Unwin, 1971) wrote: "In a line of Urdu spoken in ordinary tones a foreigner will not easily succeed in recognizing the rhythm: conversely a born speaker of Urdu, however, well-read in English, almost always finds English meter, blank verse above all, incomprehensible" (14).
13. Speaking or talking loudly may be offensive in a European cultural context while it might be acceptable elsewhere. The sense of humour and pathos is also widely different as the European is marked by understatement but this may not necessarily be so in other cultural contexts.
14. *Qita* is usually a composition of four lines but it may have many more lines as well. As in a ghazal or *qasida*, it is not required to begin with a *matla*, that is, with strict adherence to *qafia* and *radeef* in the first two lines. It is also unlike the continuous ghazal since all its lines are strung

together to create a sense of continuity with respect to the central idea. It may, however, be read alongside the ghazal to mark as to how far it bears on the ghazal as a distinct form of poetry.

15. See Aijaz Ahmad *Ghazals of Ghalib* (New York: Columbia University Press, 1971). Ahmad selected some of Ghalib's ghazals and gave their literal translations along with the explanatory notes to some American poets who, in turn, produced their own versions of Ghalib. The poets who attempted these versions were W. S. Merwin, Adrienne Rich, William Stafford, David Ray, Thomas Fitzsimmons, Mark Strand and William Hunt.
16. Some of the renderings, for example those by Adrienne Rich in Ahmad's *Ghazals of Ghalib,* are quite precise and poetically appealing, and they also read as perfect poems in their own right.

WORKS CITED

Ahmad, Aijaz, ed. 1971. *Ghazals of Ghalib: Versions from the Urdu.* New York: Columbia University Press.

Ali, Ahmed, trans. 1973. *The golden tradition: An anthology of Urdu poetry.* New York: Columbia University Press.

Matthews, J. D. and C. Shackle, trans. 1972. *An anthology of classical Urdu love lyrics.* London: Oxford University Press.

NINE

Translating Modern Urdu Poetry: Creating Canons in Translation

Translation is a way of dissemination and canon formation which works at multiple levels and in multiple ways. This is, however, subject to certain conditions and constraints. This chapter tries to posit that modern Urdu poetry calls for better dissemination into English since it has become part of a broader literary tradition and moved beyond its linguistic and cultural confines to find a space in larger and secular literary habitats.

This argument has been built and carried forward by tracing the trajectory of modernism in Urdu poetry in terms of impact and response which has imparted a certain character to this poetry over the last one hundred years. This has led to an examination of the problems and prospects of translating modern Urdu poetry into English. In order to substantiate the issues raised, some works of translation have been examined to assess how they try and familiarise the unfamiliar to a set of readers hitherto unaware of this literary heritage, and how in this process canons can possibly be created for a new set of readers who approach other literatures through translation.

All these arguments converge in formulating some propositions that chart out the future trajectory of translation and its dissemination with respect to Urdu poetry which acquired its modernity through translations of English poetry into Urdu earlier, and does so through the translations of Urdu poetry into English now.

This chapter must begin with a question of major consequences: when does a stage come in the history of a literature that the need for translating its rich heritage is more intensely realised than ever before and when does this realisation make way for the emergence and development of translational activities? This question takes in its wake several other questions that include: how does one translate and for whom, how does one choose a text and with what purpose, how does one read a translation and with what tools, and finally, how do all these engagements cumulatively contribute towards the emergence and acceptance of a literary canon within a given language and even beyond that?

Such questions may be asked and answered only at a relatively mature stage of translational activities between two or more languages. Various translations of modern Urdu poetry into English published during the recent past[1] have reached a cross section of readers and are also beginning to receive critical notice. If the number of translations already published, and others in the process of publication are any indication, we should presume that these translations are achieving a certain respectability and that Urdu poetry is making a mark beyond its spatial confines. However, the measures to evaluate these translations and their cumulative impact on an emerging literary culture are not yet available. Before these measures are made available and canons are consequently formed, it appears some more time will have to pass during which translational activities will pick up at a faster pace and a suitable critical climate will emerge. Be that as it may, the present status holds a promise for the future of modern Urdu poetry in English translation.

In view of the fact that very little has been written on Urdu–English translations so far, there is a need for critical initiation in this direction, in order to determine its worth, assess its problems and think over the prospects of canon formation. Let us focus on some of these aspects and discuss the issues related with the emergence of modernism in Urdu poetry, which led to a realisation of the need to translate it in the English language for a wider readership. In order to do so, we will trace the trajectory of modernism in Urdu poetry, then examine the specific issues involved in the translation of this poetry, and finally assess some of the translations, which would lead us to answer the larger question of whether they hold any promise for future engagements concerning the translation of modern Urdu poetry and its evaluation. We begin by tracing the trajectory of modernism in Urdu poetry and relate it to the intellectual climate that made way for the emergence of the modernist canon and its larger dissemination through translation.

TOWARDS MODERNISM: IMPACT AND RESPONSE

The study of modernism in Urdu poetry is, in a larger context, a study of English–Urdu impact and response. The first significant impact on Urdu poets has been that of the Perso-Arabic poetic tradition which may be traced from the late sixteenth century to the late nineteenth century. During these three hundred years, Urdu poetry which originated in the Deccan and flourished in northern India showed signs of the evolution and development of Urdu as a language of literary expression by defining and redefining the figures of speech, the personae of the lover and the beloved both in romantic and spiritual terms, as well as by projecting the real and surreal configurations of history. The advent of modernism in Urdu poetry may be appropriately traced to the late nineteenth century with reference to institutions, individuals, movements and modes of perception that define the post-Perso-Arabic phase of Urdu poetry. The emergence of an intellectual climate thus facilitated the rise of modern poetry.

In order to amicably negotiate with the colonial powers and policies in the late nineteenth century, certain individuals emerged as the forerunners of sociocultural transformations in the Muslim community. They acknowledged the impact of the West and believed that a liberal view towards it could bring consequential changes in their lives. In this regard, a mention has to be made of at least four extremely influential persons that include Syed Ahmed Khan (1817–1898), Mohammad Hussain Azad (1829–1920), Altaf Hussain Hali (1837–1914), and Mohammad Iqbal (1877–1938) who were well disposed towards the West and accepted its impact quite liberally. Syed Ahmad Khan who excelled in many ways as an educationist, reformer, religious commentator, historian, biographer, political visionary and institution-maker, made it possible for the literati of his times to realise the importance of political changes occurring then. He could visualise their impact on society, and think of the possible ways that could be adopted to create a better sociocultural condition for Muslims in particular. Apart from many others, three of his contributions – the creation of Aligarh Scientific Society in 1864, the launching of a journal *Tehzeebul Akhlaq* in 1870 and the establishment of Mohammedan Anglo Oriental College on the pattern of Oxford and Cambridge in 1877 – made way for liberal thinking in the field of education. He emphasised on Western scientific knowledge, promoted translations of Western literatures into Urdu, and reflected on issues relating to culture, society, manners and morals. Although his impact on poetry and poetics was not as direct as that of the others, he created fertile ground for poets and writers to reflect upon the ways that could help them imagine literature as social text.

Interestingly, while Syed Ahmad Khan launched *Tehzeebul Akhlaq* in 1864, Dr Gottlieb William Leitner (1840–1899) launched Anjuman-e Isha'at-e mataltib-e Mufida-i-Punjab, popularly known as Anjuman-e-Punjab in Lahore, the following year. Leitner, a British Orientalist who knew fifty languages, including Turkish and Arabic, authored the history of Islam in Urdu with the help of Maulvi Karimuddin, an Inspector of Schools in Amritsar, and other books on the science of languages, ethnography and the history of Dardistan, apart from travelling the Muslim countries with an adopted name of Abdur Rasheed Sayyah. In a fitting tribute, his son installed a tablet on his grave in London that bears an inscription in Arabic, *Al 'ilmu Khayrum Min al-maali,* which translates into "Knowledge is better than worldly treasures". Leitner was appointed as the first principal of Government College, Lahore, and in launching the Anjuman he aimed particularly at reviving Oriental learning and promoting critical interest in cultural, literary and scientific matters that could be relevant to the times. One of the significant contributions of the Anjuman was to create a condition for the promotion of Urdu poetry that was ameliorative in spirit and disengaged with traditional poetics. Another person to support this cause was Colonel William Rice Moreland Holroyd (1835–1913), the Director of Public Instruction in Punjab. He authored books like *Tashih-ul Kalam, or Hindustani Made Easy,* and *How to Speak and Write English: For the Use of the Natives of India* in an English-Urdu edition. Lord Donald McLeod (1810–1872) who was an ardent advocate of Oriental Studies for Europeans and European Studies for Indians, was born at Fort William in Calcutta, and served in various capacities as a Commissioner of Jalandhar, Judicial Commissioner of Punjab, and Lieutenant Governor of Punjab. He also came forward to help meet the aims pronounced by the Anjuman.

Supported by all of them, two of the canonical figures – Azad and Hali – quite emphatically promoted the idea of new poetry which greatly altered literary taste in the decades to come. On 5 August 1867, Azad made an influential presentation in the Anjuman's mushaira where he underlined his dissatisfaction with the current state of Urdu poetry, terming it essentially romantic and decadent. In his address at another historic mushaira held in the Anjuman under the patronage of Col. Holroyd on 8 May 1874, Azad reiterated his views and emphasised the need to draw upon Western sources in order to write new poetry for a new age. He lamented that the treasures of Western knowledge which were of great contemporary relevance were available to Indians but they were blissfully ignorant of them. He drew an interesting parallel by saying that English could prove to be a major influence, just as Persian did once. This helped him argue that those who could draw upon the English knowledge systems would be better placed to give a new direction to Urdu poetry. In making these points, Azad argued for the great possibility of heralding a new generation of concerned poets and writers who could revisit their poetic diction and write poetry of acute contemporary relevance. He also expressed these views through *Aaftab-e Punjab,* as well as the journal of the Anjuman, and emerged as an ardent advocate of new knowledge as against stereotypical knowledge, and socially relevant poetry as against the decadent poetry of mere emotional upsurge.

The year 1874 proved important in yet another way as Hali, who had met Azad in Lahore for the first time in 1870, recited his poems in the mushaira of the Anjuman and emphasised the need to write poetry on new themes and in a new style. Although Azad and Hali had their own limitations in reaching out to the vast resources of English poetry, they drew upon select sources to enrich their fund of knowledge for its possible application in their own context. Hali's advocacy for *nazm*, as against ghazal, which could express only romantic and decadent ideas, heralded a new age for Urdu poetry. He defined his concept of poetry and poetics in his seminal text *Moqaddam-i-Sher-o-Shairi* (Preface to Poetry) in 1893, where he made a case for "natural poetry" shorn of sentimentality and directed towards reformation, as he believed that poetry had a socio-political role to play in the age of colonialism.

Hali too can be considered as someone who tried to project literature as social text like Syed Ahmed Khan, whose biography he came to write later. Hali also translated some English poems and based some of his own poems on English models. He purposefully engaged with colonial modernity characterised by rail, telegraph, electricity, migration to city, press and western influence. Nation, community and patriotism were his major concerns and he believed that these could best be expressed in *nazm* rather than through the ghazal.

Mohammad Iqbal too negotiated with the Western world view in order to evolve a stance of his own which made him into the poet-philosopher of the East. He was much more intellectually oriented than Azad and Hali and was better equipped to reflect upon the problem of Muslim identity in larger religio-political and spatial contexts. As the West was an important point of reference for him, he also translated from English and American poetry which only underlined his desire to broaden the frontiers of Urdu poetry. His poems included in *Bang-e Dara* show the Western impact on his poetry. In fact, Iqbal stands at a very significant juncture in the history of Urdu poetry since he emerged as the first major modernist who developed serious discourse on nation, community, philosophy and faith.

Among those who accepted the Western impact and helped to create an atmosphere for the writing of new poetry and for the evolution of a new form are Ismail Merathi (1844–1917), Abdul Haleem Sharar (1860–1926), Sir Abdul Qadir (1872–1950), Tajwar Najibabadi (1890–1951), and Azmatullah Khan (1887–1923). In 1867, Ismail Merathi translated four English poems and in the following year he also wrote some of his own poems, based on English models. Deeply appreciative of English poetry as a model for Urdu poetry, he was the first to write two poems that defied the constraints of *qafia* and *radeef*, which later emerged as a movement. Merathi's was the first step towards the discovery of a form that found appeal with later poets. Abdul Haleem Sharar, who was essentially a fiction writer and interested in poetic plays also helped the cause of poems that rejected metrical constraints. He worked towards identifying a modernist style and form through his journal *Dilgudaaz*. He promoted translations from English poetry and it was at his instance that Ali Haider Nazm Tabatabai (1854–1933) translated Thomas Gray's *Elegy Written in a Country Churchyard* as "Gor-e Gharibaan" in 1897, which is considered a major translational feat to this day. He promoted a kind of poem that disregarded metre and called it *mo'arra nazm*. It was subsequently popularised by the name of "blank verse".

Two factors which clearly contributed towards the advent of modernism in Urdu poetry were the translations of a huge number of English poems into Urdu and rejection of the *paaband*, or a metrically and structurally regulated poem in favour of poems that disengaged with formal constraints. This new literary condition made way for the publication of a collection of English poems in Urdu translations called *Armughan-e Firang* by Zamin Kantori at the turn of the century in 1901.

In 1901, a journal called *Makhzan* was launched with an intention to promote translations from English poetry, and also to encourage the writing of Urdu poems on the English model. Reviewing its performance over the past three years, its editor Sir Abdul Qadir wrote in April 1904 that the aim of his journal was to draw upon Western ideas, philosophy and science in order to enrich Urdu poetry thematically and stylistically and to make it more inclusive. He drew satisfaction from the fact that his call was well received and Urdu poetry had already made a move towards incorporating modernist ideas and stylistic innovations in poetry.

While the translators chose the more popular poets like Shakespeare, Wordsworth, Shelley, Keats, Byron and Tennyson to translate into Urdu, they also chose to translate lesser-known poets like Walter Raleigh, Oliver Goldsmith, William Cowper, Walter Scott, H. W. Longfellow, Lord Lytton and several others who, they thought, would bring freshness to Urdu poetry. Sir Abdul Qadir was committed to promoting Western thought and science, and brought English-educated people together on one platform. *Makhzan* paved the way for the advent of modernism in Urdu poetry. Like *Makhzan*, many other journals, *Tanweer-us-Sharq, Deccan Review, Ifada* and *Adeebul 'Asr*, to name a few, also published new kinds of poetry. Tajwar Najibabadi, who edited *Makhzan* in 1917, also expressed his views regarding the need to modernise Urdu poetry and he continued to hold this belief even when he became the editor of *Humayun* in 1921. In January 1923, he published an article "*Urdu Shairi Mein Blank Verse*" (Blank Verse in Urdu Poetry) in *Humayun* in which he made a passionate case in favour of blank verse that had started gaining great favour with new poets. He wrote that the Urdu poets were well aware of the constraints of metrically regulated verse which could be written only at the cost of genuine poetry. His advocacy for blank verse was a definite step towards the modernisation of verse forms.

Najibabadi, another important figure in the movement, also prepared an agenda which included the task of bringing the Urdu language close to common day-to-day Hindi speech, preparing a grammar for commonly understandable Hindi, transferring Hindi metre to Urdu metre, and bringing Urdu closer to the Hindi sensibility. His efforts were supported by Azmatullah Khan who came out in favour of new nazm and, like Hali, took a stand against ghazal, saying that the new age could not afford to continue a romance with this form any further. His views were promoted by the magazine *Humayun* which was Azmatullah Khan's platform for promoting a new literary sensibility.

During 1920–35, many new poets published their work in magazines like *Humayun, Nairang-e Khayal, Paimana, Nigar, Aiwan, Yaadgar, Hazar Dastan, Aalamgeer, Adabi Duniya, Daur-e Jadeed, Shahkar, Urdu* and *Rooman*. All these journals served as sites for poets of new consciousness to come together and create a new agenda and respond to contemporary realities of life and literature. This period saw the publication of a large number of journals, the likes of which subsequent generations could never produce afterwards.

Literary thinkers like Syed Ahmed, Azad, Hali and Iqbal; benefactors like Leitner, Holroyd and McLeod; institutions like Anjuman-e Punjab, and Government College, Lahore; magazines like *Dilgudaz, Makhzan* and *Humayun*; and editors like Abdul Haleem Sharar, Sir Abdul Qadir and Tajwar Najibabadi played the most significant roles in transforming Urdu poetry since the late nineteenth century and making it what it is today. While individuals and institutions created a consciousness to engage with and incorporate contemporary reality into poetry, magazines and other publications altered its very form. The first step towards the revision of form was taken with disengagement from *paaband*, or metrically regulated poem, which adhered to *qafia* and *radeef* and maintained equal number of syllabic units in stanzas of varying length that had been practised since the late sixteenth century. The magazines created a condition for the rejection of *qafia* and *radeef* and made way for *mo'arra nazm*, or blank verse, in the 1930s, which maintained a metrical pattern, equal syllabic numbers and internal rhythm. Modernism in Urdu poetry found new expression in *azad nazm*, or free verse, in the 1950s which declared freedom from fixed syllabic numbers and opted for lines of varying length. The 1970s headed in the direction of *nasri nazm*, or prose poem, which was characterised by complete independence from all kinds of constraints – metrical, syllabic, linguistic, formal and structural. The last two stages where free verse and prose poems found favour with poets and their readers contributed significantly towards the liberation of Urdu poetry from all the established notions of poetry and poetics. It is rather difficult to determine the extent of impact and response with respect to poetry written since the 1950–60s precisely because the boundaries of the home and the world blurred post-1960s and poets extended themselves with larger catholicity to their readers who too belonged to a world of broader and secular affiliations.

TRANSLATING URDU POETRY NOW

Considering what the pioneers of modernism did to launch modernism as a movement in Urdu poetry, it should be possible for us to argue that it was with this intellectual and literary awareness of the new terms of reference for contemporary life and literature that the process of canon formation in modern Urdu poetry started in a major way. This gives us the *locus standi* to say that this literary output, which matured over the various phases of Urdu literary history, deserves to travel beyond its linguistic and cultural confines and reach out to new sets of readers in English and other languages. Just as the translations of English poetry into Urdu played a major role towards inculcating new consciousness among the Urdu poets in the past, the need for translating Urdu poetry into English in the modern times is strong enough to carry forward the Urdu literary canon and place it alongside other canons within and outside a given literary domain. While one may further assert that since the trend of translating Urdu poetry into English has shown a steady progress in recent times, there is a greater scope for its development in future. One may, therefore, argue that the project of translating Urdu poetry into English must hark back and attend to the questions raised earlier regarding the purpose, readership and methodology of translation with greater clarity.

Translating Urdu poetry now is a matter of critically engaging with a variety of issues that concern the choice of poets, texts, forms, genres and traditions. What makes the enterprise of translating modern Urdu poetry more promising today is the fact that this poetry can be profitably read and assessed alongside other modernist representations in the English language. With the passage of time and with the emergence of a secularist literary tradition, modern Urdu poetry is now becoming a part of the larger literary scene in general and the Indian literary scene in particular. Modernism in Urdu poetry, which started at the turn of the twentieth century, opened its frontiers to newer experimentations in form and technique during the 1930s, and got established as a substantial tradition by the mid-1900s. During the past six decades, it has gathered enough strength to join the larger domain of the secular imaginary and earn its readership beyond its linguistic, cultural, and literary confines. As the development of the modernist tradition in Urdu poetry has shown, it is no longer an alien or the "other" tradition; it has become a part of the larger literary traditions both in and outside India, and it is therefore closely comparable with them. With the advancements made towards the construction of an inclusive literary culture representing several sites, modern Urdu poetry has acquired enough potential now to trans-negotiate between more than two cultures, languages, and literary traditions. Added to this is the conducive atmosphere that the publishing houses have created for the dissemination of translations and the construction of a new literary culture during these decades. This has not only validated the literary text but has also authenticated the translator who has remained an isolated and unacknowledged contributor to literary knowledge all along. It may be justifiably argued that translation as a vocation and as a strategy provides a way for meaningful negotiations at the broader levels of life and literature, especially in India where its literatures have stayed together for long but only as strangers to each other.

Let us now refer to some translations in order to analyse their methodology and worth. Two respectable translations – the *True Subject* by Naomi Lazard and *The Rebel's Silhouette* by Agha Shahid Ali – have popularised Faiz Ahmed Faiz among English readers in the recent past. There were several translations of Faiz already available,[2] but these two are important for their individual qualities and for their excellence. Both translators, who are English language poets themselves, share the utmost respect for the poetry of Faiz which is, usually, a pre-requisite for choosing an author to translate. They also show a definite love for the Urdu language even without knowing how to read or write it. The inability to either read or write a language and yet translate from it might sound strange but it does not deter them from entering into the very special world of Faiz.[3] The fact that one of them is a native speaker of English while the other is bilingual and bicultural, also does not impair the quality of their translations, but gives the latter an extra advantage.

Lazard has spoken in detail about the issues involved in translating Faiz, who offered his literal translations to her to work upon and evolve her own versions. She had, in turn, the unique opportunity of consulting him on the role and nature of a particular word or phrase, an image or a metaphor. She contemplated cultural differences and the risk of the subsequent loss of meaning. More importantly, she pondered over the grammatical constructions, and thus tried to find a way of recreating a poem in English with the same spirit, feeling, tone and rhythm which Faiz might have had in mind:

> It must be faithful to the meaning Faiz has given. It must move in his own spirit, with the same feeling and tone. It must have the same music, the same direction, and, above all, it must mean the same thing in English as it means in Urdu. I have learned how crucial it is to find the verb, the active way of saying whatever needs to be said, and then to raise the verb to its highest degree, to find the most active

> verb for the occasion. And I have learned how necessary it is to throw away those crutches, adjectives on the left and the adverbs on the right. (xii)

While reading her translations one discovers that she has rendered many poems exactly as they are in words, images and form but in some others cases she has chosen to be quite liberal with the text and given a creative turn to her translations. It is precisely because translating a word for a word, or an image for an image would have made but little sense in English. As such, she has tried to imbibe the spirit of the original and recast them in a way that might suit the English reader. For her, it was an act of striking a delicate balance between the text as it was in the source language and the one that might appear through the process of translational negotiation. It is to be supposed, therefore, that a translator should bring to his/her target readers only such material that might appeal to their imagination and not be discordant with their habit of reading. This holds good in Lazard's case, as in some of the poems she seems to be interpreting the poems on her own for her readers, yet giving it an organic structure and appeal as a poem should have, in general. In spite of this, one does not notice any serious misrepresentation of thought even when she has sometimes condensed or inverted the poem either partially or fully. She has also introduced her own images and invented her own stanza patterns. Even though her translations are an addition to the rich American body of poetic literature, they may also be appreciated as one poet's compliments to another poet. They may also be read as an effort of one poet developing a kinship with the other poet which, in turn, might make that source language poet relevant to her own people.

Agha Shahid Ali's *The Rebel's Silhouette* is yet another case of passionate engagement on the part of the translator. "Would I be able to make English behave outside its aesthetic habits?" (3) was one of Ali's major concerns in approaching Faiz. However, the cause for his choice of the poet was more impelling: "To have to introduce Faiz's name seemed a terrible insult to a very significant element of my culture" (3). This does not only speak about Ali's love for the poet but also about the need of the literary world that should know Faiz the way it knows Neruda or Hikmet. Ali is aware of the problems that the language employed by Faiz might pose and, through this, of his own bilingual and cultural obligation:

> My particular problem was how to 'pretend' that I was not burdened by a dual loyalty, to ignore that I was negotiating the demands of two cultures, both of which I felt in my bones that I was responding to the sounds of two languages simultaneously.... I finally attacked the poem with no theoretical inhibition, letting each dictate its own agenda. I could always hear the music of the original, and that has been fruitful.... (8–9)

This feel for the music comes not necessarily by being able to read the language but to sense it through cultural catholicity and, added to this, through hearing it sensitively as he does by listening to Begum Akhtar singing the ghazals of Ghalib. This is an advantage he has over Lazard or those who contributed to Aijaz Ahmed's *Ghazals of Ghalib*.[4] Even though his translation process is different from Lazard's, he remarks that he was struck by her excellent work when he chanced to read them in *Kayak*. This instant liking, leading to their meeting, may be attributed to the discovery of an unexpected affinity in matters of literary choice. Ali, with his sharp auditory imagination, recognises the poetry of Faiz as an orchestration of a culture. He apprehends a poem sensually and re-composes them without any reaching after theory. A poem to him is an independent unit of idea, image and music, and he invents a befitting form in the process of re-composing it. He seems to believe what Dudley Fitts articulates thus: "the translation of a poem should be a poem, viable as a poem, and as a poem weighable" (35). In order to do so, he treats the poem at his own will, adding and discounting lines and phrases to suit his own view of the poem.

Both Lazard and Ali approach Faiz in their individual ways as poets; both re-compose the experience of the original poem and its aesthetic design, yet they create different impacts. Lazard, in order to compensate for her ignorance of the Urdu language, pays greater attention to the meaning and architectonics of the poem, while Ali who can see the poem as an image, hear it as music, and identify with it as an experience, approaches it with obvious advantages. In spite of following their own methodologies, both of them behave like natural translators and both offer inspired translations. Considering some of the common poems they have chosen to translate, one may notice their personal choice of phrases, their interpretations, additions, deletions, oddities and also their unprecedented finesse in the translation of Faiz.

Quite different from Lazard and Ali's work, we have the works of M. A. R. Habib and Frances W. Pritchett. Habib's is a case of close adherence to N. M. Rashid's poems brought together in an anthology called *Dissident Voice*. Academically speaking, this is a well-planned anthology. He takes no liberties and manipulates the complex linguistic patterns and symbolic configurations quite properly. Habib is aware of how to make an image specific, heighten the diction, eschew passive expressions and create successful cultural transference. Rashid is one of the most difficult of the modern poets to translate on account of the historical, political and religious speculations that find place in his poetry in complex ways. Habib has researched the roots of the poem, their sources, and their possible meaning. He passes through the poem as one traverses a long distance, step by step, and takes the reader along, as Rashid does in his longer poems, especially.

Frances W. Pritchett's translations of Saqi Farooqi in *A Listening Game* is another case in point. Pritchett considers Farooqi's work to be relatively easier to translate. This is taking a rather simplistic view. Farooqi, like Rashid, is another difficult poet to translate for his individual tone of voice and unusual form. Pritchett has been literal at the cost of Farooqi's sensitivity to words and nuances. At various places, Pritchett has mistaken the source-language text. This has led to loss of meaning and impaired the very basis of the poem. Pritchett has also very closely followed the text like Habib but there are several examples of literalism which make the poems mechanically successful but weak in impact, especially when one compares them with the source language poems.

Bedar Bakht and Kathleen Grant Jaeger's *An Anthology of Modern Urdu Poetry*, Mahmood Jamal's The *Penguin Book of Modern Urdu Poetry* and Rukhsana Ahmed's *We Sinful Women* are collections of modern poets that also merit mention. Bakht and Jaeger's anthology is the first volume of an elaborately planned project to present modern Urdu poets in English. It has a judicious selection of seven major poets. They tell us in the "Translators Note" that these translations "reflect one common purpose: to capture as best as we could the individual tone, mood and spirit of each poem and to go to the heart of what we felt the poet had wished to convey" (n. p.). Even though they claim that they have been careful in choosing suitable counterparts for Urdu metaphors, one notices they also have been literal in doing so. They are, however, artful in managing the rhythm and have done it without being overly deliberate. Quite unlike Lazard and Ali, they are prone to be prosaic and also choose the passive voice at times to render their lines. These have often led to ineffective renditions. There are cases of interpretation also but these interpretations are not comparable to Lazard's and Ali's in merit. Bakht and Jaeger are generally truthful to meaning, form, syntax and stanza pattern but this does not always pay, as is evident from several translations. There are successful attempts, however, at transferring the meaning, as they remain ideally intact, but poetry is not all about meaning, even in translation.

Mahmood Jamal's *The Penguin Book of Modern Urdu Poetry* suffers, first, for its selection of the poets. A translator's job, especially when he presents an anthology, is not just a matter of choosing poets but making a *valid* choice of poets and their poems. In Jamal's anthology many important poets are left out while lesser ones are included. It also defies the principle of reasonable uniformity in the number of poems selected. The introduction and notes on the poets leave much to be desired. Jamal also falls into the snare of verbalism at certain places, though he has been able to impart a rhythmic rendition to the poems. This could have been avoided by focusing more on the contextual meaning, something which Ali takes into account more successfully. Jamal, however, takes the poem independently and apprehends it liberally which often saves a translator from many failings. He has taken liberty with the Urdu stanza scheme and tried to impart an independent form to his work. While Bakht and Jaeger represent their poets faithfully, Jamal takes a little more liberty with them, though far less than Ali does. His compositions are fairly readable, rhythmic and independent.

In the line of notable translations, Rukhsana Ahmad's *We Sinful Women* is the first book of its kind to bring together a group of poets identifiable for certain common qualities. As the pioneering anthology of women poets, all of whom hail from Pakistan alone, it provides an interesting perspective. This book is a step beyond the usual frames of reference and marks the acceptance of this poetry beyond its linguistic and cultural barriers. Reading these poems is like reminding oneself of the common female predicament in the contemporary world. The issue raised earlier concerning the possible translatability of modern Urdu poetry on account of its universality, finds its illustration in this anthology. In spite of being rooted in a specific culture and socio-political set up, these poems have the potential to appeal to an impressive cross section of readers.

Rukhsana Ahmed's work has a certain flair and she succeeds in bringing about these voices together to drive home the validity of socio-political crises concerning the status of women. This anthology, however, suffers on one count: she considers these poets as feminists while some of them do not necessarily fall into this category. Her selection is justifiable only partially as there are several others who eminently qualify to be under this umbrella. Even though this anthology suffers, like Jamal's, on the principle of selection, the translations leave the reader with a considerable sense of satisfaction.

Considering the methods employed by Lazard, Ali, Habib, Pritchett, Bakht and Jaeger, and Jamal and Ahmed, we may arrive at certain broad conclusions. Lazard aims at handing over

Faiz to her readers without playing upon their preconceived notions of a poem. Her effort is directed towards the reader who is as yet alien to Faiz or his poetic tradition but she does not (mis)appropriate her poet for the convenience of her readers. Ali's readers, on the other hand, are not the same as Lazard's but his essential concerns are language, rhythm and form as they would be in the English language. In spite of their individual differences in the modes of understanding and rendering their Faiz, both Lazard and Ali internalise the poems and treat them fairly liberally. This does not happen with the rest. Habib, Pritchett, Bakht and Jaeger, and Jamal are essentially faithful translators even at the cost of being literal/ prosaic at times. While Bakht and Jaeger succeed on account of their selection of poets and poems, Jamal lags behind on this count. Ahmed's work brings other issues into focus. This is an anthology with a perspective, a clear agenda that has acquired popularity in our times irrespective of historical or cultural barriers. A valuable anthology in its aim, it suffers on account of its inadequate representation of poets. Questions as to how the translators negotiate with problems regarding language (vocabulary, diction, syntax) and style (voice, tone, poetic effect, structure, form, etc.) in the source-language text need to be analysed at individual levels with the help of concrete examples. They would, however, yield results pertaining more to the art of translations analysed above and may help us draw vital conclusions with respect to the questions raised at the beginning of this chapter.

Conclusion and Propositions

A critical survey of the select translations of modern Urdu poetry as presented above brings us to an overwhelming question: what do these works do cumulatively? Apart from offering an obvious answer that they bring a set of modernist voices to a community of new readers, one may more pertinently suggest that these works create a condition for the acceptance of a different canon by such readers who are willing to grow inclusively. This implies that these readers are keen on studying and assessing the other literary tradition to their own advantage in order to broaden the frontier of their own tradition and create a secular, democratic, literary republic of multiple traditions and affiliations. This is a possible answer in precise terms to the questions raised at the head of this chapter. This answer may be supplemented further by suggesting that with the growing number of translational engagements during these decades, the stage of an advanced Urdu–English trans-negotiation has already arrived but this can be crossed only with a set of guiding principles that would authenticate the undertaking and make it pursuable.

It may, therefore, be logically argued that the entire project of translating modern Urdu poetry into English needs to be reviewed critically and precisely. To pursue this project, the new translators of modern Urdu poetry would be obliged to spell out their choices with greater clarity than before; they would need to set an agenda and follow a methodology. Even at the risk of sounding prescriptive, it could be suggested that in order to formulate a literary culture and canon, the new translators would be obliged to define their objectives in the following terms:

1. They would be required to identify their poets/texts for translation with complete clinical detachment. The contemporary relevance of the poets/texts so identified may not be over-emphasised.
2. They would do well to plan their work carefully so as to create a perspective on poet/text/tradition in precise terms. With this aim in mind, they would do well in making their choices and selecting to translate (a) individual poets, or (b) a group of poets with certain commonalities, or (c) various trends, movements, genres that point towards the emergence of a tradition, or (d) a historical period, or (e) a thematic unity, or (f) a cluster of experiments in form, style, etc. This would help develop a broader perspective and create a larger sense of thematic and stylistic contexts.
3. They would have to be clear in the choice of their readership as this would determine the nature and worth of their work. They may work to meet the expected requirements of a

readership which may not be necessarily large. This does not, however, negate the possibility of translations catering to the need of more than one variety of readers.

4. They would have to be aware of the right sources of dissemination and be critical in approaching publishing houses that would be careful in selecting, commissioning, editing, publishing, selling and getting works reviewed in proper quarters.
5. They would also be expected to supplement their translations in order to make them accessible and useful. This may be done through providing (a) textual notes, (b) biographical details, (c) bibliographical information, and (d) proper introduction to the author, text, literary milieu, etc. It may be appreciated that a translation remains incomplete unless properly supplemented to evoke the readers' interest in the author and respect for him/her.

In spite of the fact that poetry has taken a back seat in comparison with fiction in our times, and many translations are not always meticulous, Urdu poetry in English translation has garnered a certain degree of appreciation. This translational activity is, however, yet to become a tradition. Its parameters and its canon are yet to be formed. It is looking forward to its translators; it is waiting for fuller intercultural negotiations with other canons.

NOTES

1. Some notable translations published during the recent past include: *An Anthology of Modern Urdu Poetry*, Vol. I ed. and trans. Baidar Bakht and Kathleen Grant Jaeger (Delhi: Educational Publishing House, 1984); *The Penguin Book of Modern Urdu Poetry*, trs. Mahmood Jamal (Harmondsworth: Penguin Books, 1986); *A Listening Game*, trs. Frances W. Pritchett (London: Lokmaya Press, 1987); *The True Subject*, trs. Naomi Lazard (Princeton: Princeton University Press, 1988); *The Dissident Voice*, trs. M. A. R. Habib (Delhi: Oxford University Press, 1991); *The Rebel's Silhouette*, trs. Agha Shahid Ali (Delhi: Oxford University Press, 1992), *We Sinful Women*, trs. Rukhsana Ahmad (New Delhi: Rupa & Co. 1996), *An Anthology of Modern Urdu Poetry*, trs. M. A. R. Habib (New York: Modern Language Association, 2003); *Pakistani Urdu Verse*, trs. Yasmeen Hameed (Karachi: Oxford University Press, 2010).

2. See for example *Poems by Faiz*, trs. V. G. Kiernan (London: George Allen and Unwin, 1971*)*, *Selected Poems of Faiz*, trs. Daud Kamal (Karachi: Pakistan Publishing House, 1984), *The Living Word* (Tunis: Lotus Books, 1987); *A Black Rainbow Over My Homeland* (New Delhi: Afro-Asian Writers Association); *Selected Poems of Faiz Ahmad Faiz*, trs. Shiv K. Kumar (New Delhi: Oxford University Press, 1995).
3. It would be interesting to refer to W. H. Auden's "Foreword" to *Markings* by Hammarskjold (London: Faber and Faber, 1964): "It is no secret that I do not know a single word of Swedish. When I was asked to undertake this translation, I knew I should have to refuse unless I find as a collaborator, someone who (a) was Swedish, (b) knew English well enough to give me a list of alternative words to choose between when the original Swedish word has overtones which are not exactly matchable in English and (c) would be self-effacing enough to be willing to give me a literal word for word translation without trying to do my part of the job as well" (25).
4. Aijaz Ahmad in his *Ghazals of Ghalib* (New York: Columbia University Press, 1971) conducted an interesting experiment in the translation of Ghalib when he gave literal translations of the selected ghazals of Ghalib along with explanatory notes to American poets W. S. Merwin, Adrienne Rich, William Stafford, Thomas Fitzsimmons, Mark Strand and William Hunt. They, in turn, produced their own versions of Ghalib – an exercise which opens up interesting questions about the possibility of translating a poet without knowing the language and its literary culture.

WORKS CITED

Ali, Agha Shahid. 1992. Translating Faiz. In *The rebel's silhouette*. Delhi: Oxford University Press.

——. The rebel's silhouette: Translating Faiz Ahmed Faiz, paper presented at a workshop on Language, Culture and Translation at India International Centre, New Delhi, 31 October–01 November, 1992.

Bakht, Baidar and Kathleen Grant Jaeger. 1984. *An anthology of modern Urdu poetry*, Delhi: Educational Publishing House.

Fitts, Dudley. 1966. The poetic nuance. In *On translation*, ed. Reuben A. Brower. New York: Oxford University Press.

Lazard, Naomi, trans. 2012. *The true subject: Selected poems of Faiz Ahmed Faiz*. Princeton: Princeton University Press.

TEN

Translating a Form: The Possible/Impossible Ghazal in English

Translating a text also implies translating a form which turns the entire exercise of translation into a complex affair. This becomes all the more complicated when it comes to translating a ghazal which is an entirely alien form to non-Arabic/Persian/Urdu readers and their literary history.

This chapter seeks to examine the aspects involved in translating a ghazal into English. The structure and theme of a ghazal is not easily rendered into English; yet the translator must, as far as possible, seek to retain its original form and value.

While discussing these and other related issues, this chapter examines the possibility/impossibility of translating a form from one language and culture to another, marked for their differences rather than their similarities.

An attempt has been made in the following sections to discuss the concept of form in general with a view to contextualise the form of the ghazal in particular. This is followed by an examination of the multiple contexts of ghazal, and finally the English ghazal which has been configured variously by a number of poets writing in the English language from various locations. Since the ghazal has been written widely across continents, several issues concerning text and context have come to the fore which this chapter attempts to examine in some detail with respect to the emergence of a new literary culture of impact and response.

A literary form that largely validates a text can make a significant difference in the final act of reading. It is the form that empowers a literary experience in a language, and it is the form, once again, that that gets translated in yet another language of an approximate or remote variety, with an equal measure of success or otherwise. When used in either of the contexts, it calls on its other constituents: an image, a metaphor, a symbol, a history, a culture, a tone of voice. Form also determines its stance with a language, a diction, a genre, a structure. While all the constituents may be essentially compatible with a cultural, literary or linguistic framework, they may appear incongruous, though justifiably so, in a different tradition, or in a tradition of the "other". It may be derived, therefore, that a writer in a source language operates on one level of primary representation, whereas the translator operates on multiple levels with the form and all its baggage, both in the source and the target languages. In whatever way a literary form may conduct itself (and it does not conduct itself in isolation), it is, in a major way, conditioned by all its constituents together. It may be derived further that the form, along with its constituents, creates its own modes of signification, and helps to locate a culture. This holds much more appropriately in the case of the ghazal[1] which had its origin in Arabic in the seventh century and has since been written in other languages, like Persian and Urdu, with remarkable success.[2]

THE QUESTION OF FORM

It may be easy to recognise a literary form but it is difficult to define it. A general survey of approaches to form would reveal that they broadly fall under two distinct categories. In one category, there are isolated but formal interpretations of form, while in the other there are philosophical interpretations. In the former category, we come across interpretations of form as a genre, a metrical entity, a musical whole, a diagrammatic/structural/hieroglyphic representation, a dramatic construct, a thematic unity, and a textual composition based essentially on a certain kind of language/diction. In the latter category, we have the concept of form as a manner/style of composition, a way of apprehension, an ontological entity, an epistemological creation, a statement about a subject, a dynamic and unifying factor, an organic whole, and an inner principle. There is yet another approach which resolves the dichotomy of substance and form and considers the two together.

All these concepts of form have been formulated over the ages and they have come from various literary/critical traditions. The debate has survived from Aristotle and Plotinus onwards, through Kant, Schiller, Hegel, Croce, and a host of modernists. Interestingly, divergent and sometimes contradictory views have been present during the same time, while at others certain threads of argument have been picked by different hands and argued from different perspectives. For example, when the formalists set a premium on manners in art – the polished word and stylised presentation – and cultivated thereby the "cult of form", they only reiterated Horace and the Parnassians who believed in the perfection of form as the mark of "true" art. Similarly, when A. C. Bradley put forth the idea of "significant form" in his Oxford Inaugural Lecture of 1901 ("Poetry for Poetry's Sake") as a product of the poet's amalgamating sensibility, he only harked back to the Romantic theory of esemplastic and unifying imagination, and to Schlegel (*Lectures on Dramatic Literature,* 1815) who, in turn, possibly drew from Aristotle's ontological concept of the synthesis of form and matter (*Metaphysics*). The German variant of the "organic form" was also a significant presence as "inner form" in Goethe, a concept which echoed in the writings of various other writers belonging to different times and places, like Plotinus, Shaftesbury and Humboldt. In Kant and Schiller, form received an epistemological angle as an act of mind engaged in creating an order. In another direction, Hegel added the sensuous element in the concept of matter, while Croce, in doing away with genres, considered form as an individual entity.

The modernists also continued their engagement with the form and developed both one-to-one and philosophical stances. John Hollander (*Vision and Resonance: The Two Senses of Poetic Form*, 1975) explored the visual and the auditory value of poetic form considering the eye and the ear to be the two worlds where a poem may acquire its definite appeal. Harvey Gross (*Sound and Form in Modern Poetry*, 1964) added yet another aspect to it by referring to the spatial possibilities of a blank sheet of paper which the poet could exploit with his typewriter and allow the page itself to join the composition of the poem. A different concept emerged in W. P. Ker (*Form and Style in Poetry*, 1966) who developed a holistic view of form and considered the poem as form itself and vice versa. He believed that the mind adopts the form in the same way as dance tunes become the rhythm of the dancer. Kenneth Burke (*The Philosophy of Literary Form*, 1941) also considered the subject and the form complimentary to each other and inseparable. The poem mirrored the imaginative vitality of the poet as it created its own design. R. P. Blackmur (*Language as Gesture*, 1952*)* considered form to be a mode of commencement which took into account all the constituents and activities that went into the making of the poem. It was taken as a principle of organisation which enriched the poem with the elements of consistency and crisis. He further distinguished the form, on the one hand, as related to the pursuit of craft and, on the other, as present in the body of the belief (myth, religion, insight). Georg Lukacs (*Soul and Form*, 1911) carried the philosophical interpretation still further when he said that in its profound moment form led to a great moment of silence where all chaos tended to dissolve into tranquillity. This silence, he believed, echoed music, and encompassed all that the work of art stood for.

An analysis of the approaches mentioned briefly above, would show that the question of form has engaged the attention of critics and philosophers in two different ways: one, as an idea, and the other, as a mode of expression. For the poet, in the act of writing, it may not be possible to take it as two distinct ways of coming to terms with himself/herself even while he/she may be able to distinguish between the two.

Poems acquire their own identity, which may also be subjected to a variety of interpretations like the form itself. The metrical form, as in Hopkins, may be distinguished from the musical one, as in Swinburne; just as the visual form, as in Cummings, can be rather easily discerned from the dramatic, as in Donne. It is, however, the organic/essential, inner/significant form that is more demanding, both to create and to theoretically situate. Even though a poem may be appraised for its metrical finesse, musical appeal, visual configuration or as a dramatic entity, it may at best be a partial and formal appraisal. The curious reader would like to enter the poem for its greater value. This would ultimately take him/her to explore its form with all its associations, including the visible and the invisible, the immediate and the remote, the conscious and the unconscious, in terms of the poet's personal, communal and cultural history, his/her myths, metaphors, language and frame of expression.

THE CONTEXT OF GHAZAL

Drawing from the argument above, it may be said that the ghazal has a distinct kind of form; it is a single metrical frame for the whole, a musical entity depending on the same rhyme scheme and a refrain, and a measured structural representation with each line having roughly the same length.[3] The first of the two interconnected lines known as *sheyr* (usually but incorrectly called a "couplet") features a pause in the last phrase of the line. It is then followed by the second line, which extends the idea to its completion or springs a surprise. Composed as a series of thematically independent *sheyrs*, the ghazal does not have the unity of a regular poem; yet it has a characteristic organic unity of its own. There are, however, instances where the *sheyrs* are interrelated and one *sheyr* leads to the other to complete an idea. A ghazal may have four or more such *sheyrs*. Quite often the poet uses his name to address himself or to present a persona to the reader/listener in the last couplet which imparts to the ghazal a sense of completion.

Literally, ghazal means "talking to the lady love". It is traditionally supposed to be the archetypal poetry of romantic love, both for the male and the female. Taking its cue from *nasib*, the erotic prelude to the panegyric (*qasida*) of the Arabic poetry in the late seventh century, it has incorporated complex themes, metaphysical concepts and mystical issues, as also the mundane and the ordinary. During the course of its development in the Arabic-Persian tradition, it has acquired its own features and frames of reference, and has institutionalised certain concepts like union and separation, the censor and the guard of faith, the beloved and the idol, the lover and the rival, the messenger and the confidante, the tavern and the cup bearer, and so on. As a highly concentrated form of expression, it gained in vitality through the language of indirection and understatement. Individual couplets entered the common parlance of the educated who supplemented their serious and mundane discourse by quoting couplets. The secular nature of this art form, its dissemination through the popular press, film songs, the schools of singing and the long sessions of poetry readings (*mushaira*) have helped it reach a cross section of the masses. The *mushaira*, attended by thousands of poetry lovers, held in the late evenings as a matter of tradition and carried over till the early hours of the morning, is a cultural institution of long standing; it is a certain index of social behaviour, and of the taste and tenor of a people. It thrives on the stylised recitation/singing of ghazals where poets of various hues receive an instant response, in the form of praise or censure from a lively and vocal audience. Its appeal is mysterious and the listeners are sometimes so enthusiastically involved that they repeat the first line after the poet, and sometimes they are so enraptured that the more sensitive of them chant the next line in full, or in part, on listening to the very first line, as if in instant recognition of a poetic truth. This turns the couplet into an epigrammatic expression which is retained in the listener's memory and is evoked later in the future – an appropriate reminder that art imitates life.

Even though the ghazal has been immensely popular with poets and readers in the source language, it has also received contradictory responses. There is a view that it is an offence against the innocent and the organised mind/imagination on account of its lacking in unity of subject through the entire composition. Major poets and critics like Altaf Hussain Hali, Azmatullah Khan, Josh Malihabadi, Kalimuddin Ahmad, and Zoe Ansari were much too harsh in their views about the ghazal. They believed that since there was no continuity of thought in a ghazal, there was no possibility for it to be considered a respectable form of poetry. While Azmatullah Khan pronounced a death knell for the ghazal and suggested that one should "throttle it without hesitation",[4] Kalimuddin Ahmed pronounced it to be a "semi savage form of poetry"[5]. Others defended its worth for what the purists considered its failings. They attributed to it the highest status among the forms of poetry. While Rashid Ahmad Siddiqui made a clear case for the ghazal and attributed to it a prominent place among the forms of poetry by calling it the "prestige of Urdu poetry",[6] Firaq Gorakhpuri defined it as a "series of climaxes"[7] where each couplet is both complete unto itself and a part of the whole poem. In this manner, a couplet is a complete poem unto itself and it tests the imaginative skills of the poets as also that of the reader. The fact that some of the best poets have expressed themselves through the ghazal goes to establish its worth. As a unique form of poetic expression, the ghazal reflects a certain unity of mood in spite of the couplets representing independent experiences. It is a process of creating miniatures on a single canvas and reconciling the binaries and the dualities of existence. Apart from representing the human condition, it represents a cultural condition. It shows the basic urge to connect and to locate the Eastern concept of truth within the truth. It presupposes and subscribes to the "semi-savage" in order to create a semblance of a supposed reality. The ghazal has traversed a long way, both in time and space, and has acquired its own terms of reference in various languages. The modern avatar of this art form has obliterated the distinction between the poetic and the non-poetic, the formal and the non-formal, and gone beyond the spatial confines of the East.

THE GHAZAL IN ENGLISH

The ghazal, as a literary form to which there is no other approximate form in any of the literatures, has long elicited the attention of poets writing in languages as diverse as German, French, Spanish and English. That Friedrich Schlegel (1722–1829), Johann Wolfgang Goethe (1749–1832), Friedrich Rückert (1788–1866) and Von Platen (1796–1835) have written ghazals is only too well known.[8] This practice continued in several languages, sometimes with regularity, and sometimes intermittently. What could be the reason for adopting this "alien" form, one may wonder. It could be the novelty of the form, or the great appeal of its master practitioners, or even the lure of the Orient. Quite possibly, the wish to outgrow the confines of one's literary tradition and domesticate the other, or even the literary curiosity to dabble with a new form might have been the other reason for attraction towards this form. The grounds for appeal might also vary from poet to poet, age to age, and language to language, depending on the literary climate, possibilities of acceptance and revisions in canonical formulations. The practice of writing ghazals continues even today in many more languages, and with greater confidence. The number of poets writing ghazals in the English language, especially in North America, is increasing by the day and it appears that it may soon assume the proportions of a new literary tradition.

There is an important question a practitioner of this form may need to answer: Can the ghazal be written in the same formal manner as it is, or has been written in the languages of its origin and development? The question, for the poet, as for us, is not easy to answer in clear terms of "yes" or "no". It could be said that the ghazal belongs to a different/alien culture for the poet in English and it has its own formal constraints. Furthermore, it does not have an approximate model in the English, or any of the European languages, nor does it have an oral–aural system close to English. These problems surely need the poet's attention but they do not deter him/her altogether from making an attempt. The poet may make improvisations in his/her theory and practice, try and approximate to the source models, and re-invent the form just as the haiku was reinvented in the English language.

Considering the volumes of ghazals written during the recent past, one comes across two categories of its practitioners. On the one hand, poets like Adrienne Rich, Judith Wright, Jim Harrison, John Thompson, D. G. Jones, Phyllis Webb, Douglas Barbour, Max Platter, adhere to the form of the couplet, one often independent of the other, but their ghazals do not follow the established norms of the form. They bring to use their own understanding of the form and write their own versions of the ghazal which are different from the original. On the other hand, we have a collection of a hundred and nine poets in a volume *Ravishing DisUnities: Real Ghazals in English* (2000) edited by Agha Shahid Ali. These poets follow the discipline of the form to a great extent and try to approximate to the original models for formal equivalence. The two categories do not bear upon one another, as they offer studies in contrast between considered freedom and restricted license.

In the former category of poets, a remarkable mention is that of the American poet Adrienne Rich who was introduced to Ghalib by Aijaz Ahmad when he edited *Ghazals of Ghalib*[9] and brought together seven American poets to translate Ghalib to mark the centenary celebrations of the poet in 1968. As she rendered Ghalib in her own way for this volume, she developed an immense liking for the form which she practised independently later on as well. She included her ghazals in *Leaflets* (1969) as "Homage to Ghalib" and subsequently in *The Will to Change* (1971) as "The Blue Ghazals". The seventeen ghazals included in *Leaflets* and nine in *The Will to Change* were written in a short period of time and in quick succession which explained to a great extent her new-found affair with a new mode of expression. In her *Collected Early Poems* (1993), she acknowledged her debt and wrote about her ghazal:

> My ghazals are personal and public, American and Twentieth Century; but they owe much to the presence of Ghalib in my mind: a poet, self-educated and profoundly learned who owned no property and borrowed his books, writing in an age of political and cultural breakup. (426)

Drawing upon what Rich wrote about her ghazal, David Caplan has concluded that "Rich wants poetic forms to prevent an 'equivalent' to the time's disorder. The ghazal complicates this task and makes it possible.... She employs it as a motif, a non-Western gesture, not a prosody whose requirements she must fulfil" (49). Considering her ghazal from this angle, it would be proper to evaluate them in relation to the larger socio-political predicament of the American people. I would argue that she is able to achieve the intense precision that is required in a ghazal, couplet after couplet, and this is what distinguishes a ghazal from all other forms of poetry. She creates in them an inner rhythm even while she works through free association of images in order to map out the contemporary and the topical. She thus imparts a certain contemporary relevance and identity to her ghazal which is markedly different from the ghazals of other practitioners. A ghazal from *Leaflets*, included in *Collected Early Poems* may be read along these lines:

> If these are letters, they will have to be misread
> If scribblings on a wall, they must tangle with all the others.
>
> Fuck reds Black Power Angel loves Rosita
> —and a transistor radio answer in Spanish: Night must fall.
>
> Prisoners, soldiers, crouching as, writing,
> explaining the unforgivable to a wife, a mother, a lover.
>
> Those faces are lured and some have turned away
> to which I used to address myself so hotly.
>
> How is it, Ghalib, that your grief resurrected in pieces,
> has found its way to this room from your dark house in Delhi?

When they read this poem of mine, they are translators.
Every existence speaks a language of its own. (353)

In this ghazal, as in others, the couplets stand as units of ideas and are independent of the other. Further, the ghazals comprising six couplets are untitled as the form demands and they take a leap from one miniature to another. Written in free verse, they represent a mode of apprehension, characteristic of her other poetry. The free movement of and between the lines suggests that she seems to enjoy this liberty in writing a new kind of text. This new text affords her an opportunity to speak to herself as also to address the existential dilemma she faces in contemporary life. Unlike in her poems, she assigns a new role to language in her ghazals where the connectives and the strains of an impending narrative are missing. Her tone is direct and more intimate. In "languaging" her experience, as she would call it, she takes others along with her – the reader, the contemporary writer, and the past personage – in order to create a condition for the viability and acceptance of her text.

A little removed from the ghazals of Rich are those of the Australian poet Judith Wright. The following seven couplets of a ghazal entitled "Rockpool" is an example of the continuous ghazal where one couplet enters the domain of the other and extends the idea in yet another dimension:

My generation is dying after long lives
swung from war to depression to war to fatness.

I watch the claws in the rockpool, the scuttle, the crouch—
green humps, the biggest barnacled, eaten by sea worms.

In comes the biggest wave, the irresistible
clean wash and back swirl. Where have the dead gone?

At night on the beach the galaxy looks like a grin
Entropy has unbraided Bernice's hair.

We've brought on our cancers, one with the world
I hang on the rockpool's edge, its wild embroideries:

> Admire it, pour on it, this, the devouring and mating,
> ridges of coloured tracery, occupants, all the living.
>
> The stretching of toothed claws to food, the breeding
> on the ocean's edge. 'Accept it? Gad, madam, you had better'. (419)

All of Wright's twelve ghazals put together under the title "Shadow of Fire" in *Phantom Dwelling* (1985) and reprinted in her *Collected Poems* may also be read as regular poems where couplets draw upon different perspectives, and all of them, taken together, create a multidimensional picture of a larger size. She takes a freer swing compared with Rich in this respect. Her ghazals do not have a certain beginning or end; they are like snatches from the heart of the matter. As such, "Rockpool" reflects divergent images of a nervous living, warfare, birth, growth, decay, and the inevitability of the human fate. It swings back and forth in history and religion while the rockpool, as a site, remains a silent witness to all the happenings, as if holding a mirror to life on the face of its water. What distinguishes her ghazal from a regular poem is the potential of each couplet to stand on its own even with or without other couplet(s).

Among several poets writing this variety of the ghazal in Canada, remarkably divergent voices and modes of perception may be seen in Jim Harrison, John Thomson, Phyllis Webb and Douglas Barbour. Jim Harrison, who published sixty-five of his ghazals in *Outlyer and Ghazals* (1971), put forth his creative logic in his "Notes on the Ghazal" as follows:

> I have not adhered to the strictness of metrics and structure of the ancient practitioners, with the exception of using a minimum of five couplets. The couplets are not related by reason or logic and their only continuity is made by a metaphorical jump. Ghazals are essentially lyrics and I have worked with whatever aspect of our life now that seemed to want to enter my field of vision. Crude, holy, natural, political. Sexual. After several years spent with longer forms I've tried to regain some of the spontaneity of the dance,

> the song unencumbered by any philosophical apparatus, faithful only to its own music. (26)

Harrison's ghazals, being one of the first important experiments in this form in Canada, are essentially his attempts at discovering the possibility of expressing an idea within the limits of a two-line composition. He was aware of the rich tradition of this form in Arabic, Persian and other world languages, apart from the strides made in this direction by fellow poet, Adrienne Rich, whose work he considered to be successful. Like Rich, he exploited the immense space offered by the ghazal for writing the contemporary condition. He also found it to be a mode of resorting to the queer, the unusual and the personal:

> Girl-of-my-dreams if you'll be mine I'll give up poetry
> and be your index finger, lapdog, donkey, obvious unicorn.
> (30)
>
> That girl was rended by the rapist. I'll send her a healing
> sonnet in heaven. Forgive us, Forgive us, Forgive us. (31)
>
> I insist on a one-to-one relationship with nature.
> If Thursday I'm a frog it will have to be my business. (39)
>
> I'm afraid nothing can be helped and all letters must be
> returned unopened. Poetry must die so poems will live
> again. (42)
>
> A scenario: I'm the star, Lauren, Faye, Ali, little stars,
> we tour America in a '59 Dodge, they read my smoldering
> poems (47)
>
> I was lucky enough to have invented a liquid heart
> by drinking a full gallon of DNA stolen from a lab. (57)

These couplets chosen from various ghazals of Harrison show his felicity with the couplet form and his ability to create a condition within the limits of the two lines. He attached considerable importance to form, which he thought, like many other poets and theoreticians, is conditioned by the content. In his "Notes", referred to above, he said that "form must be an organic revelation of content or the poem, however otherwise lively, will strike us false or merely tricky, an exercise in wit, crochet, pale embroidery" (26). With this awareness of how the content and the form join themselves, Harrison could write a new kind of poetry which inflamed the imagination of several other Canadian poets.

John Thompson, who did not live long enough to see the acceptance of his collection of carefully crafted thirty-eight ghazals in *Stilt Jack* (1978), had a great influence on two of his contemporaries. Phyllis Webb acknowledged his worth and attempted her own versions of the ghazal later, while Peter Sanger showed a close approximation with the poet in *Sea Run: Notes on John Thompson's Stilt Jack* (1986). Like other poets, Thompson also knew well of the delicacies of this poetic form and the demands it made on the poet. Introducing the ghazal to his readers in *Stilt Jack*, he showed his perception of this form when he discovered the link between couplets through their "tone" and "nuances" and found that the ghazal has no "palpable intention upon the reader", and that "It breaks, it has to be listened to as a song: its order is clandestine". He explains the nuances of this form and his own practice further:

> My own interest in the form lies in the freedom it allows—the escape, even from lyric 'unity'. These are not, I think, surrealist, free association poems. They are poems of careful construction performing controlled progression.
>
> There is, it seems to me, in the ghazal, something of the essence of poetry: not the relinquishing of the rational, not the abuse of order, not the praise of the private hallucination.
>
> The ghazal allows the imagination to move by its own nature: discovering an alien design, illogical and without sense—a chart of the disorderly, against false reason and tacking together of poor narratives. It is the poem of contrasts, dreams, astonishing leaps. The ghazal has been called 'drunken and amatory' and I think it is. (5)

Thompson seems to have discovered the spirit of the ghazal for himself in the way he voices it with a certain sense of confidence and belonging. The lines quoted above, read along with his ghazals confirm that he is keen on asserting both his poetics and his faith. On the one hand, he refers to the canonical authors, and on the other to the Bible and the God of his own making. The tradition of the ghazal also finds its way through his creative itinerary. Poetry was a way of belonging for him, a desperate search for a mode of sustenance. A few examples would show as much:

> I want to wake up with God's shadow
> across me: I'm a poet, not a fool. (18)
>
> Yeats. Yeats. Yeats. Yeats. Yeats. Yeats. Yeats.
> Why wouldn't the man shut up? (19)
>
> I think I hear the sound of my own grief:
> I'm wrong: just someone playing a piano; just. (24)
>
> Celebrate. Celebrate. Celebrate.
> Death cannot celebrate thee. (27)
>
> I know how small a poem can be:
> The point on a fish hook. (31)

Thompson developed a tone that has an element of desperation but also a note of certainty about it. This is the quality which distinguishes him largely from his contemporaries, particularly those who attempted writing ghazals after him. While reviewing Sanger's *Sea Run: Notes on John Thompson's Stilt Jack* in *Canadian Literature*, Webb appropriately wrote that Thompson was writing "his last will and testament" in these ghazals (156).

Phyllis Webb published her thirteen "anti ghazals" in *Sunday Water* (1982) tending towards, as she wrote in the preface, "the particular, the local, the dialectical and private". She calls them "anti ghazals" as there are "a few little jokes" although at the end, and she writes further, "love returns to sit on her throne of 'accidie,' a mystical power intrudes, birds sing, a star is plucked, and the Third Eye, opal, opens". The very title "anti Ghazals" explains her desire for seeking a subversive way of testing whether she could express her experiences in a new form. Her next collection of ghazals, *Water and Light* (1984), like the earlier one, is dedicated to Michael Ondaatje who introduced her to this new form of poetry. One may, however, mark rather easily that she is also deeply influenced by John Thompson and Ghalib. Douglas Barbour, a poet of "breath ghazal", however, in his essay on the ghazals of Webb and Thompson entitled "Ghazals in the North" included in *Lyric/ Anti Lyric* says that "Phyllis Webb has approached the ghazal tradition more as bricoleur than disciple" (108). He considers both Thompson and Webb together and asserts that one represents male romanticism and the other, female subversion. He values Thompson's ghazals for how they "transform a terribly strict and conventional form in Urdu into an open and questing one in English" (105). He considers *Stilt Jack* to be a "demanding and difficult book, one which grows richer with every reading...Chiaroscuro, richly textured, it remains one of the major texts of the seventies". (108). He views Webb's ghazals as "even more subversive of both traditional (and phallogocentric) lyricism of the essentially masculine stance of the conventional ghazal of Hafiz and Ghalib" (104). It appears that the romance of the ghazal for these poets lies in subverting the form and the traditional content and assigning a new role to it in a new context. This subversion, as it keeps to the tone and tenor of Webb's poetry, is more a matter of exploiting the possibilities of language and the form while finding expression for a new set of experiences. Two couplets from the first anti ghazal in *Sunday Water* are fairly representative of this condition:

> Four or five couplets trying to dance
> into Persia, who dances in Persia now?
>
> A magic carpet, a prayer mat, red.
> A knocked off head of somebody on his broken knees.
> (n. p.)

These two compositions amply illustrate her effort at negotiating with an experience of the other world. It tells, on the one hand, of how she views this new form in a different context, and on the other how this may possibly incorporate the burden of yet another kind of creative constraints. It would be interesting to note that "his" in the second line of the last couplet was changed to "her" when this anti ghazal reappeared in *Water and Light*. Webb is acutely conscious of her craft, as also of her need, to find a voice marked by female concern. This concern finds expression in several other ghazals of *Water and Light*:

> My dear ladies, birds of a feather,
> the astounding patience of your hatching. (26)
>
> I am apocryphal and received.
> I live now and in time past (35)
>
> The hand moved along the wall.
> I was able to read, that's all. (39)
>
> History and secrecy—that's what I said
> As member of a panel whose topic was (55)
>
> Why poetry? And why not, I asked,
> My right brain brimming sedition. (55)

Webb's ghazals are most often continuous as the idea in one couplet extends into another even though each couplet brings it full circle. In a way, she both completes and extends an experience beyond the confines of the two lines of a couplet, which underlines the possibility of writing a text variously. Susan Glickman appreciates Webb's discovery of "a kind of aesthetic androgyny in the ghazal, equivalent to its traditional ambiguity as to the gender of its subjects" (56). It may be justifiably argued that her ghazals are the extensions of her work as a poet with subjects and techniques she has been working with for long, both as an individual and an artist. Glickman acknowledges this quality that by "borrowing a structure for her poems from another culture, Webb has been able to perform an act of translation by which finding becomes making" and "shape as superinduced" becomes "form as proceeding" (59). Her ghazals, as individual poems, show her concern with the form and also as to how they emerge from the roots of her own literary heritage. Forms undergo radical transformation when treated by a "foreign" (if not "alien") hand; they carry a certain feel of the original even while they acquire a new identity.

Douglas Barbour tests the limits of sound and form in his poetry. Barbour's ghazals seek their strength from the modulations of breath as he uses them now like a counter of expression – now a word, now a metaphor, now a symbol. He creates a new code of writing by bringing language, landscape and body in constant collusion with one another. With this entirely new mode of apprehension, Barbour adds yet another facet to the fast emerging body of the North American ghazal. Barbour is continuously engaged with writing an unfinished text which extends from poem to poem and from anthology to anthology. Reading through his work, it appears that he has been engaged with discovering a form that may go well with his ghazals. The origins of this may be seen in his *Songbook* (1973) which comes very close to the expression he finally appropriates in writing his ghazals. In an unpublished interview with this author, Barbour says, "Indeed, a very particular sound, for example, caught my imagination," he says while defining his work, "when I thought of ghazals, the sound of breathing itself. There was a form and there was a breath. And there appeared what I call the breath ghazals."[10] Barbour, like Rich and Webb, is excited by the discovery of immense space that a couplet may offer. He is also one of those whose couplets become thematically connected as the composition progresses from one stage to another. In this transgression of the original form, he also realises that being an "immigrant form, it is 'alien' but very exciting."[11] The couplets of his ghazal, may be read alongside those of others, like Douglas Lochhead's (which Barbour considers ghazal-like poems) in *Tiger in the Skull* (1986), or Max Plater's ghazals in *Rain on the Mountains* as they fall in a category where one couplet is, quite often, thematically related to the other. The impulse behind these compositions is the same even though the format is different from that of the traditional ghazal but read closely, Barbour's ghazals seem to acquire their definite identity in the way he breathes his couplets and brings them closer to performance. He published eight of his breath ghazals in his *Visible Visions*

(1984), which brings about a new poetics. One of the breath ghazals may be considered in this context:

> poised on the knife edge between this line and the next
> the pulse in the base of my thumb, thumping
>
> something spills across the plate
> if you hear me, do you hear me bleed
>
> now that sound, ha huh
> if you pay attention you owe at ease
>
> so we pass thru that barrier too
> from opposite ends of the table eat (153)

Keeping in mind the fact that Barbour is a performance poet, reading these couplets, alongside those quoted above, one is immediately struck by the difference Barbour creates by making use of his breath, modulating his voice, and creating a dramatic condition of great immediacy and oneness with the reader. His breath ghazals, like his other poems, may be read as formal sequences, as he seems to be engaged in writing an unending long poem – poem after poem and breath after breath. While explaining the term "breath ghazal" and the method he adopts in writing it, he says: "I came up with the term because I was using the actual act of breathing as part of the poem's structure. The idea of doing that came to me as a way of interrupting straightforward lyric expression."[12] It would be rewarding to study it in the background of his association with the sound poetry he co-produced with fellow poet Stephen Scobie, collected on a CD called *Carnivocal* (1999). Barbour's poetry, along with his unique ghazals, may also be read with great profit in terms of their performative value: this is one quality that sharply distinguishes him from all other poets practising this form today.

Examining these ghazals, one realises that all these poets enjoy the freedom of space as they are strongly moved by a desire and need to outgrow the constraints of the regular and traditional English poem. More than mere literary curiosity, the ghazal is a way of writing a new code which assumes significant proportions in its acceptance by a liberal readership looking for newer modes of expression. The ghazals of a hundred and nine poets in *Ravishing DisUnities: Real Ghazals in English*, however, fall in a different category where, sometimes, very close proximity with the canonical form of the ghazal and, at others, a semblance, or an imitation of it has been consciously achieved by the poets. Diane Ackerman, John Hollander, W. S. Merwin, William Matthews, Paul Muldoon, and Maxine Kumin, along with every other poet in the collection, make an effort at negotiating with the intricacies, challenges and opportunities the form of the ghazal offers to them. There is no doubt that these ghazals, as opposed to those quoted earlier, are genuine efforts at following the norms of the form as also at appropriating a new-found imaginative space. This is precisely what makes them worthy of serious critical attention. One can not deny the value of the earlier examples but one may only say that those are part-efforts at writing a ghazal whereas these adhere largely to the discipline of a given form. The question that looms large is whether an "alien" form may reformulate itself strictly according to the norms of the original in the hands of such poets who have not had the chance to know its intricacies directly. The question is a major one to answer. In his introduction to *Ravishing DisUnities*, Ali is quite categorical in making this distinction: "Those claiming to write ghazals in English (usually American poets) had got it quite wrong, far from the letter and farther from the spirit.... For those brought up on some Islamic literary tradition, especially the Persian and Urdu ghazal, to have many of these arbitrary near surrealistic exercises in free verse pass for ghazals was—is—at best amusing" (1). Ali is making a case for the ghazal that he has grown up with and finds it difficult to negotiate with its new avatar. He finds the free verse ghazal "a contradiction in terms" and discovers a logical parallel for making this point that a sestina would not really be a sestina "without those six words" (2). He further quotes from a letter to him by Kelly Le Fave, one of the contributors to this collection, who is moved by "the inventive delight of the momentary" and the opportunity and ability of the poet to unleash his/her "mercurial powers" (4) even while maintaining the norms of the form like regular syllables, absence of enjambment, the individual identity of couplets, and the rhyme and refrain. He strengthens his argument by finding in the ghazal a way for the English poets who would use full rhymes and "find a formal way, a 'legal' way out, to cultivate a profound respect for desperation—something that American poetry has not altogether lost" (11). The form, he believes, liberates and surprises the poet rather than make way for arbitrariness. It is more than a matter of structural formalism; it is a way of discovering the possibilities the form may allow. Considering neo-surrealist ghazal writing in America, interacting with fellow poets, learning from his own experience of writing a ghazal, and sharing a point about syllabic length with John Hollander, he formulates a prescription, without sounding pretentious, for the practitioners of ghazal: "As a result, my suggestion to those attempting ghazals in English is that they create some system whereby some basic—but not debilitating—consistency in line lengths (inclusive of *qafia* and *radeef*) is established" (8). Ali has been clearly engaged with the problem of maintaining a formal order and his collection is a way of making this point in a certain manner. In the afterword "Ideas of Order in an Afterword", included in *Ravishing DisUnities*, Sara Suleri Goodyear liberates the form from any of its attendant constraints and hints at the way it may achieve its excellence without boundaries: "Ideas of order suggest that there is no home in which form can locate its authenticity, that it must travel and recreate its boundaries, however fragile they may be" (Ali 2000, 180–81). A reading through the collection does not, however, underline the fragility of the form discovered by the practitioners of what Ali calls the "real" ghazals; it marks, instead, its strength. This may well be noticed in Hollander who has defined in a ghazal of his own (quoted in full in note 3). Examples of couplets that observe the discipline of *qafia* and *radeef*, *matla* and *maqta* may be seen in the following compositions included in *Ravishing DisUnities*:

> Clouds of mistletoe hang in the polars, when can't survive.
> Still, decorated with ruin, they enchant our lives.

> In stone castles, cold's steel roars straight up the spine,
> and, shivering to the core, we decant our lives. (Diane Ackerman: 17)
>
> Each syllable unwinds its shy request in time.
> Speak slowly, show me what it means to rest in time.
>
> So, Kelly's really gone? Does anyone know where?
> Third hand. I heard it said she would go West, in time.
> (Kelly Le Fave: 100)
>
> How did someone come at last to the word for patience
> and know that it was the right word for patience
>
> the sounds had come such a distance from the will to give pain
> which that person kept like a word for patience (W. S. Merwin: 114)
>
> It was Aisling who first soft-talked my penis-tips between her legs
> while teasing open that Velcro-strip between her legs.
>
> Again and again that winter I made a bee-line for Ita
> For the sugar-water sip between her lips. (Paul Muldoon: 117)

All these texts may be read as meta-texts of a culture and the meta-forms of a form that is/was alien for the poets. These poets do not translate a language; they translate a form, making adjustments with the markings of their sensibility and that of the source forms. These may also be read as examples of literary hybridisation, as example of the "centre" drawing upon the resources of the "other". This entire phenomenon underlines a process of literary cross-breeding, a liberal way of enriching on the part of the culture of reference which English had become for the other world that drew upon it. While reading these ghazals it would not be entirely correct to expect exact formal equivalence with the original form of the ghazal, for differences are inevitable. The ghazal in English cannot be the same as it is in Arabic/Persian tradition; it can only be a different ghazal, a declaration of a different creative stance, a different poetics, a way of broadening the frontiers of the original. When revisionist formulations are made, variations are bound to occur and these variations may then bring about a new set of literary standards. It would be wrong, in fact, to judge the ghazal in English according to the poetics of the source form and language. The English reader, unaware of the original form and the language in which it has evolved, is likely to discover a form that does not correspond to the original, as the specialist of that literary tradition will tell. The theoreticians may be right in claiming that translating a form/text may amount to creating another form/text, but this distance has been lessened a great deal by the poets' deep engagement with ghazals, as the examples quoted show. The form of the ghazal has not turned archaic (no form does if it can persevere) as this form has been variously appropriated by the poets of the source languages through whom the ghazal has come to the English poets. It remains a virile form, both on account of its formal strength and the capacity to accommodate all possible human aspirations.

The constituents of the original form – the image, metaphor, symbol; history, culture and tone of voice – undergo a definite transformation of character when used by the poets referred to above on account of their being rooted in a different literary tradition and culture. Their cultural, linguistic and literary framework bear upon their perception of this form only too clearly. In their attempts at writing the ghazal, they wish to authenticate the form in their own language by evolving their own form. In doing so, they must maintain the formal structure, as well as the spirit of the original framework, as far as possible. It is a process of engaging with a new challenge, and of disengaging with the habits of one's own poetic principles. It is a self-imposed obligation of creating a new textual order and of institutionalising a concept by resisting the order of the regular English poem which often has a beginning, a middle and an end. The ghazal has none of these constraints as the poet is engaged in a non-finishing project, an ever-moving composition – couplet after couplet, ghazal after ghazal. It would be futile, indeed unreasonable, to expect a reproduction of the original form either in letter or in spirit. The poets writing ghazals in English can only write the other ghazal, create the other form, and achieve the other kind of excellence. Instead of rejecting, or accepting, either of the two modes of expression – of considered freedom and restricted license – rather categorically, one may appreciate the effort on the part of the poets trying to create a new order of composition, and also the readership that liberally accepts the offer of the possible/impossible ghazal in English.

NOTES

1. It has been variously spelt over a period of time as "ghazel", "ghasel", "ghuzzle," and "ghazal". It is currently spelt as "ghazal".
2. For a broader survey of the ghazal, especially in Urdu, see Carla Petievich, *Assembly of Rivals: Delhi, Lucknow and the Urdu Ghazal*, New Delhi: Manohar Publications, 1992; C. M. Naim, "Traditional Symbolism in Modern Urdu Ghazal," *Language and Area Studies*, Chicago: University of Chicago, 1967, 105–11; Frances W. Pritchett, "Conventions in the Classical Urdu Ghazal," *Journal of South Asian and Middle Eastern Studies III 1*, Fall, 1979, 60–77; "Orient Pearls Unstrung: The Quest for Unity in the Ghazal," *Edibiyat* 4, 1993, 119–35; Saleem Ahmad, "The Ghazal, Muffler and India," *Annual of Urdu Studies* #2, 1982, 53–83; Shamsur Rehman Faruqui, "Expression of the Indo-Muslim Mind in the Urdu Ghazal" and Gilani Kamran, "The Urdu ghazal as a Material for the Study of Muslim Society in South Asia," *Studies in the Urdu Ghazal and Prose Fiction* (ed.) Mohammad Umar Memon, South Asian Studies, University of Wisconsin Publication No. 5, 1–23 and 24–43.
3. The ghazal is a strict metrical composition of a minimum of four couplets. There are no enjambments between the couplets but each couplet employs the same rhyme scheme preceding a refrain. The first couplet has this scheme in both the lines but the subsequent couplets do not have the rhyming phrase in the first line. The rhyming words, as in the following couplets of Ghalib (*hua, dawa, wafa …*) are called *qafia* and the refrain (*kya hai, kya hai, kya hai …*) is called *radeef.* The lines of the couplet maintain the same length which gives the ghazal its visual consistency. The last couplet often bears the signature of the poet, with his nom de plume included in any of the two lines. Two well-known couplets from Ghalib are quoted as an illustration:

   Dil-e nadan tujhe hua kya hai
   Akhir is dard ki dawa kya hai

Hum ko un se wafa ki hai ummeed
Jo nahin jante wafa kya hai

My naïve heart, what ails you, what?
What's the cure for this ache, what?
I expect love and loyalty from one
Who knows not, what's love, what loyalty, what?

A *ghazal* by John Hollander (*Ravishing DisUnities: Real Ghazals in English*: 76) entitled "Ghazal on Ghazal" which defines the *ghazal* and approximates to the form of the original is quoted here in full:

For couplets the ghazal is prime: at the end
Of each one's trefrain like a chime: "at the end."
But in subsequent couplet throughout the whole poem,
It's the second line only will rhyme at the end.

On a string of such strange, unpronounceable fruits,
How fine the familiar old time at the end!

All our writing is silent, the dance of the hand,
So that what it comes down to's all mine, at the end.

Dust and ashes? How dainty and dry! We decay
To our messy primordial slime at the end.

Two frail arms of your delicate form I pursue,
Inaccessible, vibrant, sublime at the end.

You gathered all manners of flowers all day,
But my hands were most fragrant of thyme, at the end.

There are so many sounds! A poem having one rhyme
— A good life with a sad, minor crime at the end.

Each new couplet's different ascent: no good peak,
But a low hill quite easy to climb at the end.

Two armed bandits: start out with a great wad of green
Thoughts, but you're left with a dime at the end.

Each assertion is a knot which must shorten, alas,
This long-worded rope of which I'm at the end.
Now qafia and radif has grown weary, like life,
At the game he's been wasting his time at. THE END. (76)

4. Azmatullah Khan expressed this view in his book *Suriley Bole* (Urdu, 1940).
5. Kalimuddin Ahmad, in his widely referred book *Urdu Sheyri pe Ek Nazar* (Urdu, 1964) made this radical remark.

6. Rashid Ahmad Siddiqui assigned a respectable place to it in his book *Jadeed Ghazal* (1967).
7. Firaq Gorakhpuri has made this observation in his book *Urdu ki Ishqiya Shayri* (Hindi, 2001).
8. Interestingly, Goethe, who published his ghazal in a collection in 1819, called it *West-Ostlicher Divan* (*West Easterly Divan*). Platen and Ruckert also named their collections of ghazals in the same spirit and theme *Ghaslen*, published in 1821 and 1822 respectively.
9. Aijaz Ahmad (*Ghazals of Ghalib*) used an extremely interesting way to introduce Ghalib to the American poets (W. S. Merwin, Adrienne Rich, William Stafford, David Ray, Thomas Fitzsimmons, Mark Strand and William Hunt). He gave them literal translations of some of Ghalib's ghazals, along with explanatory notes after which they composed their own "versions" of the poet. The experiment which seemed strange to many then, now appears to be a useful source to study problems involved in translating a poet from an "alien" language.
10. From an unpublished interview with Douglas Barbour by the author, on June 19–20, 2001.
11. *ibid.*
12. *ibid.*

WORKS CITED

Ali, Agha Shahid, ed. 2000. *Ravishing disUnities: Real ghazals in English.* Connecticut: Wesleyan University Press.

Barbour, Douglas. 1984. *Visible visions: Selected poems.* NeWest Press: Edmonton.

__________. 2001. *Lyric/Anti lyric: Essays on contemporary poetry.* NeWest Press: Edmonton.

Caplan, David. 2005. *Questions of possibility: Contemporary poetry and poetic form.* New York: Oxford University Press.

Glickman, Susan. 1987. Proceeding before the amorous invisible: Phyllis Webb and the ghazal. *Canadian Literature.* 115: 48–61.

Harrison, Jim. 1971. *Outlyer and ghazals.* New York: Simon and Schuster.

Rich, Adrienne. 1993. *Collected early poems: 1950–1970.* New York: W. W. Norton & Co.

Thompson, John. 1978. *Stilt Jack.* Toronto: Anansi Press.

Webb, Phyllis. 1982. *Sunday water: Thirteen anti ghazals.* Victoria: Morris Printing Company Limited. Island Writing Series.

________. 1984. *Water and light.* Toronto: Coach House Press.

________. 1987. Ghazal maker: Review of Peter Sanger's *Sea Run: Notes on John Thompson's Stilt Jack. Canadian Literature* 112: 156–57.

Wright, Judith. 1994. *Collected poems.* Sydney: Angus and Robertson.

Bibliography

Alessandra, Riccardi, ed. 2002. *Translation studies: Perspectives on an emerging discipline.* Cambridge: Cambridge University Press.

Alvarez, R. and M. Carmen-Africa Vidal, eds. 1996. *Translation, power, subversion.* Clevedon: Multilingual Matters.

Amos, Flora Ross. [1920/1973] 1984. *Early theories of translation.* New York: Octagon Books.

Anderman, Gunilla M. and Margaret A. Rogers, eds. 1996. *Words, words, words: The translator and the language learner.* Clevedon: Multilingual Matters.

Apter, Emily. 2006. *The translation zone: A new comparative literature.* Princeton: Princeton University Press.

Arrojo, Rosemary. 1997. The "death" of the author and the limits of the translator's visibility. In *Translation and intercultural communication,* ed. Mary Snell-Hornby, Zuzana Jettmarova and Klaus Kaindl. Amsterdam: John Benjamins. 21–32.

Arrowsmith, William and Roger Shattuck, eds. 1961. *The craft and context of translation.* Austin: University of Texas Press.

Baker, Mona and Gabriela Saldanha. 2009. *Routledge Encyclopedia of translation studies.* 2nd ed. New York: Routledge.

Baker, Mona, ed. 2010. *Critical readings in translation studies.* New York: Routledge.

Barnstone, Willis. 1993. *The poetics of translation: History, theory, practice.* New Haven: Yale University Press.

Bassnett, Susan and Harish Trivedi, eds. 1999. *Post-colonial translation: Theory and practice.* London: Routledge.

Bassnett, Susan. 1997. *Translating literature.* Suffolk: Boydell and Brewer.

Belitt, Ben. 1978. *Adam's dream: A preface to translation.* New York: Grove Press.

Bell, Roger T. 1991. *Translation and translating: Theory and practice.* New York: Longman.

Benjamin, Andrew. 1989. *Translation and the nature of philosophy: A new theory of words*. London: Routledge.

Bermann, S. and Michael Wood, eds. 2005. *Nation, language, and the ethics of translation*. Princeton: Princeton University Press.

Biguenet, John and Rainer Schulte, eds. 1989. *The craft of translation*. Chicago: University of Chicago Press.

Brodzki, Bella. 2007. *Can these bones live? Translation, survival, and cultural memory*. Stanford: Stanford University Press.

Brower, Reuben A., ed. 1959. *On translation*. Cambridge: Harvard University Press.

Budick, Sanford and Wolfgang Iser, eds. 1996. *The translatability of cultures: Figurations of the space between*. Stanford: Stanford University Press.

Burger, Maya and Nicola Pozza, eds. 2010. *India in translation through Hindi literature: A plurality of voices*. Berne: Peter Lang.

Chaudhuri, Sukanta. 1999. *Translation and understanding*. Delhi: Oxford University Press.

Chesterman, A. 1996. On similarity. *Target* 8 (1): 159–63.

———. 2005. Where is similarity? In *Similarity and difference in translation*, ed. S. Arduini and R. Hodgson. Rimini: Guaraldi. 63–75.

Chesterman, Andrew and Emma Wagner. 2002. *Can theory help translators: A dialogue between the ivory tower and the wordface*. Abingdon: Routledge.

Chesterman, Andrew. 1997. *Memes of translation: The spread of ideas in translation theory*. Philadelphia: John Benjamins.

Classe, Olive. 2000. *Encyclopedia of literary translation into English*. Vol. I (A–L). Chicago: Fitzroy Dearborn.

———. 2000. *Encyclopedia of literary translation into English*. Vol. II (M–Z). Chicago: Fitzroy Dearborn.

Cronin, Michael. 2003. *Translation and globalisation*. London: Routledge.

———. 2006. *Translation and identity*. Abingdon: Routledge.

David, Bellos. 2012. *Is that a fish in your ear? Translation and the meaning of everything*. London: Penguin Books.

Davis, Kathleen. 2001. *Deconstruction and translation*. Manchester: St. Jerome.

Delisle, Jean. 1988. *Translation: An interpretative approach*. Ottawa: University of Ottawa Press.

Devy, G. 1999. Translation and literary history: An Indian view. In *Post-colonial translation: Theory and practice,* ed. Susan Bassnett and Harish Trivedi. London: Routledge. 182–88.

Dharwadker, V. 1999. A. K. Ramanujan's theory and practice of translation. In *Post-colonial translation: Theory and practice,* ed. Susan Bassnett and Harish Trivedi. London: Routledge. 114–40.

Duarte, Joao Ferreira, Alexandra Assis Rosa and Teresa Seruya. 2006. *Translation studies at the interface of disciplines.* Amsterdam: John Benjamins.

Eco, Umberto. 2001. *Experiences in translation.* Toronto: University of Toronto Press.

———. *Mouse or rat? Translation as negotiation.* 2003. London: Phoenix.

Even-Zohar, Itamar. 1978. The position of translated literature within the literary polysystem. In *Literature in translation*, ed. J. S. Holmes et. al. Leuven: Acco. 117–27.

———. 1990. Translation and transfer. *Poetics Today* 11(1): 73–78. Special issue on Polysystem Studies.

Fambier, Yves and Luc Van Doorslaer. 2010. *Handbook of translation studies.* Vol. I. Amsterdam: John Benjamins.

Fawcett, P. 1997. *Translation and language.* Manchester: St. Jerome.

Figueiria, Dorothy Matilda. 1991. *Translating the Orient: The reception of Sakuntala in nineteenth century Europe.* Albany: SUNY Press.

Flood, Finbarr B. 2009. *Objects of translation: Material culture and medieval "Hindu-Muslim" encounters.* New Delhi: Permanent Black.

Godard, Barbara. Theorizing feminist discourse/translation. In *Translation, History and Culture*, ed. Susan Bassnett and André Lefevere. London: Cassell. 87–96.

Gouadec, D. 2007. *Translation as profession.* Amsterdam: John Benjamins.

Graham, Joseph F., ed. 1985. *Difference in translation.* Ithaca: Cornell University Press.

Grossman, Edith. 2011. *Why translation matters.* New Delhi. Orient Blackswan.

Hardwick, L. 2000. *Translating words, translating cultures.* London: Duckworth.

Hatim, B. 2009. Translating text in context. In *The Routledge companion to translation studies,* ed. J. Munday. Abingdon: Routledge. 36–53.

Hatim, Basil and Ian Mason. 1997. *The translator as communicator.* London: Routledge.

Hatim, Basil and Jeremy Munday. 2004. *Translation: An advanced resource book.* Abingdon: Routledge.

Hermans, Theo. 1985. *The manipulation of literature: Studies in literary translation.* London: Croom Helm.

Hickey, Leo. 1998. *The pragmatics of translation.* Clevedon: Multilingual Matters.

Hoffman, Eva. 1989. *Lost in translation: A life in a new language.* New York: Penguin.

Holmes, James S. 1988. *Translated! Papers on literary translation and translation studies.* Amsterdam: Rodopi.

Holmes, James S., Frans de Haan and Anton Popovic, eds. 1970. *The nature of translation: Essays on the theory and practice of literary translation.* The Hague: Mouton de Gruyter.

Holmström, Lakshmi. 2006. Let poetry win: The translator as writer – An Indian perspective. In *Translator as writer*, ed. Susan Bassnett and P. Bush. London: Continuum. 33–45.

Honig, Edwin. 1985. *The poet's other voice: Conversations on literary translation.* Massachusetts: University of Massachusetts Press.

Ivir, V. 1981. Formal correspondences: Translation equivalence revisited. *Poetics Today* 2.4: 51–59.

Jakobs, C. 1975. The monstrosity of translation. *Modern Language Notes* 90: 755–66.

Johnson, B. 1985. Taking fidelity philosophically. In *Difference in translation*, ed. J. Graham. Ithaca, New York: Cornell University Press. 142–48.

Katan, D. 2004. Rev. second edition. *Translating cultures.* Manchester: St. Jerome.

Kenny, Dorothy. 2001. *Lexis and creativity in translation: A corpus-based study.* Manchester: St. Jerome.

Kirk, R. 1986. *Translation determined.* Oxford: Clarendon Press.

Kittel, Harald and Armin Paul Frank. 1991. *Interculturality and the historical study of literary translation.* Berlin: Erich Schimdt Verlag.

Kothari, Rita. [2003] 2014. *Translating India: The cultural politics of English.* New York: Routledge.

Kuhiwczak, Piotr and Karen Littau. [2007] 2014. *A companion to translation studies.* New Delhi: Orient BlackSwan.

Lane-Mercier, Gillian. 1997. Translating the untranslatable: The translator's aesthetics, ideological and political responsibility, *Target* 9 (1): 43–68.

Lefevere, André and Susan Bassnett. 1998. *Constructing cultures: Essays in literary translation.* Clevedon: Multilingual Matters.

Lefevere, André, ed. 1992. *Translation/history/culture: A sourcebook.* London: Routledge.

Lefevere, André. 1975. *Translating poetry: Seven strategies and a blueprint.* Amsterdam: Van Gorcum.

———. 1992. *Translation, rewriting, and the manipulation of literary fame.* London: Routledge.

Meschonnic, Henri. 2011. *Ethics and politics of translation.* Trans. and ed. Pier Pascale Boulanger. Amsterdam: John Benjamins.

Mukherjee, Sujit. 2004. *Translation as discovery.* New Delhi: Pencraft International.

Munday, Jeremy, ed. 2007. *Translation as intervention.* New York: Continuum.

Munday, Jeremy. 2007. *Style and ideology in translation: Latin American writing in English.* New York: Routledge.

———. 2007. Translation and ideology: A textual approach. *The Translator* 13.2: 195–217.

———. 2012. *Introducing translation studies: Theories and application.* 3rd ed. Abingdon: Routledge.

Nägele, Rainer. 1997. *Echoes of translation: Reading between texts.* Baltimore: Johns Hopkins University.

Nair, Rukmini Bhaya, ed. 2002. *Translation, text and theory: The paradigm of India.* New Delhi: Sage Publications.

Newmark, Peter. 1988. *A textbook of translation.* New York: Prentice Hall.

———. 1993. *Paragraphs on translation.* Clevedon: Multilingual Matters.

———. 1998. *More paragraphs on translation.* Clevedon: Multilingual Matters.

Nida, Eugene A. and Charles R. Taber. 1969. *The theory and practice of translation.* Leiden: Brill.

Nida, Eugene A. 2001. *Contexts in translating.* Amsterdam: John Benjamins.

Niranjana, Tejaswini. 1994. Colonialism and the politics of translation. In *An other tongue: Nation and ethnicity in the linguistic borderlands*, ed. Alfred Artega. Durham, NC: Duke University Press. 35–52.

———. 1994. Translation, colonialism and the rise of English. *Economic and Political Weekly* 25(15): 773–79.

Nord, Christiane. 1997. *Translation as purposeful activity: Functionalist approaches explained.* Manchester: St. Jerome.

Orero, Pilar and Juan C. Sager, eds. 1997. *The translator's dialogue: Giovanni Pontiero.* Philadelphia: John Benjamins.

Perez, Maria Calzada, ed. 2003. *Apropos of ideology: Translation studies on ideology – Ideology in translation studies.* Manchester: St. Jerome.

Perez, Maria Calzada. 2007. *Transitivity in translating: The interdependence of texture and context.* Berne: Peter Lang.

Pym, Anthony. 2004. Propositions on cross-cultural communication and translation, *Target* 16. (1): 1–28.

Pym, Anthony. 2010. *Exploring translation theories.* Abingdon: Routledge.

Raffel, Burton. 1971. *The forked tongue: A study of the translation process.* The Hague: Mouton.

Raffel, Burton. 1988. *The art of translating poetry*. University Park: The Pennsylvania State University Press.

———. 1994. *The art of translating prose.* University Park: The Pennsylvania State University Press.

Rahman, Anisur, ed. 2002. *Translation: Poetics and practice.* New Delhi: Creative Books.

Ramakrishna, Shanta. 2000. Cultural transmission through translation: An Indian perspective. In *Changing the terms: Translating in the postcolonial era*, ed. Sherry Simon and Paul St-Pierre. Ottawa: University of Ottawa Press. 87–100.

Ramakrishna, Shanta, ed. 1997. *Translation and multilingualism: Post-colonial contexts.* New Delhi: Pencraft International.

Ramakrishnan, E. V. 2011. *Locating Indian literature: Texts, traditions, translations.* New Delhi: Orient BlackSwan.

Riccardi, Allesandra. 2010. *Translation studies: Perspectives on an emerging discipline.* New Delhi: Cambridge University Press.

Ricoeur, Paul. 2006. *On translation*. Abingdon: Routledge.

Robinson, Douglas. 1991. *The translator's turn.* Baltimore: Johns Hopkins University Press.

———. 1997. *What is translation? Centrifugal theories, critical interventions.* Kent: Kent State University Press.

———. 1996. *Translation and taboo.* DeKalb, Illinois: Northern Illinois University Press.

Sallis, J. 2002. *On translation.* Bloomington: Indiana University Press.

Schäffner, C and Beate Herting. 1994. The revolution of the magic lantern: A cross-cultural comparison of translation strategies. In *Translation studies: An interdiscipline*, ed. Mary Snell-Hornby, Franz Pöchhacker and Klaus Kaindl. Amsterdam: John Benjamins. 27–37.

Schäffner, Christina and Helen Kelly-Holmes, eds. 1995. *Cultural functions of translation.* Clevedon: Multilingual Matters.

Schäffner, Christina, ed. 1999. *Translation and norms.* Clevedon: Multilingual Press.

Shulte, Rainer and John Biguenet, eds. 1992. *Theories of translation: An anthology of essays from Dryden to Derrida.* Chicago: University of Chicago Press.

Simon, Sherry, and Paul St-Pierre. [2000] 2002. *Changing the terms: Translating in the postcolonial era.* New Delhi: Orient Longman.

Singh, Udaya Narayan. 1990. Dynamics of textuality and configuration of space. *International Journal of Translation.* 2(2). 25–48.

Snell-Hornby, Mary. 2006. *The turns of translation studies: New paradigms or shifting viewpoints?* Amsterdam: John Benjamins.

Spivak, Gayatri C. 1993. The politics of translation. In *Outside the Teaching Machine.* New York: Metheun. 179–200.

———. 2007. Translation as culture. In *Translation—Reflections, refractions, transformations*, ed. Paul St-Pierre and Prafulla C. Kar. Amsterdam: John Benjamins. 263–76.

St-Pierre, Paul and Prafulla C. Kar. 2005. *In translation: Reflections, refractions and transformations.* Amsterdam: John Benjamins.

Tourey, Gideon. 1980. *In search of a theory of translation.* Tel Aviv: Porter Institute for Poetics and Semiotics.

———. 1987. *Translation across cultures.* New Delhi: Bahri Publications.

Trivedi, H. 1992. Omar Khayyam in India: An evolution through Persian, English and Hindi. In *Papers in Comparative Literature. 2: The Aesthetics of Translation*, ed. Amiya Dev. Calcutta: Jadavpur University. 35–62.

———. 2007. Translating culture vs. cultural translation. In *Translation—Reflections, refractions, transformations*, ed. Paul St-Pierre and Prafulla C. Kar. Amsterdam: John Benjamins. 277–87.

Tymockzo, Maria. 2003. Ideology and the position of the translator. In what sense is a translator "in between"? In *Apropos of ideology*, ed. Maria Calzada Perez. Manchester: St. Jerome. 181–205.

———. 2007. *Enlarging translation, empowering translation.* Manchester: St. Jerome.

Vanderschelden, Isabelle. 1998. Authority in literary translation: Collaborating with the author. *Translation Review* 56(1): 22–31.

Venuti, Lawrence. 1994. *The translator's invisibility: A history of translation.* New York: Routledge.

———. 2004. *The translation studies reader.* 2nd. Ed. New York: Routledge.

Vermeer, H. J. 1997. Translation and the meme. *Target* 9 (1): 155–66.

———. 1998. Didactics of translation. In *Routledge Encyclopedia of translation studies*, ed. Mona Baker. New York: 60–63.

Vieira, E. 2000. Cultural contacts and literary translation. In *Encyclopedia of literary translation into English,* Vol. I, ed. Olive Classe. London and Chicago: Fitzroy Dearborn. 319–21.

Wechsler, Robert. 1998. *Performing without a stage: The art of literary translation.* North Haven: Catbird.

Weissbort, Daniel, and Astradur Eysteinsson, eds. 2006. *Translation—theory and practice: A historical reader.* New York: Oxford University Press.

Weissbort, Daniel, ed. 1989. *Translating poetry: The double labyrinth.* Iowa City: University of Iowa Press.

Wolf, M. 1997. Translation as a process of power: Aspects of cultural anthropology in translation. In *Translation and intercultural communication,* ed. Mary Snell-Hornby, Zuzana Jettmarova and Klaus Kaindl. Amsterdam: John Benjamins. 123–33.

Yao, Steven G. 2002. *Translation and the language of modernism: Gender, politics, language.* New York. Palgrave Macmillan.

Publisher's Acknowledgements

The chapter "Translating Representation: The Problematic of Indian Literature" was earlier published as "Indian Literatures in English Translation: The Discourse of Resistance and Representation" in the *Journal of Postcolonial Writing*, Vol. 43, No. 2, August 2007, and is reprinted by permission of Taylor & Francis Ltd, www.tandfonline.com.

"Translating Modern Urdu Poetry: Creating Canons in Translation" was originally published in Sahitya Akademi's journal *Indian Literature*, Vol. XLII. No. 3, May–June 1998.

"Broadening the Frontier: Towards a Poetics of Painting and Architecture" was earlier published as "Revisiting Translation: Towards Fine Arts and Architecture" in *Literary Culture and Translation: New Aspects of Comparative Literature* edited by Dorothy M. Figueira and Chandra Mohan (Primus Books 2017), and is reprinted by permission of Primus Books.

"Author, Text, Translator, Reader: The New Indian Context" was earlier published in *Translation and Culture: Indian Perspectives* (Pencraft International 2010), and is reprinted by permission of the editor of the volume G. J. V. Prasad and Pencraft International.

Every effort has been made to trace copyright holders and to obtain their permission for the use of copyright material. The publisher apologises for any errors or omissions made, and would be grateful if notified of any corrections that should be incorporated in future reprints or editions of this book.